HISTORY OF TIPU SULTAN

HISTORY OF TIPU SULTAN

By

MOHIBBUL HASAN KHAN, C. W. MILES

GYAN

ISBN : 978-81-212-1696-8(HB)

First Published, 1864

Published, 2018

Published by

GYAN

Gyan Publishing House
5, Ansari Road
Daryaganj, New Delhi-110002
Phone: 011-47034999, 9811692060
www.gyanbooks.com
E-mail: books@gyanbooks.com

Printed at: G. Print Process, Delhi.

CONTENTS

PREFACE

In presenting this translation of the History of Tipu Sultan to the public, it may be proper to observe, that I do not consider myself responsible for any details contained in the work.

It will be seen that I have followed the rules I proposed to myself in the translation of the History of Hydar Ali—first, in the liberties I have considered it necessary to take with the language of the original, as to the construction of the sentences, &c and secondly, in allowing the Indian historian to tell his tale without the comment of conflicting authorities or a reference to the statements of persons, not so likely as himself to be well acquainted with the facts.

It will be evident to any one who reads this book, that although Tipu was an able man, and a brave soldier, still, that he was much inferior to his father in the characteristic qualities of a great man

Unlike his father, he was a bigoted Musalman, and like most of that class unprincipled and quite unscrupulous as to the means he employed to attain his ends in the propagation of his religion—with these bad qualities, his dark, suspicious, faithless character alienated those who were at first his most attached friends; and at the time Seringapatam was taken, he appears to have had scarcely one left.

The story that he was betrayed by Mir Sadik, his Dewan, to the English, or perhaps to some of the other confederated powers besieging Seringapatam, does not appear improbable, although unsupported by any evidence; but, as he was a great tyrant, there can be no doubt that his ministers were glad to get ride of him on any terms

Tipu's character cannot be better exemplified than by the cases of Muhammad Ali, Commandant, and Ghazi Khan Bede. These officers had been all their lives the most devoted and trustworthy of his father's servants, and indeed his father owed his life to them on more than one occasion, as will be seen in his history. They had been also the chief instruments of his father's elevation to the rank and power he attained, and moreover the chief means of his own accession to the throne of the Khodadad kingdom.

In return for all these meritorious services, he no sooner found himself secure in the possession of his father's authority, than he put the first to death from jealousy, because he was too just and honourable a man for the service of such a tyrant, and both were executed under circumstances of great cruelty.

It is true, Muhammad Ali, Commandant, was a violent man, that he wanted sense and entirely misunderstood his new master's character, but Ghazi Khan Bede, to all appearance, was sacrificed to mere suspicion, and put out of the way only because the Sultan chose to listen to his enemies, or because he coveted the possession of his wealth

But our sympathy is peculiarly enlisted on the part of the gallant Muhammad Ali, Commandant, when we learn from this work that he was sacrificed to his honourable zeal in resisting the infraction of the terms of a capitulation, he, as the agent of the Sultan, had negotiated with General Mathews, at Nagar. It is well known that the whole of the terms of that capitulation were shamefully violated by Tipu, and the unfortunate prisoners treated with the utmost brutality, and lastly, that General Mathews, his brother, and many officers, and soldiers were poisoned and privately murdered in prison by his orders.

It may be objected by some, that Muhammad Ali did not resist the infraction of the capitulation in their cases ;—from the man's character, however, I have no doubt but that he did, though of course ineffectually, and I think this opinion is corroborated by the charge made against him by the Sultan, "that he was in communication and in league with the English of Bombay, and about to seek their protection."

By this, and other instances in these volumes, it will be seen, that Muhammadans seldom or ever keep faith with Idolators, (among whom they reckon Christians,) when they consider themselves sufficiently strong to break it with impunity. They consider, I believe erroneously, that they have the sanction of their religion for this diabolical principle, but it is clear that Hydar Ali, Tipu Sultan, the Afghan Prince at Kabul, Muhammad Akbar, indeed, the Musalmans in general, in all periods, (with some rare exceptions) have acted in strict conformity to this most villanous rule.......

In conclusion, I trust I may be permitted to assume to myself, the merit of having made my translation as concise as possible, without any considerable deviation from the text ;—and, having done this, in humble imitation of the style of my author, I beg leave to express a hope that when my readers find errors, or inelegancies, in the language of this work, they will cast the eye of indulgence over them, and correct them with the pen of liberality and forbearance.

CHAPTER I

The accession of the mighty Prince, high in dignity, His Highness Tipu Sultan, to the throne of Mysoie, and the advance of the armies under Generals Lang and Stuart towards Wandiwash, with other events of the year 1197, Hijri—A D 1781-2.

When the sun of the Nawab Hydar's prosperity and power, which had attained its utmost height, showed a disposition to decline, and the bright star of the constellation of his Sovereignty fell from the zenith of grandeur to the depths of disease and death,[1] (in the original, affliction,) the Khans, and the Pillars of the State, that is to say, Muhammad Ali, Commandant, Budruzaman Khan, Maha Mirza Khan, Ghazi Khan, Abu Muhammad Mirdah, Purnia, Kishen Rao, &s, not relinquishing from their grasp the administration of the current business of the government; but, on the contrary, taking up the ground of loyalty and obedience, fulfilled the conditions of faith and gratitude, and continued on the same footing all the customary duties, usual during the life of the pardoned Nawab, Hydar; and, at night, after the due discharge of the officers to the dead, the coffin containing the body was filled with essences and perfumes, and despatched, without the knowledge of any other persons, to Seringapatam; and the servants who were acquainted with these transactions were seized, and confined separately, each without the knowledge of the others, that they might not be divulged.

It is proper to mention here, that at the time the Nawab determined to attempt the conquest of the Karnatak Payanghat, he also gave orders to form, or plant, the Lal Bagh or Garden, to the southward of the town or suburb of Ganjam, on this side the river Kaveri, and also to build in that garden a Masjid which, in the time of Tipu Sultan, was called Masjidi Aksa.

In front of the Masjid also, a mausoleum, covered by a dome, was erected; to superintend the building of which a Darogha was specially appointed. At the period of Hydar's death this mousoleum was finished, and his body was therein deposited.

To be concise, the well affected Khans for the present appointed Karim Sahib, (the brother of Tipu) to the office of Dewan, as the Naib of his father; and they conducted the government with such admirable policy, that not a particle of sedition or

[1] *Wa bal.*

disturbance occured, either in the civil administration of affairs, or in the army, and the officers and men of the army remained fully assured of the perfect health and safety of the Nawab, and with the sanction of the Dewan, and to quite and still the minds of the Foujdars, and other officers of the State, their monthly pay, agreeably to the Hydari regulations, was issued to all, and the same day, one thousand horse were detached to Nellore, and two thousand marched towards the English camp. Still, in the midst of all this rigid policy and secrecy, the spring and spirit of the whole army, high and low, were changed, and depressed, as it were by inspiration, to the gloom and darkness of mourning; and, at times, involuntary sighs broke forth from the breasts of both officers and soldiers

In the mean time, however, the attached and devoted Maha Mirza Khan was appointed and despatched with letters, containing an account of the death of Hydar, to the exalted presence of that offspring of prosperity and honour, the tree bearing the fruit of dignity and majesty, the conqueror of the world, Tipu Sultan, who at that time was enlightening the environs of Coimbatore and Palghat by his presence, and in earnestly requesting him immediately to direct his steps towards the camp, they made use of every expression of soliciation and entreaty

The Sultan on being acquainted with these events, notwithstanding he in private received assurances from the faithful Mirza, and had his mind set at ease by the oaths of the officers of the army, still, was much troubled and disturbed at the appointment of Karim Sahib to the high office of the Dewani, but when this auspicious intelligence reached the ears of his understanding, —*verses* "Do not listen to any one, but put thy foot in the stirrup,"—"for success and victory are hastening to meet thee,"—"a hawk cares not for a sparrow,"—"do not fear thine enemies," —"what injury can a lion receive from a lame fox."— He did his faithful well wishers the honour to accede to their requests and arrived at the camp by forced marches.

As soon as this glorious intelligence, diffusing joy, reached his hearty friends, the tongue of time sang the following verses[2]: "Come on, for the victorious ensigns of the King have arrived," —"The cry of good news and victory has reached the sun and moon,"—"The resplendency of thy good fortune has thrown off the veil from the face of victory."—"The perfectly just has arrived to redress the complaints of the oppressed,"—"The heavens gave promise of him to the people of the age."—"The time is propitious, now the King has arrived"

At once, therefore, the chiefs and officers of the government with Karim Sahib, proceeded to meet and honour the arrival of

[2] It is nearly impossible to make any thing of this poetry and the like of it in a prose translation.

Tipu Sultan, and were dignified by being admitted to do homage (kissing the ground) to that resource of the world, and after the customary demonstrations of mourning, at a fortunate hour,—*verses.* "Such as would bestow blessings on the propitious signs of heaven,"—"and make the drum of rejoicing resound to the skies,"—on a Saturday, in the commencement of the year 1197, Hijri,[3] he was seated on the throne of dignity and majesty, and the offerings of felicitation on his accession were presented.

As the throne of Mysore kingdom, from the propitious steps of that sun of the meridian of kingly power and authority, had risen in height above the heavens, and as the state and its prosperity assumed the vernal splendour of youth; in order to reward the good services of his faithful servants, the conquering Sultan made royal presents to every one separately; and having honoured them by increasing their rank and pay, he gave orders for the joyful celebration of his accession to the throne by the preparation of a feast and banquet,—*verses.* "The King arrayed the royal banquet,"—"for that is the genial spring and Paradise of master and servant,"—"The trees (flowers) of this garden are rubies, and the leaves, emeralds,"—"the sward or grass, glass; and the earth, amber. —In that assembly, melodious poets and eloquent orators, from the clouds of their invention, showered the orient pearls,[4] of prose and verse on the head of the young king, and were liberally rewarded from the table of his bounty.

After the conclusion of the feast and banquet, the Sultan, placing his fortunate steps on the throne of the regulation of the affairs of his kingdom, issued Farmans to all the commander of forts, the farmers, and collectors of revenue in the kingdom; his object being to win the affections of the whole by his kindness and regard, and by holding out hopes of future advancement,—from policy, therefore, the authority every one before possessed was still continued to them on the same footing. About this time, the commander-in-chief of the French army despatched two thousand French troops, under the command of Count Dupleix,[5] to the presence; and, after the regulation of his affairs, and finding himself fully established, the Sultan, with his victorious army, marched to Kaveri Pauk, the environs of which, from the splendour of his standards, became the envy of the starry heavens. At the same time, the English army, under the command of Generals Stuart and Lang, advanced to oppose the army of the Sultan by the route of Chungal Peeth[6] to Wandiwash.

At hearing this news, the lion-like Sultan marched with the

[3] A D 1783 There is no specification of the month in any copy of this work that I have seen

[4] Alluding to the Oriental mode of accounting for the formation of pearls in the shells in which they are found.

[5] Kun Taplis.

[6] Chingleput.

whole of his army, by the route of Doshi,[7] to Amlur, to repel his enemies, and encamped at the distance of about five miles from Wandiwash; and the next day, having formed his right and left wings, and the main body (the reserve) of his army, in order of battle, and posting his artillery in front he held himself in readiness for mortal contention. The English Officers, although they with their troops were drawn out in battle array, still, seeing the order and discipline of the Sultan's army, and the imposing appearance of the French battalions, did not think proper to engage that day, but remained formed on their own ground.

The day after that, orders were received from the Governor of Madras, recalling the English army; and the generals above mentioned, having destroyed the fort of Wandiwash, returned with their display and parade to Madras The Sultan also marched from that place and encamped at Tiruvottiyur. While at this place, the Sultan's spies brought intelligence that Iyaz Khan, the adopted son of the late Nawab, and who had been appointed by him to the government of the districts of Nagar, Gorial Bunder (Mangalore) &c., the cup of his unworthiness being at this time filled to the brim, had followed the path of treachery and ingratitude, and with the greatest perfidy had delivered up the whole of the forts of that country (Malabar) to the English of the port of Bombay; and that unfortunate man, with a great quantity of gold, jewels, baggage, and followers, had embarked on broad ship, and had taken his ill-starred route to Bombay, where he had arrived; that the English had seized the whole of that country; and that certain seditious people, (meaning the Zemindars,) who had been waiting for an opportunity to rebel, had raised the head of pride from every hole and corner, exciting rebellion; as, for instance, Anchi Shamia, a Brahman who was at the head of the intelligence department at the capital, (Seringapatam), having united in heart and hand with the governor of the fort, planned and concerted to effect the destruction of his master's house, and had excited a great disturbance; that Syyad Muhammad Khan, the son-in-law of Abdul Halim, the Afghan of Kirpa, also thinking this a good opportunity to prosecute his plans, assembled a force of horse and foot, and nad made a treaty of friendship, confirmed by oaths, with the English of Mutchlipatan (Masulipatam), with a view to the conquest of the district of Kirpa, and was the cause of great alarm in that quarter.

[7] This town is called in some MSS. Doshi Mapru, or Mamru.

CHAPTER II

The march of the Sultan's victorious ensigns to subdue his enemies and the recapture of Nagar, Gorial Bandar (Mangalore) &c—also the defeat of a detachment of the Bombay army, by the bravery of the Ghazies (Musalman soldiers), and the establishment of peace between the Sultan and the English government, also the death of that brave officer, Mahummud Ali (Commandant), in the same year, that is, A Hijri, 1197.—A D 1782

When the treachery of Iyaz, the encroachment of the English in that country (Malabar), and the rebellion of the Governor of the Fort of Seringapatam, &c,—reached the ears of the Sultan, he, making the defeat and explusion of the rebels his chief object, despatched Budruzaman Khan Bakshi with seven thousand matchlock men, Salabat Khan Bakshi, with six thousand Sillahdar horse, and Mir Gholam Ali, with ten thousand irregular infantry; all placed under the command of Mir Moinuddin, otherwise called Syyad Sahib, Sipahsalar, to defend and secure the country of the Payanghat, while he himself with all the rest of his army and departments marched towards Nagar.

When he had passed the Ghat of Chungum, the brave Muhammad Ali, commandant, with his division of troops was sent to the capital to restore order, to remove the disaffected, and replace them with faithful and loyal servants; and Kamruddin Khan with the troops of the deceased Mir Sahib, (Ali Raza Khan) was also detached towards Kirpa, with discretional powers to oppose Syyad Muhammad Khan, and the Sultan then marched by the route of Devanhalli, Mudgiri, and the Suba Sura, and encamped in the environs of Chitaldrug

The Foujdar of that place, Dowlat Khan, to manifest his loyalty and obedience attended the Sultan with his dependants and was received with great favour and honoured with a dress of confirmation on his reappointment to the Foujdari

When the Sultan moved on and encamped under the Ghat of Nagar, Muhammad Ali, commandant, who had been despatched to the capital, proceeded thither by forced marches by the route of Bangalore, and encamped under the Karighat hill, on the bank of the river. —According however to the rule,—*verse,*[8] "O wise man fear him who fears thee,"—"although thou mightest be able to conquer a hundred such in battle"—and after the fashion of wolf courtesy, began (following the path of intimacy) to show great regard and friendship towards the rebel

[8] *"az un kaz tu tarsad bitars ai hakim
wa gar ba chu u sad bariye bijang."*

governor of the capital, and sent a message to him to the effect, that if permission were accorded, he would enter the Fort alone, and sleep one night at his house, that he might have the pleasure of seeing his family and children, and that the next morning, according to the orders of the Sultan, he would proceed by the route of Coorg to the attack of Nagar

The Killadar lent a willing ear to the deceiving words of the commandant, and gave orders to the guards of the fort that he should be admitted; and he seeing all things favourable to his views and hopes, at night held his detachment in readiness, and crossing the river placed his men in ambush near the walls of the fort, and gave them orders that when he should enter the fort, and his Turee or trumpet sound the charge, they were immediately to enter and man the walls, bastions and gates. Accordingly he, accompanied by fifty brave and experienced men as a gaurd, immediately after entered the gate of the fort and sounded his trumpet, and having seized and bound the guard, posted his own men at the gate. In the meantime at the sound of the trumpet, the troops in ambush swiftly advanced from their concealment, and entered the fort and extended their guards and sentinels on all sides.

The brave commandant now quickly advanced to the houses of the Killadar, and his deputies, and to that of the Anchi Shamia and his coleagues, and before they could open their eyes from the sleep of neglect and folly, they were dragged out of their beds and put in prison. The next morning, with the sanction of the Sultan's mother, some of the rebels were blown from a gun, the companions of Shamia impaled, and he himself loaded with irons and confined in an iron cage—a fit punishment for his villainy

The office of governor of the capital was now transferred to Syyad Muhammad Khan Mehdivi, a friend of the Sultan's, and the defence of the city was entrusted to the care and responsibility of Asad Khan, Risaldar, a brave and very able man and who was also an old servant —Muhammad Ali having effected this, immediately marched with his troops by long stages, taking with him the letters of the Sultan's mother, and his report of the arrangements made at the capital, and arrived in camp at Nagar, and detailed all the circumstances to the presence.

The Sultan was well pleased with his services and presented him with a gorget and a Khillat or dress of honor.

The next day the Sultan ordered the passage of the Ghat; and his troops with the greatest gallantry quiting the roads of the mountain, where detachments of the English with guns and musketry were posted, ascended by a route on the opposite side in the rear of the enemy, and commenced firing on them.

The parties of the English before mentioned now to save themselves from being cut off, assembled in one place and bravely fought their way into the fort.[9] —The brave and faithful troops of the Sultan now immediately surrounded the fort, raised batteries against it, and used their best endeavours to batter down its walls It happened however one day during this period, that a stone which was thrown from a mortar into the fort, fell on a part of the wall, under which was a well full of water, and breaking down the wall filled up the well with its rubbish. From this cause a scarcity of water arose in the fort, and the want of water carried away the strength and constancy of the hearts of the garrison

One night, therefore, near one thousand musketeers with two or three thousand pioneers and inhabitants of the place with brass and earthen vessels came forth from the fort, and taking as much water as they could bear away from a tank near the walls, carried it into the fort. The Sultan being informed of this, the next night stationed guns, musketry and rifle men on the mounds, or banks of the tank, and when on that night they came as before rolling on like a dark cloud full of rain, the lightning and thunder of the guns and musketry, drowned some in the sea of their own bood, and some washing the hands of their presumption with the water of despair, and breaking the vessels of their good fortune with the stone of flight, sought the protection of the fort; but notwithstanding this extraordinary states of things, the thirsty garirson held out for two days, but at length the officer commanding in the fort through the medium of the brave Muhammad Ali, proposed conditions of surrender, and gave up the fort to the servants of the Sultan, and was placed under the protection of his government,—thus by the aid of the Sultan's good fortune, this fort was taken in eighteen days, and some person present on the occasion gave the date impromptu in the following words *Hydainagar griftah* [10] 10 or 1197 Hijri.[11]

From this place the Sultan proceeded without delay towards Gorial Bandar (Mangalore), and on the road fell in with and surrounded a body of English troops, which under the command of Colonel Campbell, was advancing to the relief of Nagar with supplies of all kinds

The horse of the Paigah being encouraged by the promise of free plunder, and the Kuzzaks and Silahdars stimulated by the promise of one hundred rupees for every horse killed in action, were ordered to attack this force and destroy it It happened that in the field, where this action was fought, there were two tanks, or ponds of water, at a distance of about a mile and a half from each other

According to orders, therefore, the Risalas of musketeers

[9] The seige of Nagar.
[10] Hydai Nuggur taken.
[11] A D 1782

and irregular foot (brave as lions), the rocketeers and artillery were posted on the road to these tanks, and they kept up a continual fire on their enemies

The Kakur and Chapao horse[12] were sent to throw the enemy's baggage and followers into confusion, while the Sultan with a select few and his body-guard, made desultory charges and attacks on the main body. The Colonel above mentioned, however, kept the ground with great constancy and valour until mid-day, when at length his ammunition failing by degrees the order and courage of his force, which consisted of four thousand (Indian) infantry, twelve hundred Europeans and seven guns was broken, and a terrible shock and great disgrace fell on them and they were destroyed.

Hussain Ali Khan the Bakshi of the Paigah (or body guard), the brother of Asad Ali Khan, the chief of Bhikanpilly, at the commencement of the action had given up two guns to the English, and after losing most of his best men was obliged to retreat.

The Sultan being much grieved at this loss, told him, if he had any of the honour or courage of a gentleman left in him, to recover the guns. To retrieve his honour and character, therefore, he with seven hundred men lightly equipped, advanced and fought so energetically against the English, that he was the chief cause of their defeat and destruction :—at length having received eleven musket and bayonet wounds he left the field grievously wounded, but victorious.

But to return,—The Sultan having taken possession of all the warlike stores and equipment of the defeated army, presented to his own brave soldiers armlets, gorgets and strings of pearls, and then without the least delay, marched on and at one assault took Pettah, or suburb of the fort before mentioned (Mangalore), and directed the commencement of the siege and conquest of the fort; in a very short time, therefore, notwithstanding it was the depth of the monsoon, and that the rain fell in torrents, so that a man could not put his head out of his tent, or his feet on the ground; and that casts or models of animals might have been taken from the impressions of those dead lying in the mud; heavy batteries were thrown up, approaches pushed on, and a continual fire of guns, musketry and rockets maintained, and some vessels being seized, the passage to supplies by sea was blocked up. The besieged also, who were well known for their hardihood and constancy in braving the labours and hardships of war, crowded the walls and bastions of the fort and for three months

[12] A parenthesis in the original :
Although these are included in the Bede tribe, they carry off the palm even from them in the arts of robbery and oppression, and are the most notorious thieves of the world; for with their bamboo spears, they will risk their lives for a sugar cane.

defended themselves valiantly.[13] At last, however, from the length of the siege and the want of provisions, they were reduced to great distress, and they then sent a messenger to the presence to ask for quarter, and they were received under the protection of the Sultan.

Every one, therefore, according to his merits received a respectable command in his service, and the foreheads of their attachment were made resplendent by the symbols of faithful service. (From this it appears, that those who joined the Sultan were Hindus)—Mangalore, Hunawar, &c. having been taken by the victorious Sultan, he determined to return to Mysore by the route of Coorg and Bul It happened by a melancholy fatality, that in the course of this journey, the brave Muhammad Ali, commandant, for a trifling fault, and for showing too much obstinacy and presumption threw away his life. The detail of this event is as follows, that a certain Kasim Ali,[14] governor of the fort of Nagar, a servant of the late Nawab, and who, during the government of Iyaz Khan had charge of that fort, had colleagued with that traitor, and followed the path of perfidy and rebellion; and when the English troops arrived from Bombay, gave up the fort to them without resistance, he accepting the post of Lieutenant-governor:—When the fort however was recaptured, he, seeing the road of safety shut against him, sought the protection of the brave commandant before mentioned, and having taken from him assurances for the security of his life and property, took up his residence in his tent. The Sultan, therefore, one day inflamed with anger, sent for this Governor of the fort to the presence, and when he arrived he addressed him to the following effect:—that the fort of Nagar being full of provisions, the means of defence and a good garrison, how was it possible it should fall into the hands of the enemy? That allowing a mean, ungrateful slave had traitorously rebelled, he (Kasim) who was a man of good family and appointed to the charge of this strong fort, what did he do, that for only one day he did not perform his duty as governor, and try to resist and repel his enemies.

He in reply said that, although there were abundance of stores and provisions, still, the Naikwars (Hindu chiefs apparently), and the chiefs of districts at the suggestion of the traitor,

[13] The First Grenadier Battalion of the Bombay army formed part of the garrison at Mangalore on this occasion, and gained great honour by its gallantry during the siege

[14] It appears from this, that Muhammad Ali, commandant, lost his life for insisting that the terms of the capitulation made by General Matthews at Nagar, should be observed in the case of Kasim Ali, he, being the agent employed in its negotiation It is well known that it was most shamefully violated by Tipu and that both the General and his brother, with many other officers and men were barbarously murdered by that tyrant's orders.

Iyaz, acted contrary to his, Kasim's wishes, and having made a secret agreement with the enemy, without his knowledge, admitted them into the fort, that he, the Sultan's slave, being without remedy, determined to proceed to the presence, but that his enemies prevented him The Sultan then said to him,—"allowing the truth of what you state, why were you not prepared against the arts of the Naikwars, or Nairs, and why did you not send intelligence of this to the presence; and besides, when you thought your best policy, present and future, lay in the surrender of the fort, why did you allow the money and property of the state to be gratuitously plundered by the enemy, and why did you not take as much care of it as you did of your own?" that in this matter he was undoubtedly an ungrateful faithless servant,—to conclude, the Sultan having established his guilt, by the advice of his council of state the delinquent was sentenced to be impaled. The next day Zain al Abedin the Bakhshi of the Kutcheri of regular infantry (the son of Asad Khan, Mehkurri; Foujdar of Kishnagiri), received orders to put the sentence in effect, and other officers of horse and foot were attached to the Bakshi above mentioned to be present at its execution. The Bakshi, troops &c. having assembled at the place appointed, they sent for the prisoner who was under a guard of the commandants, when he himself accompanying the prisoner came to the place of execution and said, this man has claimed my protection,[15] you must forgive his offence, or you must first put me to death and then execute him.

The Bakshi and the rest of the officers reported this in detail to the presence, and the Sultan said we will spare the criminal this day for the sake of Muhammad Ali, but let him be placed under our own guards and this therefore was immediately done.

The Sultan now sent for Muhammad Ali in private, and repeated his determination to execute the prisoner, and told him that his opposition in such a measure tended to disturb and interrupt the operations of government, the regulation of the different departments of the state, and to do away with the example necessary to be shown to others—that he, the Sultan, in punishing this man only acted as directed by the provisions of the divine law, in order that other governors of districts and towns of the kingdom, might in future avoid the commission of such crimes; but, that leaving that alone, punishment was indispensable in a newly established government; that the control and regulation of the troops and country might be ensured, for that it was a saying of the wise "in order to confirm or establish your government you must give the sword no rest"—But notwithstanding the Sultan for two hours expostulated with him, and

[15] In virtue of the capitulation and surrender of the fort of Nagar apparently.

advised him not to oppose the execution of a convicted malefactor, still he, with his original obstinacy, which indeed belonged to his nature, and because his last day had arrived and the hand of death was striking the drum of his departure on his shoulders, paid no attention to the commands of the Sultan, but rose up and went away without asking leave—*verse*—"advice makes no impression on crooked minds, or obstinate men"—"the branch of the stag's head is not made green by the rain." —The Sultan was much displeased at his disrespectful conduct, but, on account of former acquaintance and services, took no notice of his insolence, and remained silent that day. The next day the fire of the Sultan's wrath flamed violently, and he again gave the same orders to the Bakhshis as before :—but when they took the prisoner to the place of execution, the idiot before mentioned from excess of folly or presumption, not knowing that (*verse*)—"to seek an opinion contrary to that of a king (tyrant), is to wash your hands in your own blood," arrived on an elephant and taking the prisoner from that fatal place and mounting him on his elephant called out,—"any one who will join and support me let him follow us ,"—two or three hundred musketeers of his own Risala therefore joined him, and altogether they took the road to Seringapatam (Seringaputtun). As soon as this had taken place, certain persons who were his enemies, and who during the whole of his life, had been seeking epportunities to effect his destruction, represented this circumstance to the Sultan, the reverse of what was intended, as that Muhammad Ali had rebelliously taken the criminal and was proceeding to the port of Cochin, and there was no doubt but from that place he would proceed to Bombay, and that in such circumstances to allow him to remain alive, was in fact to give up the whole of his kingdom and authority.

Hearing this story, the Sultan despatched horse and foot to trace his steps, while he himself, troubled and agitated, mounted his horse and followed them , and Syyad Hamid, an officer from Arkat, a man of great stature, and strength, and of great abilities, was sent on in advance with Ghazi Khan to compel him to return. These two officers, therefore, with a large body of troops pressed on and overtook and surrounded him on a hill, about four *kos* from the encampment of the victorious army , and with soft words and threats brought him round to the right path

As the foolish fugitive was now ashamed of his conduct, he dismounted from his elephant and stood alone, when the Sipahdar, or commander before mentioned, laid hold on his hands and he with the criminal doomed to death, and the soldiers who had followed them, were presented by him to the Sultan, who without any delay ordered Kasim to be impaled and the commandant to be heavily ironed and placed in a covered palankin and despatched to Seringapatam.

The Sultan after this returned to his tent, and to punish the contumacy of the men who had followed the commandant, some were put to death, and some after having their hands and noses cut off were turned out of the camp. These poor men, who had been punished for their companionship with the prisoner in irons, followed him for two stages, crying out to him, "Oh thou vile incendiary, thou art the cause of our ruin, our hands and noses have been sacrificed to our senseless love of thee."

When these cries reached the ears of the commandant, his feeings of honour and compassion were violenty affected, but he repressed his agitation as best he could until night, and at mid-night having performed his ablutionary duties he cut out his tongue, or rather drew it out by the root, and like a lamp at the approach of morning, died. Some say that he had a diamond ring on his finger, and that having taken out the diamond and rubbed it on a stone, he swallowed it and so died.[16] Some one found the date of his death in the following words *Rukn-i daulat biuftad.* The prop or pillar of the state is fallen, 1198 Hijri.

When the people of his escort the next morning found him dead in the palankin, they took him up and returned with him and his horses to the presence, and all the furniture and move-ables of his house were one by one examined by the Sultan. Among the articles was a small box, locked and on its being opened and examined, several letters from English officers were found, written and sent to him during the expedition to the Payanghat to induce him to join them, and promising him in that event large Jaigirs, &c. which letters, although that faithful servant had answered by scornfully rejoicing their offers, still, from his extreme simplicity he had neglected to tear up,—these, by accident passed under the angry inspection of the Sultan and when therefore the contents were explained, they became, or were made, the grounds of obloquy and reproach and the suspicion which had been entertained of his disaffection and treachery was confirmed.

The Sultan, therefore, gave orders that the commandant's corpse should be dragged outside the camp and there left, and his sons were made the Sultan's slaves, and his Khadima or wife, was given as a wife to one of his (the Sultan's) slaves, a worthy and excellent man, who kept her in respectablity and honour to her death, and never addressed her by any other name than mother, and indeed treated her in every respect as if he had been her son.

The mother of the Sultan on hearing of these events, which arose entirely from misunderstanding, was much grieved, and

[16] Colonel Marriott's copy says his grateful master assisted him in his departure for the next world, by the administration of a dose of poison.

cursed the hasty anger of her son, and sent for his, the commandant's, widow who resided at Seringapatam to live with her in the Harem Sera, or Seraglio.

The deceased commandant, although a man of blood, and very intemperate, still, was universally known for his liberality and generous support of the poor, and monthly and yearly forty or fifty Fakirs, or religious medicants, spread their carpets in his tents, and resided there, and often elephants, palankins and horses presented to him by the Nawab, were given away by him in charity to these men to that extent, that the deceased Nawab, knowing his liberality, frequently repurchased them from them, and when occasion required bestowed them again in presents on the commandant. The fame of his generosity to the poor extended so far, that whenever a party of these religious beggars assembled at the gate of the palace, calling out for charity, Hydar Ali was accustomed to send word to them to go to that low or vulgar fellow, (meaning the commandant), and he, pleased beyond measure at the compliment, gave up to them whatever he had of money, plate, utensils, clothes, &c.

After his death, when his property was examined in his own chest, they found nothing but some old clothes, a religious mendicant's cap, and a coat or frock presented to him by Amin Sahib a Mushaikh of Arkat, who was his Murshud, or spiritual guide, and forty cash or copper coins with the impression of an elephant upon them. But to return :—After these events, the Sultan having consigned the charge of the forts of that quarter to the most faithful and distinguished men among his servants, Budruzaman Khan, who left the force of Syyad Sahib after the battle of Cuddalore,[17] which circumstance will be mentioned hereafter, was now summoned by the Sultan, and appointed to the Foujdari and government of the district of Nagar, and the Sultan then marched towards Coorg, when at this period arrived Sadleir, Colonel Dallas &c, on the part of the governor of the port of Madras, in order to renew and confirm the relations of peace,[18] and, with expressions of friendship and regard, they presented rich dresses, and a profusion of gold and jewels, to the servants of the Sultan ; and with well weighed words or explanations cleared away the dust of enmity from the mind of the Sultan , after therefore the preliminary arrangement of the conditions of peace, and amity, and the accomplishment of their objec-objects, they with Abdul Wahab Khan, (who had been a prisoner in Seringapatam), and certain European prisoners returned to Madras

The governors of the forts and districts in the territories of each of the opposing nations were now recalled.

[17] Some words left out in all the MSS here ; but this appears the meaning as they stand.

[18] *dar sadad.*

The Sultan's mind being now set at ease by the establishment of peace, he determined to revisit has capital, and he therefore marched and encamped with all his retinue and army in the vicinity of the Bul district, and having named that fort Munzirabad, he gave it in charge to a brave officer as governor, and selected and appointed Zain-al-Abedin Mehdivi, who was a favourite servant, to the entire government of Coorg, and gave him strict orders to displace, imprison, and punish all the rebellious and seditious people of that district; and the capital of that Suba, which was before called Markera, was named Zaffarabad.[19] The Sultan after this dismissed him, and about the conclusion of the year, at a fortunate hour entered his capital Seringapatam On this occasion the chiefs and nobility, such as the Sadaut and religious chiefs, according to custom, went out of the city to meet him, and had the honour to kiss the victorious stirrup, they being also received with distinguished marks of favour

When the kingly throne became enlightened by the resplendent countenance of that sun of the firmament of victory, (the Sultan), he addressed himself seriously to the regulation of the country, his army and all the departments depending on his state, and revised and altered the rules and principles of the protection and defence of his kingdom after a new form :—for instance, in former days, that is in the time of the deceased Nawab, the exercises and manoeuvres of the regular troops were arranged and performed, and the word given according to the Fench system of military evolution or tactics,—but, now, the Sultan drawing the pen of examination or correction through that system, with the advice of Zain-al-Abedin Shustri, (the brother of Abul Kasim Khan, Hydarabadi, who was also honoured with the title of Mir Alam Shustri), he changed the military code of regulations and altered the technical terms or words of command, above mentioned, (the French), to words of the Persian and Turkish languages; and a separate treatise called Futtah al Mujahidin,[20] was written by Zain-al Abedin and his system was confirmed. From the regular infantry, five thousand men being selected, they were named a Kushun, and the officer commanding that body was called a Sipahdar In each Kushun were four Risaladars or colonels of infantry, and one of cavalry, and under the orders of each Risaldar or colonel, were ten Jowkdars or captains, and on that scale or proportion one hundred men being a Jowk, the chief of them was called a Jowkdar, every Jowk or company included two Sur Kheil, ten Jemadars, and ten Duffadars. —In the regiments of troops or regular horse,[21] which

[19] The abode of victory

[20] *Fateh u'l mujahidin.* (Persian)

[21] Teepdar, equivalent to Risaldar, and Teep Risala, according to Kirkpatrick.

were formed and appointed after the manner of the Europeans, the Teepdar and Subadar who, in the French and English languages are called major and adjutant, were called Youzdar and Nakib In distinction to the Nakib of the Kushun and Risala, he, who was called Yussakchi[22] had his name changed to Shurbushurn. The officer commanding three or four Teeps, (regiments of cavalry), was called Mokubdar. In this mode he invented new terms in all departments as will be succinctly mentioned hereafter.

The Shustri before mentioned was now appointed to command the Kushun of the deceased commandant, and after some time he was known to every body by the sobriquet or nick name, of "Chup gir Dumuk"[23]—"shoulder, or carry arms"

About this time the Bar or regular infantry, Kutcheri, was called the Jysh Kutcheri;[24] the troop or regular horse Kutcheri, the Uskeri Kutcheri; and the Bundeh, or Slave Kutcheri, was called the Asad illahi Kutcheri.

[22] Adjutant or Brigade major, there is much confusion in this detail in all the copies.

[23] *Chup gir dumuk* (Persian)

[24] The Kutcheri consisted of from five to six Kushuns or Brigades. The word originally appears to have been applied to a hall of audience.

CHAPTER III

An account of the operations of Mir Moinuddin, otherwise called Syyad Sahib, the Sipahsalar of the Sultan in the Payanghat province, and a description of the battles fought between Syyad, the French, and the English troops, and his return to the presence, also, the conclusion of peace in the same year, that is to say, the year 1197 Hijri, or A D 1782.

When the Sultan marched towards Nagar, Syyad Sahib, with his own dicision of troops, was encamped on the Walpundul river, and while there, spies brought intelligence, that Colonel Lang with his force had proceeded suddenly by forced marches from Trichinopoly, with the intention of taking possession of Karur and Dindigul

The moment the Syyad received this information he despatched Budruzaman Khan, with all the musketeers and artillery in advance, to oppose him, while he himself followed after him with the rest of his troops. When, however, the above mentioned Khan had arrived at Tarwar Palah, Osman Khan Turin, the Governor of the fort of Karur, notwithstanding he had a very strong garrison, and abundance of warlike stores, resigning his courage and confidence, gave up the fort to the above mentioned Colonel, and he himself went and joined Roshan Khan and Sripat Rao, who had been appointed to reduce the rebellious Naimars. The Colonel, in the mean time, leaving a garrison in this fort, marched on and laid seige to the small fort of Arawa Kurchi, and was using his best endeavours to take it, when the Khan above-mentioned arrived in his neighbourhood, and encamped on this side the Amaravati river.[25] The Colonel, as soon as he was aware of the arrival of the victorious army, left his batteries and encamped on the opposite bank of the said river. The next day, however, seeing the small number of the Sultan's troops, he gave up the idea of attacking them, and recommenced the siege of the fort; repaired his batteries, and renewed his fire on the walls. The Khan, therefore, having consulted his Risaldars, selected a certain Jowkdar, named Kamruddin, and his Jowk or company, completely armed, and appointed him Killadar, or Governor; and despatched him at night to the fort under the escort of the Risala of Himat Khan Bukhturi, (the nephew of Payinda Khan), and the Risala of Babar Ali Beg, with orders to attack the enemy. As soon as these Risaldars received their orders, they advanced with the greatest bravery and attacking the advanced or outlying pickets of the British troops in flank,

[25] The Mysore side, apparently.

and dispersing them, they escorted the Jowkdar and his company to the fort and then returned. The Colonel, the next morning, finding a reinforcement had reached the fort, in the greatest rage imaginable, ordered his artillery and musketeers to fire at a particular part of the fort, from the morning until midday; at which time, the wall on one face being levelled with the ground, his troops made an assault.

The garrison, notwithstanding they bravely exerted themselves to beat back the storming party, and for two or three hours handled their arms manfully; still, as the hand of death was striking the drum of their defeat and destruction behind them, they all lost their lives.

The English troops victorious, therefore, after taking possession of the fort, turned their faces towards the attack of the Khan's camp; the Jowkdar, however, who has been before mentioned, having crept out by a water drain, escaped and joined that force. The Khan, now finding his troops unable to cope with, or oppose the English army, retired by a night march to the vicinity of Dharapur.

Roshan Khan, however, and the before mentioned Rao, remained hovering round the English army, making Kuzzak, or desultory attacks, when Syyad Sahib arrived,[26] and after a period of five or six days, and the treachery of Osman Khan Turin, the Killadar of Karur, being established, he was impaled. The troops were now formed to attack the English army, when a letter from Monsieur Bussy, the commander-in-chief of the French army, arrived, stating that the whole of the English army had advanced to the vicinity of Cuddalore, to give battle and the Khan, with his force, was to return, and after the defeat of their proud enemy, they would together proceed to make all necessary arrangements in the quarter in which he then was. Syyad Sahib, therefore, immediately on receipt of this letter, appointed his own Dustadars, (colonels or generals of cavalry[27]), to remain behind, giving them strict orders that to the utmost of their ability, they should prevent the soldiers of the enemy from plundering the peasantry and inhabitants of that quarter; and he himself marched by the route of Tatingar Putti, to Totum Musli, and there halted one day, when his spies brought him intelligence that a great quantity of stores and provisions belonging to the English army, were deposited in the fort of Kurtullum, and that it was guarded by a few foot soldiers only.

The Khan, therefore, accompanied by the Risalas of infantry alone, marched and commenced the siege of this fort;—it happened however that the site of the fort was surrounded by

[26] This relates to the former passage regarding Syyad Sahib

[27] A Dusta is, or was formerly, a body of twelve thousand horse; latterly, however, the term was applied to a much smaller number by Tipu

the running streams of the river Kaveri, and the irrigated fields near it were deep mud and covered with green crops The garrison, which consisted of not more than twenty or thirty men, withstood gallantly the multitude of their assailants, and prevented their effecting an entrance, and indeed exerted themselves with such energy in the repulse of their enemies, that the Syyad after attacking and fighting the whole day returned at night to his encampment, and appointed a number of Kuzzaks to watch the fort, for this reason, that the next morning he intended to attack with artillery and to carry ladders with him, and after taking the fort to put the English garrison to the sword, in revenge for the loss of his men slain in the fort of Arawa Kurchi.

The garrison, however, not thinking themselves safe, the same night taking what articles they could with them, and burning the rest, marched off to Trichinopoly, which was distant about five fursungs, or nearly eighteen miles. The Syyad, therefore, now marched from that place and proceeded to Cuddalore by the route of Durwachal, or Wardachal, and the Khan before mentioned, with the artillery and Risalas, was despatched to the fort (of Cuddalore), to the aid of M. Bussy, while he himself (the Syyad) with the remaining horse and foot marched towards Selimbur.[28]

But to return : The English army under the command of General Stuart, by forced marches, arrived by the route of Pondicheri, and Bagore, and encamped on the river Kurth, on the western side of the fort of Cuddalore

The French at this time kept five hundred men with twelve guns, equipped after the manner of the English, in readiness as an advanced picket,[29] and the Hydari Risalas agreeably to the orders of the Khan, were posted on the right of the French and strengthened their position there by raising batteries for their support. After a period of three days the English General, during the night, took possession of a hill in front of these bodies of French and Mysorians, posted guns on it, and made all ready to open his fire, when very early next morning, the commander of a ship which had arrived from Madras, fired three shots at the fort, and the men in the batteries left them to see the ship[30] and what she was about to do ;—at this period the fire of the guns from the hill suddenly opened one after another The English regiments, (European), marched to attack those of the French, and the battalions of Sipahees also marched to attack Hydar's Risalas and had arrived very near ;—In this situation of affairs the French being formed, retired towards the fort leaving their guns ; and the Mysore Risalas not having time to withdraw their guns, and

[28] Called Chillumbrum by the English.

[29] *Manghalay* signifies the forehead in Turkish—also an advance guard

[30] The sight.

not waiting until they received orders from their commanding officers, turned their faces towards the sea and took to flight.

A certain Bahadur Khan Risaldar and Babar Ali Beg, however, with the greatest gallantry and presence of mind, retired facing the enemy, taking with them the guns of their own Risalas, and brought them to the ditch or glacis of the fort, and there halted.

The English troops, therefore, took the batteries and remained conquerors. In these circumstances the commander-in-chief of the French troops assembled fifteen hundred Frenchmen, without artillery, and placed under the command of Monsieur Dupleix and Colonel Ambeau, (perhaps Rochambeau) to repal the English :—As soon, therefore, as the French troops received their orders, they in excellent order, their arms carried and their line well formed, marched and stepping out boldly entered the field of battle.

The English European troops, who amounted in all to three or four thousand men, with their ranks closed, by a sharp cannonade killed a great many of the French, but the French officers without flinching, advanced close to their enemies and poured into their ranks a most destructive fire, and for one Pher, or more than two hours, the battle raged unremittingly, for as soon as the brave fellows had done what they could with their fire, they rushed on and engaged hand to hand, and shoulder to shoulder with their bayonets. On both sides, therefore, such a furious struggle ensued, that at seeing it, the hearts of the clouds of heaven became water, and from the concussion of the fierce charges of these iron men the earth shook to its centre.

Time, that tyrant, hard hearted as he is, at seeing the killed in this hard fought battle, shed showers of tears, and Behram (Mars), the blood drinker, from fear at the blood shed by these valorous men, fled to the fifth blue fortress of the skies, (the fifth heaven). For two hours, therefore, during this mortal strife, those present in the battle, saw and heard nothing but the smoke and thunder of the guns and musketery , but at length the English European troops lost all power to keep their ground, and they, therefore, retreated.

At this conjuncture, the Karnatic battalions (the Madras native regiments)[31] formed up quickly from the right and left, and covered the backs of the European soldiers[32] with their own bodies and gained the day, for they most gallantly drove the

[31] The translator regrets much that he has no means of ascertaining the number of the Madras native regiments, who this nobly distinguished themselves.

[32] The Colonel of one of the retiring regiments is said to have expressed his surprise at the unsteadiness of his men, they being as he said all *tried* men, that is, men tried at the Old Bailey.

French before them. The French troops therefore, of whom only five or six hundred remained, reareated and gained the fort. At this time one thousand Frenchmen, who in daring pride and intrepidity carried their heads to the skies, formed and advanced from the fort to repeal their adversaries, when at this critical moment, the English troops retired to their ground of encampment, and the battle was left for the decision of the next day.

The French troops halted and bivouacked at about the distance of an arrow shot from the fort After two or three days, during which the English were marking out or raising batteries, and the French were occupied in endeavours to frustrate their plans, a treaty of peace which had been made between the French and English governments in Europe, arrived :—the two armies, the French and English, now, therefore became one, and all enmity and contention ceased. The officers of both armies met and ate, and drank wine with each other at the same table. At the same time, therefore, by the mediation of the French and with the consent of Muhammad Ali Khan, Suraj ud Dowla, a treaty of peace and friendship was established between the Sultan and the English.

But to return : Badruzaman Khan, and Syyad Sahib, having effected a junction, marched towards Turwadi, but after the conclusion of peace, with the permission of the Commander-in-chief of the French army, they proceeded onwards and encamped near Bilpur. After halting there a month, they again marched and encamped on the river Walpundul, on account of the abundance of forage there to be obtained. One day however, while halting at this place, a storm suddenly arose at an unseasonable period, and fell with great violence on the Hydari camp, and the river swelling at the same time carried away and destroyed the property of the merchants and poor people of the camp, and many men and women were carried by the force of the stream to the sea and drowned. Most also of the merchants and artizans of the camp were reduced to poverty—the camp, therefore, was immediately changed, and the troops marched and encamped to the northward of Arni. At this place a Risaldar named Hari Singh was assassinated by his own soldiers in some dispute regarding their pay, and from this place also Badruzaman Khan proceeded to the presence.

During this period Muhammad Morad, the civil governor of Rai Vellore, after having collected about sixty or seventy harse, and two or three hundred foot, made excursions on the country surrounding, to the distance of six or seven *kos* (ten or eleven miles), and exacted supplies of provisions from the Hydari and Sultani districts, (those of Mysore) and extending the hand of devastation, frequently set fire to the houses and habitations of the poor inhabitants, and reduced them and the produce of their fields and gardens to ashes. It happened one day that he made a forced march by the route of Kiriatum, with the intention to attack the fort of Sautgarh, and at night having by great exertions climbed up one side of the mountain, to the top, arrived at the gate of the fort It happened at that time that the wife of a foot soldier of the garrison, being about to cook her morning meal, was standing on the wall pouring out the water in which she had washed her rice, and seeing the ranks of the assailants advancing, set up cries of "they are come,"—"they are come," and immediately threw the vessel containing the rice, on their heads. The sleeping garrison at this, awaking and springing up from their slothful sulmbers, immediately seized their arms and with the bow, musket rifle and rocket, steadily opposed the storming party, so effectually indeed, that the governor before mentioned being foiled, was obliged to take to flight, and arrived a fugitive at Belinjpur, but as these happened to be a picket or outpost of the troops of Shah Murad Risaldar, (the military commandant of that quarter), stationed in a temple of the town, they immediately attacked him, and he was abliged to retire from thence also, but not until he had plundered the town and taken much spoil. He however halted for a short time in the river Belinjpur,[33] when the Risaldar above mentioned, who was stationed near Ambar Garh hearing the vollies of musketry immediately got his men ready, and following the footsteps of the officer before mentioned, (Muhammad Murad), rapidly advanced, overtook and surrounded him in the bed of the river, and in one vigorous attack put the whole of his soldiers to the sword, taking all the property they had plundered to his own charge and keeping.

The unlucky Muhammad Murad, therefore, with only fifteen or twenty horse, returned and entered his fort, (Rai Vellore).

At this time an order from the presence was issued directing that the country of the Payanghat should be delivered up to the English, also detailing the terms of the treaty of peace, and recalling Syyad Sahib In obedience to this Firman therefore, all the governors of forts, collectors of revenue, &c of parts of that country, (the Payanghat), were recalled, and some of the strong hill forts with the fortress of Alumpunah of the Suba of Arkat, which had been restored and repaired, were again dismantled and broken down, and the Syyad with all his troops and followers having crossed the Ghat of Chungum, arrived at Tripatur, and from that by the route of Hulidrug and Punglur joined the Sultan. at this period the address and ability manifested by Mir Sadik in the intelligence department, during his official duties as Kotwal of Arkat, and of the army;—having well pleased the Sultan, he was at once raised to the dignity of Sahib Dewan, (Prime

[33] Written in some copies Berinjpur.

Minister). At this period also, ambassadors arrived at the presence, with letters and presents of great value from the chiefs of Poona, and the Nizam of Hydarabad, containing congratulations on the Sultan's accession to the throne, and (the former) requiring him to send the horse shoe[34] tribute in arrears for two years, and these persons having discharged their commissions, they demanded the Chouth or fourth of his revenue.

At this demand, the world-conquering Sultan, being exceedingly excited, addressed the ambassador to the following effect. "Do you not know that our deceased father, may his sins be forgiven, spent all the money laid up in his treasury, with the revenue of his kingdom for three years in the expedition or war of the Payanghat,[35] and that by the advice, and at the instigation of your governments (the Mahrattas and Nizam) having exerted himself faithfully and nobly in conquering that country, he stepped from the throne of his world to that of the next?—that with all this exertion, you notwithstanding your engagements, to assist him, gave him no aid whatever, as by your treaties you were bound to have done.

"Nevertheless, by the favour and blessing of the Almighty, and by the fortune of our victirious arms, in all this time we have not been compelled to seek the indulgence or favour of any one, little or great;—for the mighty and true giver of victory made us conquerors in every battle. —After the death also of Ali Hezrat (Hydar), the traitor Iyaz, the slave of our house, who had risen to great honour by the kingly benefits and favours he had received.—*Verse*—"Too much kindness from a master is the enemy of a servant." —"Excessive rain is as bad as lightning to the crops or harvest." —From the impurity of his wicked disposition determined to destroy the foundations of the prosperity of his patron and master as quickly as he could, and his head being filled with the vapours of pride, from his possession of money, jewels, rank and dignity, he gave up all the towns, villages and forts in his charge to the English. Notwithstanding this, by the blessing of God, with very little labour that country has been all reconquered by us and the troops of the enemy destroyed. This is well known to the world at large. You will, therefore, tell your masters that at present we have no treasury (money) that we should pay the horse-shoe tribute, but that we have a number of guns and muskets inherited from our pardoned father (Hazruti Marhum) and they are ready at their service However, after the settlement and regulation of this country, orders will be given to the treasurers of the Khodadad to send the customary amount payable to you." After this address to the ambassadors, containing rules and instructions, for their guidance; from motives

[34] *n'al bahay.*

[35] Coast of Coromandel.

of policy and precaution, he despatched a certain Muhammad Osman, a servant of the late Nawab, a discreet person well acquainted with the forms of courtesy and the etiquette of society, to Poona, with money and valuables, and certain curiosities from the country of the English, plundered by his troops in the province of the Karnatak, merely as a lesson or warning.

CHAPTER IV

The marriage of Burhanuddin, the most worthy of the sons of Lalamea (who was the brother-in-law of the Sultan, and slain at the battle of Churkuli), with the daughter of Budruzaman Khan, the Foujdar of Nagar, and his appointment and mission to conquer the Hill Fort of Nurgunda—also the insubordinate conduct of the Chief of Punganur, and the appointment of certain kushuns, or brigades, to punish and reduce him to subjection—also the repair of the Fort of Ruhmaun Garh—Occurrences of the year 1198, Hijri—A D 1783.

After the Sultan had arrived at his capital, and had completed his arrangements for the regulation of his army and kingdom, his enlightened mind determined on the celebration of the nuptials of Burhanuddin Khan, and by the counsel and advice of his ministers and chief officers, he selected the lady of the Serai of nobility and virtue, the vergin daughter of Badruzaman Khan, Nayut, Subadar of the district of Nagar—a man whose loyalty was well known to,and appreciated by the Sultan ; and the Khan was therefore summoned from his government at Nagar. When therefore the Khan arrived at the foot of the throne, he was honoured with princely gifts, and apprised of the views and intentions of the Sultan, and the Khan seeing opposition to this commands would involve his detriment and disgrace, and notwithstanding his wife and children were averse to the marriage, he determined to agree to the Sultan's proposition The officers consequently who had the charge of preparing the banquet, and on whom devolved the responsibility of the royal feast, according to the orders received by them, arrayed the joyful banquet, and in a very short time by the performance of the established customs of felicitation and invitaton, obtained the approbation of the Sultan ; at that time the spies and newswriters on the banks of the Tungabhadra river, wrote to the Sultan, that most of the tributaries of the kingdom of Mysore were disaffected and ready to break out in open rebellion, and that they had put forth the hand of violence from the sleeve of rancour and infidelity, and that their cruelty and oppression had caused great misery, to the whole of the Sultan's subjects ; and not only that, but from the vice of their dispositions they intended ulterior mischief, as for instance, Kalia Desye, that is, the chief of Nargunda had opened the doors of fraud and treachery on the peasantry of the country, and the sighs and complaints of the poor and afflicted had ascended to the heavens—that he, day by day advanced his foot beyond the limit of his ability, and like the Punganur Poligar, moved by the devil, had lighted up the fire of revolt and rebellion —that he had neglected to discharge the Paishkush or tribute due to the Sultan for two years, and had most insolently attacked the Fort of Sudam, a dependency of the Sirkar of Kurum Gunda, and had plundered the towns belonging to that fort,—that he had several times attacked the said fort. and had made many of the officers or dependents of the Sultan drink the cup of martyrdom,—also that the Poligar of Madanapalli had joined him heart and hand, and was also the cause of great tumult and disturbance

At hearing this news, the fire of the Sultan's wrath flamed high, and considering the safety and comfort of his subjects as inseparable from his honour and responsibility, he immediately dispatched Syyad Ghaffar, the Sipahadar with his Kushun or brigade to Nargunda, to ascertain the state of affairs there; the Sipahdar therefore marched, and having after many stages arrived there, soon obtained a perfect knowledge of the whole affair. It appeared certain that this man (the Chief of Nargunda) devoted to villainy, was instigated and aided in his rebellion by Parasuram the Chief of Mirch, whose son was bethrothed to his daughter, and that being vain and conceited at this connexion, he had raised his head to the clouds and was possessed with the vain desire to be the ruler of the districts, lying between the rivers Kishna and Tungabhadra, and hearing of the arrival of the Sultan's troops, from the natural malignity of his disposition took the path of ingratitude, and advanced to oppose them The Sipahdar above mentioned on discovering his intention, and while he was selecting a secure position for his troops, wrote to the Sultan acquaint him with these circumstances.

Burhanuddin, the Sipahsalar, therefore, with five thousand horse and three Kushuns, the Sipahdars of which were Syyad Hamid Shaikh Onsar, and Ahmed Beg, was appointed and marched to take the fort, and make the rebellious chief a prisoner. —Shaikh Omr the Sipahdar, also with a Kushun two thousand irregular foot, (Ahsham) and six guns was appointed to root out the Poligars of Punganur and Madanapalli.

When the said Shaikh Omr marching by Panglur, and Devanhalli, arrived near the mountainous district of Gywar, which lies to the east-ward of Nandi Drug, and encamped there, he heard from some of the chief landholders and government guards of the roads and passes,[36] that among these mountains was one very high and on its sumit a wide plain, that it possessed a fountain or reservoir of water, the depth of which could not be fathomed, by the line of science that on this mountain was the foundation of walls built with stone, and that they appeared to have been in old time a fort but long since in ruins—that if the walls were rebuilt, they would afford a strong defence and refuge to the

[36] *Minwar* persons who receive a stipulated allowance for the care and protection of the roads and mountain passes

Sultan's troops, and that a force stationed here would undoubtedly ensure the obedience of the country in the neighbourhood. The Sipahdar, therefore, with some of his officers and those who made this statement went up the mountain and examined the place and much admired it, and then wrote a description of the mountain and the representations of the friendly people of that district to the presence. He then marched on, and encamped in the neighbourhood of Punganur, and notwithstanding he strove to advise and guide the chief, he still rebelliously advanced to oppose him, and with twelve thousand foot occupied the posts on his route, ready for action In consequence, in the neighbourhood of Rama Samudram, a town on his frontier, a very sanguinary battle was fought between the two parties. The trops of the Sultan, however, like lightening daily burned up the harvest of the infidel array, and with the bayonet, musket, and the keen sword, gashed the heads and breasts of their misguided opponents.

At length the brave Sipahdar in one attack with his sword cut down the commander of the enemy's troops, and immediately separated his head from his body , and the infidels seeking this, lost the footing of stability and confidence, and turned their faces to flight, and they made the Hill Fort of Bhui Kunda, which is surrounded by a dense and impenetrable forest, their place of refuge.

The Sultan's troops having plundered and destroyed all in their way, and taking the fort of Rama Samudram at one assault, marched towards the said Kunda, and after the labours of five days that fort was also taken from the enemy, and the Sipahdar and his Kushun obtained great honour and having thus defeated the infidels at all points they marched on. The Poligar of Punganur whose name was Shunkh Rayel or Rawul,[37] hearing of the defeat of his troops, and being in great trepidation, gave up the fort of Punganur to his confidential servants, and sought refuge on the top of the mountain of Awul Pilly, four *kos* distant from the above town and surrounded by a fearfully thick forest, where he collected together three or four thousand brave foot soldiers.

When the Sipahdar had defeated the Infidels he pursued them, and besieged the fort of Punganur, occupying himself in opening trenches and approaches, and raising batteries, and in a very short time having battered down the walls by the fire from his guns took it, and then committing it to the charge of his own brave troops, he like a raging lion turned his face again to the field of battle, that is to the conquest of the Hill Fort before mentioned, but as this hill was surrounded by a frightful desert, and as the density of this forest was such, that no living creature

[37] The ancient Kuchwasa Rajput chiefs of the eastern part of Gujarat, the brothers or relations of the Rana Chitore or rather Udaipur, were called Rawul.

could pass through the trees and bushes without the greatest difficulty and danger ,—and, moreover, as the enemy had occupied the roads or paths on all sides, and had built towers from which they were ready to discharge their arrows and musketry, and make a vigorous defence , the Sipahdar during a month, and after the greatest labour and exertion, was unable to get even a glimpse of the cheek of the object of his desires (that is he made no progress), and on account of the insufficiency of his force, being without resource, he addressed a letter to the Presence and requested assistance. A Sipahdar of the name of Imam Khan with his Kushun was therefore appointed to his aid On the arrival there of the Khan above mentioned, both the Sipahdars consulted, and under the guidance of some of the inhabitants of that part of the country, they entered the forest or jungle on two sides, and carried death and destruction on the enemy, and they being defeated and dispersed, the hill was surrounded , and after incredible exertions for seventy days, the fort was taken The Poligar, however, with a number of his men previous to this, avoiding the conflict, had fled and sought refuge in the district of the Poligar of Chitore, and thereby escaped the vengeance of the Sultan's troops In about two or three months, the two forts of the fugitive Poligar and all his dependencies were taken, and committed to the charge of the able servants of the presence, and the two Sipahdars having returned, and being admitted to an audience of the Sultan, all the plunder and the elephants and camels were passed in review under his own inspection ; and the Sipahdars were honoured by the receipt of royal presents and favours.

As the description of the mountain of Gywar had been previously received from the Sipahdar by the Sultan, he determined at this time to inspect the hill himself, and therefore with his body guard,[38] certain of his friends, and the infantry of the guard, he proceeded to Pungalur, and a week after to the hill, and having examined it, as he was well pleased with its situation, the pioneers, able stone-masons, and builders, were appointed to raise the walls and buildings of a fort, which was named Rahman Garh.

Returning from this place, he honoured Nandi Garh with a visit, and named it Gurdun Shukoh,[39] or the Terror of the World. The Sultan thence proceeded to Devanhalli, and as that town was the place of his birth —*verse*—"The earth of one's own country is better than the throne of Solomon"—that distinguished town, therefore, was named Yusufabad, and a faithful servant was left in charge of the fort, and strict orders were given to him to repair the walls and buildings with stone and mortar,

[38] Julow.

[39] *Gardun shukoh.* (Persian).

and thence by pleasant easy stages, in one month and fifteen days the Sultan returned to his capital

It is proper to mention here, that, as the Poligar of Punganur, by his evil fortune, according to the saying—*verse*—"If thou contendest with thy Lord and Master,"—"wert thou the heavens thou wouldest be turned upside down,—had been severely punished by the Sultan's victorious troops, and was now wandering in the desert of disgrace and degradation, so in the same way the Poligar of Madan Palli (Madanapalli) not well considering his future prospects, followed the same path, and his territories were also added to those of the Sultan.

CHAPTER V

An account of the conquest of the Mountain Fort of Nargunda by the brave exertions of Kamruddin Khan, and his return to the presence, with other events of the same year, A D 1784

As soon as Burhanuddin, the Sipahsalar or commander-in-chief, had taken leave of the Sultan, he marched by Chitaldrug and Sanur, and joined Syyad Ghuffar the Sipahdar in the vicinity of Dharwar, and having committed the charge of his right and left wings to his bravest officers, he encamped in the vicinity of the hill fort of Nargunda, and apprized the mountain chief of his arrival, to take possession of that fort, and also sent word to him by messengers that if he was desirous to preserve his country and property, he should immediately quit the fort, and deliver it over to a Killadar appointed by the Sultan, and then by manifestations of regret for his misconduct enlighten the forehead of his obedience, and by employing Burhanuddin's mediation, and every influence, and setting forth his loyalty, his districts and property might be restored to him—that otherwise he might be certain he would give his life gratuitously to the lower regions.[40] As he Kamruddin however received a scornful and bitter answer to this proposition, the fire of his pride and anger flamed violently, and he marched on and encamped on a river running south-west from the mountain, but at the distance of seven or eight miles, and issued orders to the faithful Sipahdars, that is to Syyad Hamid and Syyad Ghaffar to advance, and they with great bravery moved on and enclosed the mountain in a circle, and the infantry like mountain lions ascended and commenced the attack of the fort on all sides, and by the fire of musketry and artillery battered down the walls.

The mountain chief was however a brave man, and his troops often sallied forth, and attacked the batteries, and killed many of those defending them. As an example of their courage, one night finding an opportunity, a small but brave detachment of the garrison descended from the top of the mountain and attacked the pickets of the Sipahsalar's army, stationed at the foot of the mountain, so vigorously, that they killed the Bakshi, Salabat Khan, and two hundred horse The gallant Sipahdars, notwithstanding their increasing exertions to take this hill fort, still made no progress, and several assaults were made but without success. As this happened to be the period of the hot season, the want of water was felt to that degree, that water-carriers brought water from the river on which the army was encamped,

[40] *Mamalik nairan.*

on bullocks and camels to the batteries at the foot of the mountain, and on account of the distance, also, in time of need the men in the batteries could receive no succour from the army. Notwithstanding this, the experienced Sipahdars and the officers of the Ahsham or irregular infantry, exerted themselves in the most zealous and honourable manner, and carried on the batteries to the very foot of the walls The chief or Poligar of the fort, therefore, being alarmed for the result, despatched on account of the critical situation of his affairs to the chief of Mirch, and to the Poona authorities, and requested their aid

The Mirch chief accordingly sent five thousand horse to his assistance As this body of horse, however, had encamped on a river, swelled by the rains, and were waiting for a force of ten thousand horse which had been despatched from Puna (Poona) also to the aid of the chief of Nargunda, the Sipahsalar fearing the strength of so large a force of the enemy, wrote a detailed account of their movements to the Presence The Sultan's ambassadors who were stationed at Puna (Poona) also made him acquainted with these circumstances. The Sultan, therefore, despatched orders to Kamruddin Khan, directing him to proceed with his force to the aid of the Sipahsalar Burhanuddin to oppose the Mahratta horse and to take the fort.

It is proper, however, here to mention that Muhammad Pir Zadah, the son-in-law of Halim Khan, the chief of Kirpa, finding an opportunity and having by the pledge of valuable jewels obtained a large sum of money, assembled a body of four or five hundred horse and two thousand foot and having made an agreement with the English of Mutchli Bandar (Masulipatam), and taking with him a battalion and two guns from Kuttur, he determined on attempting the re-conquest of the districts of Kirpa, and the reduction of the castles and forts of that country. He therefore advanced and placed a garrison in the fort of Kuhmam, and slaying and plundering proceeded to Budweil (Badvel). A party of infantry belonging to the Sultan were stationed in that fort, but they having been made favourable by bribery, with their permission or connivance he was allowed to send a party of his own men into the fort, and then he marched on to Kirpa At this time Kamruddin Khan, by the orders of the Sultan arrived in that neighbourhood, and in consequence in the vicinity of Phul Mamra, a severe battle was fought between the two parties which continued vigorously contested from the morning to midday, and the brave men on both sides exerted themselves with the utmost gallantry. At length the Khan, Kamruddin, determined to deceive and circumvent his enemies ; and of a sudden retired with his troops from before them and concealed himself in a wood, in front of which was a tank full of water, and a small hill in the midst of the tank, and here he remained looking out for opportunities. The Syyad before mentioned, therefore, giving himself great credit for the victory he had achieved, halted and encamped on the same spot of ground, and the English officer commanding the battalion, also discharging all apprehensions of his enemies from his mind, and flattering himself they had no power to oppose his attack and that they had fled, encamped in the rear of the Syyad's force. When, therefore, two or three hours after this period, the Syyad's cavalry unarmed mounted their horses without saddles, and took them to the tank to water them, and were each occupied with his own business, of a sudden, the Kuzzaks of the brave Khan (Kamruddin) taking advantage of this favourable opportunity, charged them and gashed their breasts with their swords and spears, and they, therefore, fled towards their encampment and gave their troops warning of the Khan's arrival, but the horse of the Khan followed so close on their heels that the whole of the force was trodden under the hoofs of his cavalry, so that not a single man of them remained alive, except the Syyad and the English officer, who with a thousand difficulties escaped with their lives from this place of slaughter The victorious Khan now took possession of the forts of Budweil (Badvel) and Khummam, and having settled the affairs of that quarter in the best manner possible, he remained with his troops and artillery ready to chastise his enemies when the Sultan's order arrived The moment, therefore, this was received, he marched with his troops and with four thousand horse, forded the river Kishna, and in one night attack on the Mahratta horse, who were just ready to cross over, drowned them in a sea of their own blood, taking many of them prisoners. He then victorious marched towards the fort of Nargunda, when he pitched his tents between the mountain and the encampment of Burhanuddin, and a Sipahdar named Shaik Imam, one of his own officers, was sent to the assistance of the Sultan's faithful servants. When the chief of the mountain heard of the arrival of this force with its distinguished commander, and the defeat of the Mahrattas, the loins of his courage were broken, and as most of the bravest infidels had been killed or wounded he was unable to oppose further effectual resistance to the army of Islam, and therefore weaning his heart from the desire of possessing wealth and dominion, and fearing for his life, after a week's delay he despatched a message of peace and an offer to surrender the fort to the Khan before mentioned He therefore apprised Burhanuddin of this message and having, obtained his concurrence, they in concert the next day despatched a Kowl Nama, or the conditions of agreement, by the hands of Syyad Hamid and Mirza Hydar Ali Beg, Risaldar, to the chief of the mountain and he was brought down from the fort, and immediately with his family and children placed in confinement, and under the guard of the Kushuns of the Mirza and Ahmad Beg sent to the presence. Some however say that the daughter of the Poligar who was one of the most beautiful women of her time, after she was honoured by reception into the Musalman faith and the performance of the marriage ceremony was received into the Harem of the Sultan. In short after the hill and fort were taken, the Taluk was committed to the charge of an Amir, a faithful servant of the Sirkar

The Sipahsalar Burhanuddin although he openly appeared united and friendly with the Khan, still in secret entertained great enmity and hatred towards him, and used all kinds of arts in effecting the overthrow of his rank and dignity, and first because he had with his own troops defeated a large body of Mahrattas, and next because the fort of Nargunda had surrendered after his arrival :—while he the Sipahsalar with all his exertions in six or seven months had done nothing. For these reasons he determined to accuse him of a violation or defection of his duty to his sovereign, and thereby make a display and merit of his own loyalty and zeal, and he therefore addressed a letter to the Sultan, stating that Kamruddin Khan, was a disaffected person, and that it appeared that he through the medium of Malik Esau Khan, alias Esau Meah Mehdivi, who was his secretary and counsellor, secretly maintained a correspondence with the Nizam of Hydarabad and Mushirul Mulk Sohrab Jung—that besides this he was openly building a very large house in the Chaddar Ghat of Hydarabad, and that it was most likely he in a short time would abandon the service of the Sultan.

The Sultan without discriminating between friend and foe as soon as the letter above mentioned arrived, recalled the Khan with his secretary and troops to the presence. This foolish man (the Khan) however did not like to bring his secretary to the Sultan, because during the period of his Dewani or agency he had done many unworthy acts, and had greatly oppressed and plundered the poor, so much so indeed that the whole of the peasantry weeping and wailing had fled to other countries from his exactions and cruelty, for he had taken all affairs of revenue or government under his own direction, and decided on them without asking the consent or pleasure of his master. Of this the Sultan was aware. When therefore the Khan proceeded to the presence, he being afraid that some misfortune might befall him in the event of an investigation into his conduct, conceiving that all had been done by him from pure zeal for his (the Khan's) service, he presented him a gift of a lakh of rupees, and without the knowledge of any one sent him off by night to Hydarabad, while he with his troops marched and joined the Sultan When however after his arrival the Sultan called for the Dewan, the Khan answered that he had taken leave to bring up his family and dependants from Hydarabad.

This answer confirmed the bad opinion the Sultan previously entertained and the brave Khan was placed in confinement and his troops incorporated with the Sultan's army.

CHAPTER VI

The rebellion of the people of the district of Coorg, and the march of the victorious standards of the Sultan to punish the insubordinate inhabitants of that quarter, and the capture there of eighty thousand men and women, with other occurrences of that year, 1198, Hijri. A D. 1783

When Zain-ul-Abedin Khan, Mehdivi, the Foujdar of Coorg, from his intimacy with the Sultan, and the confidence he reposed in him was placed in uncontrolled authority there, he filled all parts of the kingdom with rebellion, and regulated the affairs of the government according merely to his caprice and folly—insomuch that from the inherent vices of his disposition, he extended the hand of lust to the women of the peasantry, and compelled the handsomest among them to submit to his will and pleasure. In consequence of this tyrannical conduct, the whole of the people of Coorg advanced into the field of enmity and defiance, and every one in his own district prepared for battle, and Momuti Nair and Ranga Nair, the ministers of the Poligar of that place, who eagerly looked out for such an opportunity to attack the Sultan's troops, assembled all their retainers and peasantry, surrounded and besieged Zafurabad, plundered all the country in its vicinity, and had reduced the besieged to such extremities, that even during the light of day they were afraid to quit the walls of the fort. In addition to these misfortunes, they had neglected to provide themselves with a sufficient stock of provisions and ammunition. The Khan, who was the source and origin of these troubles, at these occurrences began to be ashamed of himself, he being shut up with the rest; however, by disguising a Jasus, or spy, he despatched him to the presence, with an account of what had occurred and the insolence of the besiegers.

When the Jasus had delivered the letter, and had detailed the situation of affairs, the Sultan determined himself to punish the people of Coorg, who had frequently before rebelled against his government, and had blocked up the path of duty and obedience with the thorns and stakes of sedition and rebellion, and had also given the troops of the Sultan unceasing trouble

He therefore issued orders to the quarter master general, to proceed with the Tiger standard and the blue Pavilion, and pitch them in the vicinity of Sultan Peeth, a town lately built at the distance of one fursung and a half west from the capital, and Zain-ul-Abedin Shustri, Sipahdar with his Kushun and abundance of stores, and two thousand Ahsham or irregular foot was sent in advance as a warning to the rebels The Sultan giving him orders to proceed without delay, by forced marches to the fort of Zafarabad, and give the rebels such a lesson as would in some measure restore the peace of the country until the arrival of the royal army, and likewise to inform the inexperienced Foujdar there of the speedy arrival of the Sultan, and to give him every assurance of succour and support.

The Sipahdar above mentioned, who was a notorious coward, although, according to the Sultan's orders he marched on quickly, and arrived at the gate of the Ghat, still, as the rebels, as soon as they became aware of his arrival attacked him on all sides with their arows and muskets, they soon dissipated his senses and manhood. He, therefore, being a person who had never before seen fighting, but had spent his life in religious studies, lost all confidence, and retired under the protection of the Kotul or pass of Sudapur; and there fortified his encampment, and notwithstanding all the Risaldars and Sipahdars accompanying him, men who had been trained to war under the instruction of the brave commandant, Muhammad Ali, could say, in prompting and urging him to move on, still the Sipahdar, struck with fear, made the ague and fever and a pain in the stomach his excuse and refused to move forward a step. "Truly, how can the hard duties of soldiers be expected from luxurious and effeminate men :"— When these circumstances became known to the Sultan, he bestowed a few maledictions on his worthless officers, and after making his arrangements and paying his troops all which took up a fortnight, the dispenser of justice with twenty thousand regular infantry, twelve thousand irregular foot, ten thousand good horse, and twenty-two guns on the fifteenth of the month of Zihuj, with all the pomp and circumstance of war marched towards that quarter

After the Sultan had arrived and encamped near the stockade, or bound hedge of the Coorg district, leaving all his horse at the ghat of Sudapur, Puria Puttun and Munzurabad; he with his irregular foot, Kushuns and artillery, crossing the Ghat, threw himself like a raging lion into the midst of that frightful forest, the Coorg country—*verses*—"What can I say of this wonderful wilderness"—"The pen trembles at its mention alone." Its bamboo brakes intricate as the wooly curls of an Abyssinian ·— the roads or paths as confused as the lines of the galaxy[41]." The high and low lands of that country unequal as the souls of the generous and miserly. The hills and valleys impassable. The low grounds covered with rice crops as high as the waist. The elephant of fancy is here immersed in its quagmires to the breast. The boughs of many kinds of trees such as the teak, the tall sandal, the white gun and the ood (a sweet smelling wood) reach with their highest branches the Palm tree of Toba (in Paradise), and the tendrils of the black pepper vine spread the net of deceit over all other shrubs and trees. The fields of Kakila,

[41] Some copies of the work have—"as the curly ringlets of a bride.

that is to say, cardamums, like fields of wheat and barley blooming over the hill and dale,—cinnamon trees, also, like the light and clouds of the heavens distilling life and vigour over all the herbs of the field—and the fruits of the gardens, such as falsa, (a berry used in making sherbat) citrons, the custard apple, the Burheil, and jamoo, (a kind of plum) the plantain, are the dispensers of honey and sugar, to the bitter palates of the unfortunate. The rivers in that country like the eyes of the sorrowful, always overflowing. The tanks and reservoirs on the roads like the eyes of the forsaken, full day and night. The bride of the verdant earth drowned in the dew of modesty, veils herself from the eyes of the sun in the dark shades of the forest; parterres of the buds, or flowerets, of the Mehdi, Velvet, and the hundred-leaved, roses, always blossoming, like wanton girls, take off their modest veils to show their beauties. Wild elephants resembling mountains, both male and female, like troops of buffaloes wander about at their perfect freedom, and the young elephants like young Abyssinians making chowkans (a kind of cricket bat) of their trunks play at ball.[42]

Most of the towns and villages of that country are placed under hills, or are concealed among the trees,—they are surrounded by strong walls, in which many apartments and houses are built, and also in the enclosed space, and they are secured by a deep ditch dug all round—this is to protect their houses, for in the dark nights the elephants frequently make an attack on their villages and plunder and destroy them;—this, therefore, preserves the inhabitants and their property in safety. The men are mostly of a brown complexion, or the colour of wheat, but some are black—they are tall in stature, their clothing consist in a very dirty shirt, double, reaching from the neck to the ancles, and until this shirt is worn to rags, they never think of changing it;—they use a handkerchief, black or white, tied round their loins, and wear a leathern cap on their heads. The soldiers, however, never stir out of their houses or towns without a matchock with the match lighted in their hands, and a broad knife which they call kurkutti, fastened round their waists The women are beautiful, and in bloom and delicacy, the envy of the beauties of China and Choghul, and in elegance of form and gait, silvery complexions, and loveliness of feature, they rival the maids of Turkistan and Persia. In that wild country, which is however, beautiful as the garden of Paradise, they move about gracefully as the divine Huris—they, however, are very ill and indelicately clothed—one cloth about ten or twelve feet long, is wound round them, reaching from the navel to the knee, and a white handkerchief about three feet square is thrown on their tender breasts, the treasury

[42] I should have left out most of this poetical description of Coorg, but that I did not consider myself justified in curtailing the work.

of love. This dress destroys the effect of their beauty. The men of this country are cold, and passionless, in regard to women; but the women on the contrary are eager and ardent in their intercourse with men Historians of old relate that formarly in the neighbourhood of Akrubnar, (*Nar*, or rather *Nad*[43] in the language of that country, signifying a town), it was a foolish custom, but one considered in their pagan religion both proper and meritorious, that if there happened to be four brothers in one house, one only of them married, and the other cohabited with the woman so married by turns, one every night, and some even say, that all four remained with her every night[44]—the offspring of these marriages were divided among the brethren

When, however, the deceased Nawab (Hydar) conquered this country, he abolished this abimonable custom, and seizing many of the women, he gave them to his own soldiers.

But to return,—a description of the cold here makes the pen before it begins to write, stiff, as if it were plunged into the frozen sea— and the tongue of truth at describing the temperature is with fear and astonishment congealed like ice, notwithstanding it is covered with the posteen of the lips,[45] what can it say therefore. The sun with all its heat fearing the influence of the cold, every day covers his head with a counterpane of clouds and hurries away from this country[46]:—the fast travelling moon also every night from a similar fear hides her face in the blue veil of the heavens. This, however which has been written, is the description of the summer. God protect us from the winter and rainy seasons,—for during six months in the year, the clouds of Azur (the ninth month), pour their showers over the whole of that country, and the earth like the eyes of the oppressed, is filled with water, and from the evening, until two hours of the day have arisen, (seven or eight o'clock in the morning), the vapours of the falling dew, like the sighs of the afflicted, cover hill and dale, and many straight well made active young men from the violence of the cold having lost the warmth or use of their limbs, sleep in their narrow huts like a bow with their feet and breasts doubled up together. For six months the labourers or cultivators of the soil of that country, covered from head to foot with an old cloth or blanket, work for nine or ten hours a day, but all this time they are subject to the bites of leeches which are produced from the roots of the trees by excessive rain, and remain among the leaves and branches, and these in number, like locusts thirsting for blood, rise and fix themselves on the bodies of men and cattle to their great injury, and never quit them until they are

43 Nad as Ramnad &c.

44 Julius Cæsar says the same of the Ancient Britons

45 Moustaches

46 In the original this is written merely to show the ability and learning of the author.

filled with their blood; besides these, there are an infinite number of serpents of all kinds, and the most poisonous scorpions, and if these bite any living creature, its life quits the body so instantly, that even the Angel of Death is not prepared to receive it.

But to proceed:—when the pious Sultan entered that Jangalisthan or country of forests, by the route of the Turkul Ghat, he encamped on this side the gate of the stockade, called Mandal. The next day he gave orders to his two Sipahdars with their Kushuns to assault the stockade gate, before which the infidels had dug a deep ditch and had built a wall on each flank, and from these with their arrows and matchlocks they completely blocked up the road:—they accordingly commenced the action, but on this day the infidels displayed the utmost intrepidity and not only repelled their assaults, but drove the two Kushuns before them and killed and wounded the greatest part.

The conquering Sultan however with his victorious troops by a route by which the wind and rain could scarcely penetrate, now with the rapidity of lightening fell upon the infidels, and despatched a great number of them to the infernal regions. On the other side, the French under Monsieur Lally and the Asad Ilahi Risalas or regiments of Chelahs[47] made numbers of these Pagans food for the musket and bayonet, on the other flank also, the infantry of the body guard[48] with the greatest intrepidity took up their enemies one by one on the points of their spears or bayonets and threw them head foremost into the depths of hell, and many of the infidels were made prisoners. Notwithstanding all this, they still stood firm and made many vigorous attacks on the Sutan's army and dispersed them. At this time, therefore, the select of the body guard and certain of the Sipahdars seeing the bravery of the enemy, assembled those who still remained and determining by successive charges to make an impression, threw themselves at once on the enemy In the twinkling of an eye, therefore, the bonds which kept together the infidels were broken and they lost their stability and firmness, and placed their feet in the desert of flight.

The soldiers of the Sultan's army now, therefore, closely pursued them and troops of them were slain with the unpitying sword. When the Sultan had thus conquered his enemies, he advanced and encamped in the vicinity of Hulkulinar, and the Shustri who has been before mentioned, when he saw the plain cleared of the enemy, to do away with the impression of his former misconduct made an attack on the village of Khushalpur and plundered and burned it, making prisoners of a great number of the infidels, with their wives and children;—he then returned to the presence From this place now, agreeably to the Sultan's

[47] Slaves brought up by the late Nawab and trained for service by the Sultan, and when formed into regiments called by him Asad Ilahi

[48] Julowdars

orders, four Risalas, or regiments, with a large supply of stores and provisions, marched to the fort of Zafarabad (Mudgiri), while the Sultan himself remained encamped where he was until the thirteenth of the month of Mohurram il Haram. On the fifteenth of that month, A H 1199, the Sultan marched by several stages to the capital of Coorg, and encamped on the eastern side of the town, by the road, by which according to the orders of the Sultan, the Amirs and Khans had entered the jungles, and with hatchets and saws had daily cut away and burned the jungle to the distance of three miles, and in this way had cleared the country to the distance of seven or eight miles. In these operations the tenants of the jungles had been reduced to great extremities and in different battles also of the infidels two or three thousand men had been destroyed.

When, therefore, the chiefs of Coorg saw the signs of weakness and debility on the forehead of the condition of their men, and and that they no longer had the power to oppose the army of Islam, they dispersed to all parts of the mountains and jungles and sought refuge in the most difficult inaccessible parts of the country.

The conquering Sultan now therefore appointed and despatched his Amirs and Khans with large bodies of troops to punish these idolaters and reduce the whole of the country to subjection As for instance, Monsieur Lally was sent for that purpose to the Ilaichee or Cardamum Ghats, (the western Ghats according to Colonel Marriott) and the Kushun of the Shustri with another was sent under the command of Hussein Ali Khan Bakhshi towards Akrubnar. The rest of the Sipahsirdars that is to say Mir Mahmud, Imam Khan &c. were despatched to the Thul Kaveri, and Khushalpura, and for two or three months, the Sultan remained encamped on the same ground. The Bakhshi before mentioned however by good management and exertion carried distress and confusion among the rebels of that quarter (Akrubnad), and in a short time attacked and destroyed many of their towns, returning with eight thousand men and women with their children prisoners. In the same way Monsieur Lally collected from the Ilaichee Mountains an immense crowd of these wild men like flock of sheep or a herd of bullocks, and returned with them to the presence The Sultan after this moved forward and pitched his tents and standards on ground to the southward of the hill of Thul Kaveri, (the fountain or source of the River Kaveri arising from the same hill) and despatched his troops in advance giving them orders to pursue the rebels, that is to capture their chiefs.

The brave Sipahdars in consequence advanced to the attack on all sides, and as they knew that to cut off these infidels, the seed of disobedience and rebellion, was the policy of the Sultan's Government, and likewise that most profitable to themselves, they with great labour and exertion captured and brought in troops upon troops of the rebels, and in the course of seven months and a few days eighty thousand, men, women and children were made prisoners. At length both the before mentioned chiefs were taken on Ilaichee Mountains by the exertions of Monsieur Lally. The war, therefore, was now at an end and the rest of the disobedient being humbled, became enrolled among the faithful servants of the Sultan. The Sultan after making arrangements for the security of his conquests, and the erection of several wooden or stockaded forts (called in this country Lukkur Kote) being now free from all apprehension, returned victorious to his capital by the route of Sudapur.

Of the two chiefs, one Mumoti Nair in a short time died,[49] and Ranga Nair was honoured by being circumcised and made a Musalman by the Sultan, and named Shaikh Ahmad, and appointed a Risaldar. The Sultan also adopted him as his son Ballia Banu the Queen of Kunianore (Cananore) who was of the Mapilu tribe, paid her respects to the Sultan while he was encamped at Thul Kaveri, and brought with her the tribute due for two years, with elephants, horses and other valuables as presents:—and she in return was dismissed with dresses of honour and other royal presents.

When the Sultan arrived at Seringapatam, the prisoners taken in the country of Coorg, who had been all made Musalmans and were styled Ahmadees, were formed into eight Risalas or regiments, and veteran officers were appointed to train and discipline them, and they with very little labour having instructed these wild men, soon made them perfect in their military exercises and movements. About this time the Sultan caused gorgets of gold, silver and jewels to be made, and they were presented to the officers of horse and foot, the Assad Ilahi and Ahmadi regiments, according to their different ranks, and the uniforms of these regiments being also made up of tiger cloth, (a new invention in weaving) they were clothed in it The names of the twelve months and the cycle of sixty years were changed in contradistinction to the Arabian names, all which however shall be detailed, please God, on some future occasion The names also of a number of forts were changed in the same manner;—as for instance—Chital Drug, was called Furrokh Yab Hissar; Gutti, Fyze Hissar; Bullari (Bellery), Sumr Puttun; Punugundi, Fukhrabad; Pao Garh, Khatmi Garh—The Suba Sura Rustumabad—but this being the old name was, therefore, merely renewed, or restored—Nandi Garh, Gardun Shukoh; Devanhalli, Yousfabad; Pungalore, Darussurrur; Makri, Sawan Garh. The fort of Bul, Mankurabad; Coorg Zafarabad; Kalikote, Islamabad, Dindigul, Khalikabad; Sunkli Drug, Muzuffarabad; Kishingiri, Fulk il

[49] Not a natural death I fear.

azum ; Mysore Nazzarbar—and in this manner in all matters new terms, or new inventions were introduced. About this time also, from the whole of the Sultan's servants, six or seven thousand men of the Shaikh Syyad tribes were selected and despatched to Kurg to re-people that district. The air and water, however, not agreeing with them, some fell sick with fever and ague, and after repeated applications to the presence were allowed to return—but some with whom the climate agreed, remained there.

CHAPTER VII

The invasion of Mysore by the Mahrattas and the chief of Hydarabad with the intention to subdue the territories of the Khodadad Kingdom, and the conquest by them of certain forts of that State in their neighbourhood, and the march of the victorious Sultan to repeal his enemies by the route of Adhuni (Adoni), and the conquest of that place in the year 1199 Hijri, with other matters, A D. 1785.

When the Ambassadors of the Sultan, who previous to this time had proceeded to Punah with presents and ten lakhs of rupees, in money, arrived there, and had visited the chief (the Paishwa) and the minister, Nana Furnavis and had made an offer of the foregoing presents and money, they refused to receive them and peremptorily rejected the whole.

The reply of the Sultan which has been before mentioned, "that he had inherited a few guns and muskets from his father and had always kept them in readiness," remained fixed in the Paishawa's heart like a thorn, and he, therefore, in these plans (the rejection of the presents, &c) united in heart and hand with Nizam Ali Khan and despatched orders to all parts to collect his Amirs, or chief officers. Accordingly in a very short time all the Amirs of Punah with their contingents of troops and warlike stores assembled, and Nizam-ali-Khan conformably to his agreement, with his chiefs such as Mashir-ul-Mulk, Syfe Jung, Teigh Jung, &c. and the whole of his army consisting of forty thousand horse and fifty thousand foot, marched from Hydarabad and by the route of Bidar proceeded towards Badami, the fort of which is the frontier station of the Sultan's dominions in that direction.

The Mahrattas also with eighty thousand horse, forty thousand foot and fifty guns of heavy calibre and vast quantities of warlike stores, being all in readiness, marched and arrived at Badami. The Ambassadors of the Sultan therefore received their dismission, from that place, and the two Potentates (the Paishwa and Nizam) now met and having consulted together determined to attack the forts of Mysore, and first gave orders to besiege the fort of Badami which was however held by a brave officer The Amirs therefore of these Princes exerted themselves strenuously in the attack of the fort, and in raising batteries and battering down the walls, and also by continually repeated assaults,—but notwithstanding they lost thousands upon thousands of brave men in these operations, it was taken at last by capitulation only, after a siege of nine months. The confederates, however, after repairing the fort still remained there, in order to collect supplies and stores, despatching their Amirs to all quarters to reduce and take possession of other forts and towns, and accordingly the said Amirs with a large force marched and obtained possession of Dharwar and Jalihul, by a bribe of thirty thousand rupees It is proper to mention here that the governor of these two forts was a certain Hydar Buksh, Rafizi or Shia, a man who had but a short time before been Khan Saman or house-steward to the Amir-ul-Omra, the son of Muhammad Ali Khan, Suraj-ud-Dowla—and at first was a confidential servant, but at length having misapplied and stolen a large sum of the money of his master, and being consequently afraid of punishment, he deserted from him and sought refuge in the protection of the Sultan, and was appointed to the command of these forts ,—this man following the path of ingratitude gave them up for the amount specified, to the Sultan's enemies , while, he himself with his followers and property took the road to Punah. In the same way Gujindar Garh, Nolegunda, Nargunda &c. indeed the whole of that side of the River Tungabhadra was surrendered to the enemy. The commanders of these forts being treachrous scoundrels, who seduced from their duty by the promise of increased rank and pay and the payment of ready money in bribes, joined the enemy. The Poligars of that quarter as the chief of Sir Hatti, Damul, Kanakgiri and Anigunda, also joined and assisted the enemy. When the Sultan's spies reported these circumstances to him, and his faithful Amirs and chief officers, advised and entreated him to march to oppose his enemies, he immediately ordered the assembly of his army and the different departments, and on the sixth of the month of Shaban-ul-Muzam of this year, with a fine well-disciplined army consisting of six Kushuns or brigades of regular infantry (a Kushun is about two thousand men) three Mowkubs of horse, (the Mowkub is a regiment of regular cavalry of about four hundred horses and men according to Kirkpatrick[50]) ten thousand irregular foot, thirty thousand good horse and a park of twenty-two heavy guns, marched to Bangalore and ordered the attendance of the Poligars. The Munshis or secretaries therefore quickly wrote out orders directing them to join immediately with their troops, provisions and stores, and promising to remit their tribute until the conclusion of the war (with the Mahrattas and the Nizam). The Poligars of the different countries, such as the chiefs of Rai Drug, Harpanahalli, and others despatched their contingents of troops to the presence according to custom, but the chiefs themselves pretending to be sick remained at home.

But to return,—after the conclusion of the festival of the Lilut ul Barat,[51] and the payment of the whole army, the Sultan marched by great Balapur, Hindupur and Pao Garh to the river

[50] For a more detailed explanation of these terms. I beg to refer to the select letters of Tipu Sultan, translated by Col. Kirkapatrick, p. 958 of the Appendix.

[51] *Lallatu'l barat.* (Persian).

Makri where he halted two days, and leaving his heavy baggage and followers to the care of Purnia, the Mutsuddi or clerk of the Toshu[52] Khana, the Sultan with his horse lightly equipped by a forced march moved on to the vicinity of Hunur where he encamped. The next day he marched on to the town of Kubkul, two *kos* east from Bullari (Bellery), where he encamped part of one night, but moving on during the night, at day break the next morning his advanced guard suddenly appeared in front of the hill of Adhuni (Adoni), and the Sultan and his cavalry halted and rested themselves at the village of Gulbayen. The governor of Adhuni (Adoni), Mohabat Jung, (the son of Shuja-ul-Mulk Busalat Jung), who was married to the daughter of Nizam Ali Khan (the Subadar of the Dekhan) had his family with him having been lately appointed to the government of that part of the country.

As soon, therefore, as he heard of the arrival of the victorious army, being greatly alarmed, he deputed his minister Assad Ali Khan to the presence, and in the meantime taking advantage of the opportunity, despatched the whole of his wealth with his women to the mountains. When the envoy presented himself to the Sultan he in the name of his master entreated the Sultan would desist from his purpose to injure or molest him The Sultan replied, that in his heart he had entertained no enmity to his master, but, that as the Nawab (the Nizam) without cause had manifested hastility towards him, and had joined the Brahmans (the Paishwa, &c.) and was seeking the overthrow and destruction of his state, he would soon see the difference between his (the Sultan's) friendship and fidelity and their treachery and violation of treaties—that, independent of this, they (the Nizam) had abandoned the ties of faith and religion, and had joined the ancient enemy of his house, and with a large army had invaded and taken possession of the territories of a Musalman Sovereign, and had carried their enmity to that degree that idolators had plundered and burned the Masjids or mosques and houses of Musalmans and the poor people of the country, and had raised the flag of rapine and desolation in the territory of the Khodadad; that it would be good policy, therefore, that they (the Sultan and Mahabat Jung) should strengthen the foundations of friendship and unite in repelling and doing away with those who were shaking the chain of hatred and enmity—(in the original an allusion to the chain of gold in front of Noushirwan's palace, shaken by those who demanded justice) or that they should meet and consult in this matter, and if he Mohabat Khan chose, he might remain where he was, sending a body of his best troops under the command of his own officers to join and aid the

[52] *Tush* is synomymous with *zad* and signifies the wallet or provisions of a traveller.

Sultan's forces For that he (the Sultan) had bound up his loins in this religious war in order to establish Islamism on a firm basis, to obtain the favour of God, and ensure the peace and safety of God's people. As the governor (Mohabat Khan) did not however agree to the Sultan's propositions and failed in coming to present his respect to him, and also prepared to resist and defend himself, the Sultan to give him an example of what he could do and to frighten him, the morning after that day, gave orders to the Sipahdars to attack the town, and they assaulted and took it, and swept it with the besom of destruction, they did not however succeed in bringing the governor to the right path, and, therefore, on both sides the fire of war was kindled, and the soldiers of the victorious army and the chief of the ordnance department, turned their faces to the reduction of the fort, high as the heavens, and having encompassed it on all sides, raised batteries, dug their approaches and pushed on their attacks chiefly from the garden containing the tomb of Basalat Jung, and from the tank at the Tomul gate,—from thence they kept up a continual fire of cannon and mortars;—still however, the Sultan's compassionate heart never intended the conquest of this fort, but what he did was merely to awaken the solicitude of the chief of Hyderabad (the Nizam) for the honour of his relation and the safety of his daughter, shut up in the fort and the siege of the fort was undertaken in the hope that by this means he might be induced to offer terms of accommodation and desist from the ruin of the poor people of the country. Otherwise if the Sultan had seriously intended to take the fort he could have taken it with ease the first day, and also the governor with his women and wealth, as will be seen from the following statement; for when, in the morning, the Sultan's army attacked, and entered the city and penetrated, firing vollies to the gate of the fort, it was open for any one to enter, and when the inhabitants of the city, who fled to the fort from fear of losing their lives like so many crows or kites, were shouting, screaming and crowding to get to the gate of the garrison not a single man was to be seen either on the bastions, or walls—the fear of the lion-like Ghazies having seized on them. At seeing this, some of the Sultan's friends, and Amirs represented to him that this was the very time to take the fort; that he should not allow his enemies leisure to rub their eyes and awaken from their sleep of neglect, and, that if he would give orders they would take the fort, and bring Mohabat Khan willing or unwilling to the presence.

Rustam Jung, that is to say Monsieur Lally the French Officer, also repeatedly submitted this to the Sultan. The Sultan, however, pretended indifference to the matter and said do not attempt it, on any account; please God to-day, or to-morrow, or perhaps in a week, or at furthest a month, he Mohabat Khan will come out and surrender himself with his hands tied. The writer of these lines was present at this siege; but to return—after mid-day the besieged governor gave orders for the regulation and security of the fort, and assembling his soldiers, amounting to near seven thousand men, horse and foot, took the duties or direction of the defence upon himself Lal Khan and Sadullah Khan, Surkheil of the Kaim Khanis, who had command of four hundred Jaunbazes, were stationed at the gates and kept themselves ready to repel the assaults of the victorious army, and each side laboured hard in all warlike arts to deceive the other. When the Nizam of Hydarabad heard of these occurrences he refused to eat or sleep, and the forced march of that lion of the forest of valour (Tipu Sultan) and the attack of Adhuni (Adoni) deprived him of his senses. Having therefore apprised the Paishwa of these circumstances, they held a consultation on the subject;—some of the more experienced and wise among them, said that seeing that the frontier fort Badami which was not very strong was taken by capitulation only, after the labours of two armies for nine months, during which the smoke of the guns and muskets had been sufficient to dry up the brains of those employed in the siege, and that in one year they had actually done nothing more—what could be expected from their future operations? that since the troops of the Sultan in the absence of their master were not slack in fighting, what would they do in his presence? that the best thing they could do, therefore, was to appoint a number of officers with troops to lay waste the country and that the two princes should return to their capitals. This advice of the Amirs being approved by the princes, and their policy highly applauded, the Nizam of Hydarabad on his part appointed Mashir-ul-Mulk, Syfe Jung and others with a large body of troops to the relief of Adoni and the chief of Punah, (the Paishwa) appointed Yuswant Rao Holkar, Parasuram the chief of Mirch, Hari Pant Phurkia, Rastia Mahratta and other Amirs, with all the horse, foot and artillery to the aid of the Amirs of Hydarabad and the devastation of the Sultan's territories, and the two princes under pretence of ill health returned to their own capials, that is to say Hydarabad and Punah (Poona).

The Sultan at hearing this intelligence was much encouraged and determined now to take the fort of Aduni (Adoni) and to punish the governor who had so contumaciously refused to listen to his suggestions or advice, and in consequence issued orders to his officers to breach the walls, and they occupied themselves in battering the defences and assaulting the fort, one month and twenty days.

The site of the fort, however, and the strength of the walls (which was built by Musaud Khan an Amir of the Adil Shahi dynasty, as has been detailed in the author's work, *Tuzkirut il Beladwa il Ahkam*, in the second Ourung) were of that description, that the dust was not shaken upon one of its dunghills by the fire of the guns, nor were the walls to be breached by cannon or mortars, the fire therefore was of no avail. After some parts of the walls, however, were in a slight degree injured by the fire of the guns, the lions of the forest of valour, according to the Sultan's orders, made a vigorous assault on several sides, that is to say, Syyad Sahib and Kutabuddin Dowlat Zai, from the burying ground of Busalat Jung, Monsieur Lally and Imam Khan Sipahdar from the Tamul gate, and Hussain Khan, Buzai, and Muhammad Hulim from the hill Huzar Zeena. These having planted ladders against the wall attempted to escalade the fort. The garrison who were famous for the obstinacy of their resistance, and for their hardy endurance of the labours and hardship of the siege, crowded round the works to oppose them and manfully repelled their assailants, and a great number of them fell by the sword; the cause being that the ladders which had been made according to the instructions of the Harkaras, or spies, were found too short compared with the height of the walls, and the brave soldiers, although they abandoned the ladders, and strove to mount the walls by driving in iron pegs or spikes, still failed, and that day were entirely unsuccessful, for the garrison with the sword, arrow and musket, effectually stopped their progress, and near two thousand brave soldiers lost their lives on that occasion. At the result of this assault the Sultan was much grieved, and several of the Harkaras and spies were put to death

For some days after this, therefore, the troops did nothing but light up the fire of war, and from morn till night the flames of contention blazed high and again ladders were prepared long and strong, and they with iron pins and ropes were all in readiness, when Mashir-ul-Mulk and Syfe Jung &c. accompanied by the Mahratta army, arrived to the succour of their fort The Sultan on becoming aware of their arrival, not liking war on both flanks (or rather in his front and rear) abandoned his batteries, and changed his ground, encamping with his rear to the Black mountains, and there having stationed guards and pickets on all sides, remained in readiness for action. Two days after a severe action was fought between the outposts, or advanced parties, of the Sultan and the Mahrattas—the cause being the folly and incapacity of Hydar Husain, Bakshi Silahdar, who with a body of seven hundred horse belonging to Ghazi Khan, Bede (an officer who never authorized any such movement), from conceit attacked a force of ten thousand Mahratta horse, but at length finding he could not resist this mighty force, he was obliged to retreat

The brave Ghazi Khan, however, with the same body (seven hundred horse), still kept his ground against the ten thousand and for two hours displayed the utmost gallantry, but from apprehension of disgrace, he despatched the rash Bakhshi to the presence, in charge of his son Kadr Khan, and in the mean time, after distinguishing himself in the most heroic manner without aid or succour, and being wounded, he was obliged reluctantly to quit the field The Mahrattas, however, followed him and killed some of his party, and two or three hundred of his men with their horses were taken prisoners by them, and they then returned. Kadr Khan, however, with two hundred Janbazes, after escorting the Bakhshi to the camp, charged the enemy and recovered eighty horse of his own troop, and made prisoners of fifty of the enemy's horse and brought them to the presence. In the course of this action, Lumchur the Kuzzak, and Manna Choudhuri, made a sudden Chuppao attack, and captured two elephants, eight camels, and fifty ponies, from the Mughals of Hydarabad The Sultan on hearing this, immediately beat to arms, and with all his troops marched rapidly, on their heels the fire of his artillery opening so suddenly that the outposts of the enemy fell back on their main bodies, and both their armies fell into great confusion, and sought refuge under cover of the city and fort, and from that time never returned to the field of battle. The Sultan, therefore, remained until evening, with his troops formed in order of battle, expecting their advance ; but, at length, leaving two Kushuns as pickets in front of the enemy, he returned to his ground of encampment

The morning of the next day, Mashir-ul-Mulk and the others having consulted, after a great deal of contention, took the governor of Adhuni (he being persuaded to consent) with his property and family to the fort of Raichore (Raichur)—when the spies reported this to the presence, the Sultan immediately detached Mir Sadik with a body of troops to take possession of the fort and stores, while he himself followed the steps of the confederates to the river Tungabhadra, eight fursungs distant, and took some of their stragglers prisoners, and some baggage which had been left behind ; and then returned and encamped on the north side of the fort. The Mir before mentioned, having taken possession of the fort and the palace of Mahabat Khan, placed all the valuable property left by that chief with some boxes locked up with great care, on his camels and elephants, and sent them to the presence. When, however, the Mutsuddies (civil servants) of the Tosha Khana opened these boxes, they found nothing in them but old slippers and shoes (intended as a manifestation of contempt for the Sultan) they, therefore, surmised that perhaps the governor of the fort, among his other avocations exercised the profession of a churum doze or cobler, or that he had collected some tax (in kind) from the houses of the shoemakers ; or perhaps that he had collected them in the way of trade to send them for sale to Hyderabad.

On the representation of these circumstances to the Sultan, he was much displeased at the stupidity and folly of the Mir, and ordered him to examine with his own eyes, all the property and articles of value, and select only such as were worthy, and send them to the Sultan, and to leave those belonging to the shoemakers or leather dressers where they were. The whole, therefore, of the wardrobe, the armoury and the tents &c of Basalut Jung, were taken and deposited in the stores of the Sultan. After the accomplishment of these measures, the lower fort was laid in ruins, and Kutub-uddin Khan Dowlat Zai, was appointed to the charge of that Suba.

CHAPTER VIII

The march of the victorious army to the discomfiture of the Mahrattas then plundering and laying waste the country on the other side the river Tungabhadra, and an account of the capture of Kanchan Garh and Kupli or Kopli, the passage of the river by the victorious army, and the battles there fought with the Mahrattas in the same year, Hijri, 1199

As soon as the Sultan was set free by the conquest of Adhuni, he having in view the chastisement of the Mahrattas, marched by the route of Kanchan Garh, and despatched a party of horse in advance, to take prisoner the widow of the Poligar of that place—the Poligar himself having died a short time previously His wife, therefore, whose name was Tunguma, governed in his place, but at that time had taken her feet out of the circle of obedience, and loyalty to the Sultan, and sometime before this in the hope of an increase of territory and wealth had entered into neotiations for herself, with the chief of the Mahrattas, through the medium of Hurri Pant Phirkia—when, however, this woman heard of the Sultan's intention, she immediately fled by night, with a few slave girls and servants and crossing the river Tungabhadra, escaped. Her son, however, whose name was Mudkum Kur, and about ten or twelve years of age, was taken prisoner in the small fort of Surkah, his residence, and was honored by being circumcised and made a Muslim, and he thenceforward received the name of Ali Mardan Khan, as will be seen in the account of his family given by the author of these lines, in his work called the *Tuzkirut il Belad wa il Ahkam*[53] in the eleveth Ourung :—It will be seen there, that the above named (Ali Mardan) after some time was married to the daughter of Khan Jehan Khan, who also was an adopted son of the late Nawab, and originally the son of a Brahmin, the Deshpandia of Kolar, who in his youth being ill treated by his school master, of his own pleasure, the great and true guide shewing him the way, reached the presence of the deceased Nawab, and became a Musalman and his wife also, after arriving at the years of discretion, of her own free will, and after obtaining permission of her father and mother, embraced the religion of her husband, and thereby secured to herself happiness in both worlds.

The Sultan from this place marched on and arrived in the neighbourhood of Sundur,—the governor of that fort was named Govind Rao, the nephew of the celebrated Morar Rao, who after the capture of his uncle, had retired to Punah (Poona), and there

[53] *Tozkiratu'l Biladwa'i Akham* (Persian).

representing to the Paishwa the ruin that had defallen him, solicited a recommendatory letter in the name of the Nawab, and having obtained it, returned to the presence The Nawab being naturally compassionate and indulgent and desirous also to oblige the Paishwa, after taking security that he, Govind Rao, should in no circumstances violate his engagements with the government, contained him in the presence of the fort of Sundur At this time, however, he had quitted the path of rectitude, and had united with the Mahrattas, but when he heard of the march of the Sultan's troops, the flight of the lady before mentioned (Tunguma) and the condition of her son, he lost the use of his senses, and fled to the Mahratta army with his servants and dependants. Taluk Sundur with its dependencies was, therefore, taken possession of, without opposition by the servants of the Sultan After the necessary arrangements for the security of this place, the Sultan exalted as the heavens, with his army, in number, equalling the number of the stars, marched towards Kopli The governor of that place who was a relation of the rebel Poligar of Kanakgiri, strengthened his fort, and remained ready for the attack, and notwithstanding the Sultan's Amirs strove to advise and direct him ; it was all of no use[54]—according, therefore, to the orders of the Sultan, the brave Sipahdars and the French Officer M. Lally assaulted the fort on both flanks and took it by storm,—and for an example to the rest of the infidels it was sacked, and the women, both Musalman and Hindu, violated by the soldiers, and money and valuables to a great amount taken from the houses of the merchants, bankers and weavers or cloth makers, of the people of Islam, who are called Momin, and many also of the women of that tribe, from fear of violation by the soldiery, threw themselves into the river Tungabhadra, which at that time was raging with the violence of the rains, and perished , the governor of the fort was also killed.

When, however, the Sultan heard of the violation of the women he punished his soldiers severely, and issued orders, strictly prohibiting such excesses in future. From this place the Sultan now marched on to the neighbourhood of the town of Haspeenth depending on the Poligar of Harpanhalli and halted there four days In these marches and halts the month of Ramzan (the lent of the Musalmans) was completed, and after the fulfilment of the devotional duties of the Id ul Fitr, or the conclusion of the fast and the customary banquets and rejoicings, the Sultan marched and pitched the tents of his army on the bank of the Tungabhadra even with the Ford or Ghat of Gorokhnath—as it happened, however, to be the period of the swelling of the river, some delay took place in crossing it ; in that time, therefore, the Mahrattas subdued and took possession of all the country.

[54] He knew the value of their advice

on the other side of the river ; and with the intention to attack the Sultan, raised their inauspicious standards opposite to him, and fortified with guns and musketry the ford of the river against the passage of his army, and they also despatched an officer with a large body of troops to capture the Hill Forts of Gopal and Bahadur Bandah. This officer, therefore, marched and besieged both these Hill Forts, and after a siege of two months Bahadur Bandah was taken, it not being a very strong fort. The commandant of the Fort of Gopal was not however to be deceived by the enemy, and vigourously defended himself, and moreover frequently attacked their batteries, and drove the infidels out of them

The river, however, still continued to swell to that degree, that even the basket men, (or Watermen) were unable to cross it, and the passage was therefore unattainable by the Sultan's troops. In consequence, therefore, thirty boats were assembled from the districts of Harihur, Horul (Hurrial), &c and three or four hundred large baskets were also collected, and near two months were expended in waiting for the decrease of the waters, even then, the water, instead of falling, daily rose higher. The Sultan, therefore, ordered that twenty-one guns of heavy calibre should be ranged on the banks of the river, and that ten cartridges should be fired from each The artillery men having executed these orders, from that time the water decreased, and in two or three days fell to half its former height The Mahrattas at hearing the report of the guns, imagining it was a salute for good news, and that it must be either because a reinforcement of French troops had joined the Sultan's army, or that the Kuzzaks had made an incursion into the Hydarabad territory, and had defeated the Nizam, they therefore determined that to stay any longer, where they were was unworthy of their military[55] character, and accordingly marched off to Shanur, they left, however, ten or twelve thousand horse, encamped on the bank of the river.

When the water had sufficiently subsided, the Sultan ordered his army to cross over, and first at night two Kushuns of the Jysh, and two thousand horse with the artillery, the wind being favourable were ferried over in boats and immediately fell upon the Mahratta horse who were entirely unprepared for their arrival, and with sword and musket drove the dust of existence of their bodies, and seven hundred horses with the flag elephant, and a number of camel drums[56] were taken on his occasion. Those of the Mahrattas who escaped, leaving their horses, arms, and property behind them, fled towards the main body of their own army, and informed their chief of the passage of the river by the Sultan's troops. The next day, therefore, the Sultan himself with

[55] In derision
[56] Kettle drums carried on camels

his army of heroes crossed over the river and pitched his tents on the opposite bank, where he covered the front of his army with redoubts, and halted there for the space of a month—during this period, the provision, treasure, artillery, and indeed all the departments with the followers, &c had crossed over, and the enemy also, with the design to attack the Sultan, advanced with their troops and artillery, and encamped four farsangs distant.

In a few days, therefore, the Sultan (the destroyer of his enemies) with the whole of his horse, four Kushuns and his guns and stores, left his encampment, intending to try the strength of his enemies, and advancing towards them two fursungs, formed in order on the plain. The Mahrattas being informed of this movement turned out in good order, and also formed in order of battle. The Sipahdars of the Sultan's cavalry according to his orders on seeing the approach of the enemy, posted a body of infantry in the low grounds, the guns attached to them being loaded with grape, were kept in readiness, while the household cavalry accompanied by the horse of the Paigahs, and the body guard, with great show paraded over the higher ground. The Surkheils or commanding officers of the Bede, or - irregular horse; that is to say, Ghazi Khan, Wali Muhammad, Ibrahim Khan &c., agreeably to the Sultan's orders, formed their lines to the front and advanced to attack the Mahrattas, when, however, the Mahrattas charged them in turn and they were within arm's length of each other, the Kuzzaks very bravely after their mode, wheeled off from the flank, and retired towards their own army The infidels fully armed and equipped, now therefore, pursued them without any consideration or apprehension, and suddenly presented themselves to the muzzles of the guns"[57]. The infantry in ambush, therefore, now immediately rose and advanced, and with the fire of their guns and musketry, soon took off the edge of their enemies' valour; and the horse charging them from the rear raised the clamour of the day of judgement, until the troops of Islam and the infidels were mixed and confounded among each other like light and darkness Whatever of manhood and courage, therefore, existed in them was now brought forth, and in the heat and press of the battle, the rocketeers having lighted their rockets, threw confusion and dispersion into the masses of the Mahrattas, and the artillery men from the flank of the line by a continual fire from their guns, scattered their ranks like as the leaves of trees are scattered by the cold blasts of autumn. The officers of the Mahrattas, seeing the signs of defeat and the indications of flight and dispersion on the foreheads of their dispirited soldiery, immediately fled, and the victorious army pursued them to the distance of two farsangs (about seven miles) and crowds of these dark minded infidels were slain and taken prisoners.

[57] Hydar Ali's old manoeuvre

The Sultan after this victory, marched on and encamped his victorious army at the distance of four measured farsangs, in an open and extensive plain. The plan of the encampment of the conquering army on that day was as follows. The Kushuns with their guns were drawn up as a fort or in square, (on the flanks, front and rear), and in the centre were the Sultan's tents and those of the Darbar, (this I think shows that even after his victory, the Sultan was afraid of the Mahrattas), on the right were posted the regiments and Dustahs of cavalry, and on the left the Sillahdar and Kuzzak horse; surrounding the Sutan's tents and Durbar, the infantry called Assud Ilahi and Ahmadi were stationed The rear guard was composed of the Ahsham and Gundehchar[58] infantry, also the pioneers, Komattied, (Palankin and Duli bearers), and the contingent troops of the Poligars &c The horse of the advanced posts, or the ground guards were stationed one farsang distant to furnish videttes.

The enemy likewise their troops now got themselves ready and advanced to the river of the town of Kudduk, with the intention to give battle The Sultan, therefore, after the lapse of four or five days, one night formed his Kushuns under Shaikh Imam, Shaikh Omar, and Imam Khan, Sipahdars, with the guns and rocketeers, and Ghazi Khan, with two thousand horse under the command of Husain Ali Khan, Bakhshi, and Maha Mirza Khan, with an intention to make a night attack on the Mahrattas, and they were marched off towards the Mahratta camp while the Sultan himself, remained in the centre of his camp with the Paigah horse, and the rest of the cavalry.

The Sipahdars and Bakhshis, therefore, proceeding by the road pointed out by the guides, marched on, and at about four o'clock in the morning, arrived near the Mahratta camp. They had, however, mistaken the road, and now fell in with the pickets of the enemy, who had lighted fires here and there about their posts, and Shaikh Omar who was with the leading division, seeing these, and fancying also he saw before him the lines of the Mahratta army, without informing the other officers of his intention, opened a fire from his guns and rockets. The report of the guns, rockets &c., soon awakened the Mahrattas and some sought the road of safety, and some of the Mahratta chiefs attacked the assailants The Bakhshis of the Sultan's troops, however, being experienced men, now quickly wheeled about, and under the cover of the hills and jungles, avoided their enemies and returned to the presence, and reported to the Sultan the whole of the circumstances The Sultan exceedingly angry at the failure of the expedition, immediately dismissed from his service Shaikh Omar, and gave his Kushun to a man named Fazil Khan, a Risaldar. The Sultan next day marched and encamped on the river Bola, and the

[58] I do not know what description of troops is meant under this name

Mahrattas also at the same time changed ground, ane encamped at the distance of about nine miles, with their rear resting on a thick jungle. Two days after the Sipahdars or commandants of regiments or brigades, Imam Khan, Fazil Khan and Mir Mahmud, with two thousand Kuzzak horse, and one thousand rockcteers, under the command of Kadr Khan, the son of Ghazi Khan, were again despatched at night to surprise and plunder the camp of the Mahrattas. The able and experienced Sipahdars having clothed all their men in Kumlis (a kind of blanket mostly of a black colour) they wound their devious way, like a black snake through the turnings and windings of the hilly road

After undergoing the labours and fatigues of a long march they at length arrived in the rear of the Mahratta camp, and when the pickets of the Mahrattas aware of their arrival prepared to oppose them, they in the Mahratta language gave themselves out to be a detachment from the Mughal (Hydarabad) army sent to their aid from Raichur (Raichore), and without stopping, marched direct into the midst of their camp, where they raised a terrible storm with their musketry, rockets and keen swords, and the bands of the order and discipline of the Mahrattas were broken asunder, and on all sides the field of battle was straightened on these infidels. The chiefs of their army, however, with the cavalry, jumping on the backs of their horses without saddles or clothes, fled towards their park of artillery, which was at a considerable distance.

The able Sipahdars,[59] victorious, with much plunder, both in money, valuables, arms and fifteen hundred mares, having also taken prisoners many women and children belonging to the Mahratta chiefs, returned to the presence, and in reward for their labours were honoured with presents of jewelled gorgets, strings of pearl, and gold and silver armlets. The Sultan, however, the emblem of mercy, despatched the women taken prisoners with presents of honorary dresses and robes, in palankins, and under charge of a party of rocketeers to the Mahratta camp. The Sultan also secretly despatched four elephants, and eight beautiful horses, with a sum of money to Hari Pant, Rastia and Madhuba Bini, through the medium of these ladies, and thereby made them the slaves of his commands and munificence.

But to return; the Mahrattas left their ground where they then were and marched to Sirhutti, where they encamped.

[59] The Sipahdars commanded a brigade or Kushun.

CHAPTER IX

The retrograde movement made by the Sultan, from motives of police or convenience, and the pursuit of the Mahrattas—also the arrival of Burhanuddin Sipahsalar, with his troops and the arrival of a convoy of provisions from Nagar in charge of Budruzaman Khan Foujdar, also the seizure of the district of Sanore, and the flight of Hakim Khan, and a description of the battles fought between the Infidels and Moslems in the same year 1199, Hijri—A D 1784

The Sultan after the night attack made a night march, and the next morning pitched his camp in the Jungle where he remained the whole day. The next night he again marched to the junction of the river Bala with the river Tungabhadra, and there encamped.

It is not to be concealed here, that the cause of these night marches was this—from the filth accumulated from the great numbers of horses and bullocks in camp, and from the carcases and stench of those which died, and the multitude of people in camp, flies were generated in such numbers that they became a pest to the whole army, to such a degree that the soldiers at night even, could neither cook nor eat their victuals, the Sultan, therefore, gave orders that they should dissolve sugar and sweetmeats in water and sprinkle it before their tents and this being done, when the flies settled upon this sugar and water, he marched off and left the ground At this time Burhanuddin Sipahsalar with his division of troops, arrived from the neighbourhood of Anuti, and Budruzaman Khan with an immense convoy of provisions also arrived from the district of Nagar, and was admitted to the honour of an audience When, however, intelligence of these night marches reached the Mahrattas, they immediately fancied that they arose from fear of their mighty army and that the Sultan was returning to his capital, and that he had no power any longer to withstand them—they, therefore, with the whole of their force followed quickly and encamped at the distance of two farsangs in the rear of the victorious army, so near that the pickets and outposts of both armies were stationed at the distance of an arrow's cast only from each other, and at this distance repelled the different attacks made by each other. The Sutan, therefore, having formed his plans, morning and evening had his Kushuns out in the plain, under pretence of exercise,[60] manoeuvring about and firing from daylight in the morning to eight o'clock; and in the evening from five until it was dark—and this was done continually. After manoeuvring five or six days after this fashion,

[60] This is one of the stratagems recommended in the *Futtah il Mujahiddin.*

the Sultan one evening, leaving the baggage and followers of his army in the same place gave orders to his Amirs, to make a night attack from different points in the mode following: Mir Moinuddin with two Kushuns, five guns and the French regiment was ordered to attack the right flank of the enemy, and Burhanuddin with two or three Kushuns and six guns marched towards the left wing of the enemy for the same purpose, while the Sultan himself with two Kushuns, the horse of his Paigah, and the Ahsham foot, advanced with a determination to attack the main body of the enemy

The night was, however, without moonlight, and so excessively dark, that the troops with the greatest difficulty and labour made their way to the point of attack [61] By the light of the false or earliest morning, Burharuddin, first among them all, attacked the troops of Hari Pant and Rastia, and opened the gate of dismay and calamity upon them, Mir Moinuddin, embarrased by his guns, which, owing to the deep mud of the roads could not be got on, left them behind and with two light French guns marching quick fell upon the troops of Syfe Jung, (in some copies he is called Subkut Jung)[62] or, the right wing of the Nizam's army, (the symbol of flight) which was entirely unsuspicious of such tricks of the night,[63] and caused the confusion of the day of judgement to fall among them.

At this time, the Sultan himself with the greatest rapidity moved on to attack the main body of the enemy These attacks on all sides having compressed the Mahrattas in a small space, the chiefs of that army, who were bound to the service of the Sutan, keeping aloof from the action, the Mughal army was entirely overrun and plundered, and all their baggage and property trodden under the hoofs of the Sultan's horse. For the rest, the chiefs of the Mahrattas mounting their horses fled to the Tope Khana, or park of artillery, which was about one farsang distant. The baggage of the army and the stores and wealth of the Urdu Bazar of the Mahrattas, fell, therefore, into the possession of the servants of the Sultan, and the tents, camels, standards and horses with their head and heel ropes, &c were all taken The Sultan remained to rest and refresh his troops the whole day in the Mahratta camp, after midday, however, the troops of the Mahrattas assembled and advanced with their heaviest guns, about a farsang, and taking possession[64] of some high ground, placed them in battery there, and opened their fire with such precision, that they greatly distressed the Sultan's army and broke the arms and legs of many of his soldiers

[61] *Subh Kazeb.*
[62] *Sabuqat jang* (Persian)
[63] *bazi-e-shab* (Persian).
[64] A mistake here

The Sultan's anger now flamed violently at the insolence of the Mahrattas, and he ordered that they should be driven from their position, and Syyad Hamid, Shaikh Onsur, and Ahmad Beg, Sipahdars, therefore, with the regiments of Monsieur Lally, marched, following the low grounds to attack the Mahratta park of artillery—it happened, however, that on their way thither they fell in with a large body of the Mahrattas; estimated at thirty thousand well appointed horse, who had concealed themselves in the dry bed of a tank[65] near their position, and were lying in wait of an opportunity to attack the Sultan's troops The brave Sipahdars and gallant Frenchmen immediately levelled their muskets and poured forth their fire in vollies with such effect, that the enemy from the tumult and throng, could not wheel about without difficulty, and therefore, of necessity presented their breasts as a mark for the bullets and bayonets of the musketeers, and they were consequently pierced with as many holes as a net, two officers of the Mahrattas, who each rode an elephant, were killed, and the rest leaving their horses and arms escaped with their lives only In fine, in the twinkling of an eye, seven or eight thousand horse of the Mahrattas were destroyed and their bodies scattered upon the plain

When the chief of the Mahrattas saw the marks of fear and despondency on the foreheads of his soldiers, he turned away from the fight, and his courage failing him, he withdrew his guns, and retreated to the distance of two stages. The Sultan, now therefore victorious, with the spoil of the Mahrattas, his drums beating for joy at his success, returned to his tent and the next day marched further on towards Sanore.

It is not to be omitted here, that Abdul Hakim Khan, the chief of that state, after the death of the Nawab, without reason estranged his heart from the Sultan, indeed from his (the Sultan's) youth even, he had been his inveterate enemy;—moreover after the accession of the Sultan, he sent neither letters of congratulation, nor presents of cloths, &c courtesies which are esteemed the pledges of friendship and good-will. His agent, however, Chintu Pandit, on his own part, and merely to pay court to the Sultan, made some presents, but although these circumstances hurt and aggrieved the feelings of the Sultan—still on account of the ties of relationship which existed between them, the Sultan gave him no molestation, but on the contrary, overlooked some very unworthy actions done by him

Notwithstanding all this, this unlucky man never put any confidence in the Sultan, and had now leagued and intrigued with the Mahrattas When he found, therefore, that the Sultan was approaching him, reflecting on his own unworthy conduct, he trembled like a reed at the sound of the hoofs of the Sultan's

65 It must have been a large tank

horse, and with certain of his friends, and the dependents of his household, that is his women and a small sum of money he had by him, he at night fled and joined the army of the Mahrattas, leaving Abdul Khira Khan alias Khira Mean in the city. The date of this flight is given in the following Hindusthani words, *Hakim Khan miyanah Sab Ko Chhor Ke ap bhaga*[66]

When the Sultan heard of his flight, and his junction with the Mahrattas, he was astonished, but at night despatched Syyad Hamid, and Syyad Ghaffar Sipahdars to take possession of the city, and in the morning he himself marched and encamped before the place, and then despatched Mir Sadik and Mahdi Khan, Bakhshi, with orders that all the property and wealth of the state of Sanore, which the Khans of former days had collected at a vast expense, should be sent to the presence, and all this Hakim Khan by his foolish enmity gave gratuitously to the winds. The officers sent, agreeably to their orders, without opposition from any one, took and despatched to the presence whatever they found of gold, silver, carpets, or tents, vessels, arms &c as for instance in Abdul Hakim's wardrobe, they found fifty turbans of different colours, of the Burhanpur chintz kind, hung upon pegs in the wall, and honorary dresses of great splendour and value, of the same colour corresponding to the turbans, under cloth covers or in packages ; but besides these, articles of great value brought from all countries laid about in heaps and these with lists of all of them were sent to the Sultan, and after being inspected by him were deposited in the Tosha Khana.

The light guns were all added to the Sultan's artillery and one gun composed of five metals,[67] twelve legal guz in length was broken up and sent to the mint to be coined into halfpence. In fact all the valuables, among which were carpets of the most elegant patterns with gold and silver flowers, each the load of four or five camels, and the Kalecchas and Sutrinjas, (other kinds of carpets) of which each was the load of an elephant, were all siezed by the Sultan's servants A short time after this, Khira Meah on horseback, and accompanied by two or three servants arrived, and was honoured by being admitted to an audience ; at this audience the Sultan addressed him and said "what has befallen your father, that he should have run away in this manner ? we ourselves in no matter, and in no mode, ever interfered with or molested him, but on the contrary, our favour towards him increased daily ; but setting this aside, shame on your relationship, that without any injury or breach of engagement on our part, your father should have joined with the Mahrattas, the enemies of our house and openly displayed his hostility. Depend on it that he will never be the better for it, nor ever see

[66] Hakim Khan Meeana, left all and ran away.

[67] *Panras.*

the days of prosperity." Khira Meah in reply, said, "that undoubtedly his father had acted unwisely, and that the bread of his fortunes had been dried up in the sun of despair—that he, the Sultan's ransom, or sacrifice, was ignorant of what had been done, or he would have opposed it to the utmost of his power." After this the Sultan placed him near his own tent, and sent him twice a day wishes from his own table—he, however, kept him under strict restraint or surveillance in the same way that he kept Kamruddin.

CHAPTER X

An account of another night attack, the last battle and the defeat of the Mahrattas by the victorious army, and the establishment of Peace between the Lion conquering the world, the Sultan and his weak incompetent enemies the Mahrattas, also the regulation of the districts of the Poligars, with other events which occurred in the year 1200, Hijri—A D. 1785-6.

The Sultan after the capture and regulation of Sanore, leaving a garrison in that city, marched to the northward, and encamped near Jobun Garh, and halted there for thirteen days of the month Mohrrum il Huram He now also distributed his army into four divisions ; each consisting of four Kushuns, five thousand irregular foot, five thousand Silladar horse,[68] and fifteen guns. The first division was placed under the command of Mir Moinuddin, otherwise called Syyad Sahib—the second division was placed under Burhanuddin—the third was committed to the charge of Maha Mirza Khan , and the fourth to Husain Ali Khan, the Mir Bakhshi.

Having done this, the Sultan ordered them to march on and directed that the aforesaid divisions should encamp at the distance of three miles from the remainder of his army The Sipahsalars, therefore, in obedience to these orders, took up their ground, and employed themselves in preparing their troops and arms for immediate action, while the Sultan himself with two Kushuns, the Assad Ilahi and Ahmudi , three mokubs or regiments of horse, eight Dustas[69] of the Paigah, or household horse, four thousand Kuzzaks and ten thousand Ahsham infantry, remained encamped where he was. On these arrangements, it was currently reported by him, that of the Sipahsalars, (the officers commanding these divisions,) the first was commissioned to the conquests of the dependencies of Hydarabad , the second to the conquest of those of Puna ; the third to the maintenance of order at Raichur (Raichore), Kottur, &c. ; and the fourth to the capital, Puttun, to subject and control the different forts and districts of the Poligars—while the Sultan himself was to attack the Mahrattas. The commander of the Mahratta army at hearing this news became like quicksilver, restless and uneasy, when of a sudden Mir Moinuddin, with his force, at the instance of Syyad Hamid, and Syyad Ghaffar, marched at night and attacked the hill fort of Mondergi Drug, which was garrisoned by the Mahrattas, and at one assault took the fort and passed the garrison under the edge of the sword. The town was also pillaged, and he returned

[68] *Khwud aspeh*

[69] A Dusta was about twelve hundred, in Tipu's army.

with stores of provisions and much gold and jewels. In the same way Burhanuddin marched towards Binkapur and Misri Kote, which were in the occupation of the Mahrattas, in a way that no one could be aware of his arrival, and unfurling the standard of enterprize, carried exceeding terror and dismay among them, and lighted up the fire of plunder and slaughter in all that quarter. The Sultan also now advanced straight towards the enemy, the sign or symbol of defeat.[70] In that march, however, the Mahrattas attacked the rear-guard of the victorious army, and brought a storm of evil on its followers, and plundered the Banjaras of ten thousand bags of grain, which they carried off. The Sultan now, therefore, despatched a message to the Commander of the Mahratta forces to this effect, that it was unworthy of noble generous minds to injure or distress God's people without cause, and that if he (the Mahratta) had the breath of manhood still remaining in him, their dispute might be settled in an hour, that his wish was, that in a well fought battle of one day, they should finish the book of strife and contention. As the chief of the Mahrattas well knew the valour, (meaning the reverse) of his own troops, and that without peace, he could not expect to save himself from destruction , he declined to agree to the Sultan's proposition. However, by the advice of certain of his servants, who recommended war, he agreed to an action to be decided with the sword alone. The Sultan, therefore, one day assembled his four divisions on the rives Guduk, and arranged them in order of battle, and having appointed his Kushuns to the right and left wings, he himself mounted on an elephant with his guard, took his station on the field, and first ordered the brave men of his Paigah, or household cavalry, to commence the action and accordingly each Dusta galloped forward and having formed in close order took possession of the field.[71] The Mahrattas also armed cap-a-pie, now charged the Sultan's troops, and between them a very severe action ensued It was, however, determined, that each Dusta should fight only half an hour, that the devotion and bravery of the whole army, officers and men, might be fairly tested. Every brave man, therefore, made the utmost display of his courage, and many by their prowess effaced the renown of the great actions of Rustum and Isfendiar, and until mid-day, the clashing of swords, the whilstling of arrows, and the rustling of the spears[72] continued so great and so constant, that the gallant

[70] In contra-distinction, the Sultan's army being invariably the victorious army

[71] I should have attempted a description of Tipu's military regulations from the *Futtah ul Mujahiddin*, and other works but there is not sufficient interest in such details to repay the trouble

[72] The noise made by the strokes or cuts of the sword, is represented by the word *Shaha shah* , that made by the striking or whilsting of an arrow, *chaqa chaq* and that made by the piercing of a spear, *khapa khap*.

troopers at length quitted their swords and spears, and laying hands on each other had recourse to their poignards and daggers, and on every side lay heaps of slain. After the brave men of the Paigah, the Silladars, next stretching forth the arms of manhood, made the face of the plain as red as the rosy morn, with the bood of their enemies The chiefs of the Mahrattas, however, aware they were not able to resist the swords of the worshippers of fame, in the pride of superior numbers determined to charge with their whole force, and thus ride over the Sultan's army, and accordingly with this intention, they with all their troops, amounting to seventy or eighty thousand men, moved forward. The Sultan, now seeing that the Mahrattas had violated their agreement, immediately gave orders to his artillery, and they moving forward quickly from the flanks with the Sipahdars (and their Kushuns) by their heavy fire of musketry and artillery, soon compelled the unfortunate Mahrattas to taste the sherbet of flight. As soon, therefore, as they were scattered and dispersed, the regiments of horse, and the Kuzzaks, of the victorious army followed them for two farsangs, and took from them to the amount of two or three thousand horse, a quantity of baggage, stores, and arms; as arrows, swords, and two pieces of cannon, and ten returned. The Mahrattas on the contrary, for three stages never looked behind them and fled without halting even for the night Hari Naik the Poligar of Kanak Giri, who at first had attached himself to the Mahrattas, seeing at this time the irregularity of their measures and movements, now finding an opportunity, left them with his troops and offered his services to the Sultan, who received him with great favour.

The Sultan after this marched with his army to Binkapur, and encamped eighteen kos to the northward of Sanore; at this place a party of Kuzzak horse left the army with an intention to plunder the villages in that vicinity. It so happened, however, that the outposts of the Mahrattas obtained information of this movement, and posted themselves on the road by which they (the Kuzzaks) marched and at one charge surrounded and killed every man of them. The Sultan hearing of this was greatly incensed, and issued orders to the other Kuzzaks, with his army and to his own horse, that no one should proceed beyond the limits of the outposts, or grand guards, without pemission. In this encampment the Sultan remained one month, and in that time, by dispensing gold and sending honorary dresses and presents of all kinds in the way of courtesy and friendship, made several of the chiefs of the Mahrattas obedient, and the slaves of his commands, and all operations were undertaken by the advice and instruction of these men, until one day, when, according to the hints and directions of these chiefs, all four divisions of the army were made ready, and marched off for a night attack, and the Sultan having assembled a number of hermaphrodites[73] belonging to his camp, to the amount of about one hundred and fifty, he gave them painted sticks and placed them in front of each division.

The pickets of the Mahrattas who were the servants of Hari Pant Phirkia, seeing and knowing the Sultan's troops, allowed them to pass When, however, the Sipahsalars arrived near the Mahratta encampment, one of the Mahrattas becoming aware of their approach, apprised Holkar, that they had entered the camp through the villainy and collusion of the officers in command of the pickets; Holkar, on hearing this, left his tent on foot, and he had no sooner quitted it than the fire of the rockets and musketry blazing close to his eyes, he immediately ran away leaving his favourite wife asleep in the tent, and the rest of the Mahratta chiefs followed his example. The whole of the camp, therefore, after this was plundered, and the half alive Mughal camp, was also completely pillaged, and eighteen women, the wives of the Mahratta chiefs, with their gold and jewels were taken. As soon as the morning dawned the Sipahsalars, victorious, with the captured baggage of the Mahrattas, their standards, tents, elephants, camels, treasure and four guns, marched on their return, and notwithstanding the Mahrattas rallied those of their army spared by the swords and that they seized and occupied the road by which the Sultan's troops returned, and fought desparately to cut them off—still, it was of no avail, and they were compelled to retire, and the Sipahsalars on their arrival were honoured by admission to the presence, and they presented the plundered property and the women taken to the Sultan; the liberal Sultan to every officer and soldier who had distinguished himself on this occasion, gave two months' additional pay, besides other honours and advantages.

The women taken prisoner were dismissed as before, after making an agreement, which they confirmed with solemn oaths to the effect that by every art and means, they would prevent their husbands from continuing the war, and that they would never withdraw their hands from importunity and solicitation, until their husbands laid their heads in submission on the orders of the Sultan. On the arrival of the women in the Mahratta camp, their husbands fearing they had been polluted, and the veil of their honour had been rent by the rude hands of the Musalmans who made them prisoners, placed them all in a tent pitched separately for them, and did not allow them to enter their tents

The women, therefore, now opened mouths to reproach and revile the illiberality and want of shame manifested by their husbands, to extol their own purity; to praise the kind and honourable treatment they had received from the Sultan; and lastly pertinaciously to insist that peace should be made.

[73] *hizan*

The chiefs of the Mahrattas, therefore, now cleared their minds of the bad opinions they had formed, and discharged from their hearts the deep-rooted enmity in which they had indulged, but still from a sense of duty exerted themselves in the execution of the orders of their chief—however, on whatever side the Sultan's troops advanced to the attack, they as constantly retired. When the Sultan, therefore, found there was no readiness for action on the part of the enemy's troops, after the lapse of a month, casting the eyes of compassion on God's people, according to the hints and instructions of the chiefs of the Mahrattas and Mughal armies, he commenced to set on foot negotiations for the establishment of peace, and Budruz-aman Khan and other Khans, with friendly letters, a sum of money, some raritise, valuable cloths and jewels, among which was one diamond necklace, worth five lakhs of rupees[74] were despatched to Puna.

Holkar and other chiefs of the Mahratta army, who had been often defeated by the Sultan's troops, and whose women and wealth had been so often pillaged and violated by them, now reduced to extremities, detailed the bravery and enterprize of the Sultan's army in their letters to Puna, and strenuously advocated the conclusion of peace When the chief of Puna, (the Paishawa) and his minister consulted with their chief officers,[75] on this measure, the latter said, our best policy apparently is, that we should also send embassadors with rarities and presents to the Sultan, and thereby wash the dust of enmity from off his offended mind with the pure water of conciliation, and refresh and revive the garden of our territories with the flowing stream of amity and concord ; for this reason that the impression and effect of an association with the Musalman King, would be the source of order and strength to our state, and even if it were not so, that the character for courage and prowess of that great man the Sultan, was so well known, that should he turn the reins of his operations to our quarter, he would inevitably conquer the whole of our country, and the hereditary possession of the Mahratta empire would be taken out of the hands of their race. As these words of advice took effect on the hearts of the chiefs and as they had also heard that a body of French troops had arrived to the aid of the Sultan, the offer of negotiation on his part was considered by them as a most fortunate occurrence, and they accepted the ambassadors and presents and the dust of enmity existing on both sides was washed off by the water of friendhip, and they also despatched an ambassador with presents of rarities, honorary dresses, gold, jewels, fine horses and elephants to the presence of the conquering Sultan.

They requested, however, that the Taluks of Nargunda, (Nalgonda), and Jalihul should be presented to them as gifts. The

[74] 500,000

[75] *Karpardaz.*

Sultan, the asylum of the world, from policy and according to the verse—"be generous, be generous that the stranger may become thy slave,"—agreed to their request, and forwarded the Sanads of those three Taluks to them It is not to be omitted here, that as the chief of Puna (the Paishwa) gave the Sultan's ambassadors the district of Kuslapur in Jagir, so that in return, the Sultan gave him these three Taluks.

The forts and towns in that neighbourhood which by the neglect and villainy of traitors, had fallen into the possession of the troops of the enemy, were now restored to the Sirkar Khodadad —included in these negotiations was the petition of Hari Pant for the pardon of all the offences, great and small, of Hakim Khan, which was obtained by his mediation, and the Suba of Sanore was again restored to him as before. When the Sultan's mind on the score of peace was fully satisfied and at rest, he returned victorious to the town of Sanore. Hari Pant Phirkia who had placed the ring of obedience in the ear of his existence, and who was the origin and founder of the peace, had the Taluk of Gujindar Garh, with dependencies, and several towns of Kanchan Garh, presented to him in Jagir to furnish his Pan and Betel nut expenses[76] The Sultan then marched on by the route of Gopal and Bahadur Bundah, and crossing the river (Tungabhadra) encamped on the tank of the Darjee Mahal which lies two kos to the eastward of Anagundi, and in order to complete the repairs of this tank, halted there some time During this period, the Poligars of Rai Drug, Harpanahalli, accompanied by a number of their dependents, entered the Sultan's camp in the hope of being admitted to an audience. The Sultan, however, bore a violent hatred to these chiefs for this reason, that whenever they were summoned, they declined to attend, owing to their ill will towards him, and therefore, all wish to accept their services, or admit them, was totally rejected from his mind.

He at night, therefore, despatched his Kushuns and making prisoners of them and their dependents, put them in irons and sent them prisoners to Bangalore,[77] and all their territory, wealth and property of all kinds were seized, and their districts and forts assigned to able civil officers, and brave military governors, a brother of the chief of Harpanahalli, however, who was residing in some town of that district in ill health, when he saw the torrent of tht Sultan's anger and the waters of calamity surrounding him, fled at night with his wife, family and dependents, and leaving the latter at Dumul proceeded to Mirch, and he, therefore, escaped with his life and property The Sultan after this marched and entered his capital, Seringapatam.

[76] Pan is a leaf eaten with Betel nut, well known in India called by Indians Tambul Patra

[77] One died at Seringapatam, and the other was poisoned by Tipu, according to Col Marriott.

CHAPTER XI

An account of the re-establishment of order in the City of Seringapatam, the regulation of the whole of the Sultan's territories and the dismission from office of Mir Sadik, Dewan, or Minister of state, also, the completion of the Ali Masjid—the return of the Ambassadors from the presence of the Sultan of Room, or Constantinople, sent thither in the year 1198 Hijri, and the despatch of an Ambassador to Hydarabad with other events of the year 1202, Hijri—A.D. 1787.

When the capital of the kingdom was enlightened by the respledent countenance of the Sultan, the dispenser of justice, his world conquering mind occupied itself in the regulation of his kingdom and army At this time also the exactions and tyranny of the Dewan, or minister of state (Mir Sadik) who according to his caprice and will oppressed the people of the Suba of Adoni (Adhuni) and Sanur, having been represented to the Sultan his services were dispensed with, that is he was dismissed, the property in his house being seized according to orders, two lakhs of rupees the currency of Adoni (Adhuni), which is called Chulaoni, and one lakh of huns or pagodas, Muhammad Shahi, were found, and he was put in irons and imprisoned, and Mehdi Khan Nayut, the Jagirdar of Awulgunda, was appointed to the Dewani (in his place). At this time the Sultan determined to recommence the building of the Masjidi Ala, the erection of which had been suspended since the year 1198 Hijri, and the Daroghu Public buildings, according to the plan, which will be mentioned hereafter, completed it in two years, at the expense of three lakhs of rupees, and the prayers of the Eedi Fitr, in the year 1204, Hijri, were the first said in that mosque, and it was named by the Sultan Masjidi Ala.

A concise account of the cause of the building this mosque is as follows :—it is known, that when the vile and rejected Brahman Khunda Rao with the intention of uprooting the fortunes of his Master, began to excite disturbances, and the late Nawab fled alone to Bangalore, and that villain imprisoned the Nawab's Zanana and the Sultan (who was then a boy of six or seven years of age,) in a house in the fort, near the gate of the Deorai Peenth, which at present is called the Ganjam gate—at that period, before this house, there stood a Hindu temple, the area or space round which was large. The Sulan, therefore, in his infancy being like all children, fond of play, and as in that space boys of the Kinhiri and Brahmin castes assembled to amuse themselves, was accustomed to quit the house to see them play, or play with them. It happened one day during this period, that a Fakir (a religious mendicant) a man of saint-like mind passed that way, and seeing the Sultan gave him a life bestowing benediction, saying to him, "Fortunate child, at a future time thou wilt be the king of this country, and when that time comes, remember my words—take this temple and destroy it, and build a Masjid in its place, and for ages it will remain a memorial of thee." The Sultan smiled, and in reply told him, "that whenever, by his blessing, he should become a Padishah, or king, he would do as he (the Fakir) directed." When, therefore, after a short time his father became a prince, the possessor of wealth and territory, he remembered his promise, and after his return from Nagar and Gorial Bundar, he purshased the temple from the adorers of the image in it (which after all was nothing but the figure of a bull, made of brick and mortar) with their goodwill; and the Brahmins, therefore, taking away their image, placed it in the Deorai Peenth, and the temple was pulled down, and the foundations of a new Masjid raised on the site, agreeably to a plan of the Mosque, built by Ali Adil Shah, at Bijapur, and brougth from thence.

As, however, the regulation of the kingdom, the chastisement of the rebellious, such as the people of Kurg, the Mahrattas, and the Poligars were the first objects in the mind of the late Nawab —the work fell into delay for a time, but now, when from the blessing of God all these difficulties had been removed, the work was resumed.

The Sultan now divided the whole of the territory under his authority into three parts, each of which he distinguished by a different name; as for instance, the country on the coast was called the Suba Yum, (the sea); the cities and towns of the hilly and woody country, the Suba Turun; and the open and level or champaign country, the Suba Ghubra (the earth). The chief Officers of Parganas also received the title of Asaf. About this time also, round every city, town and fort, at the distance of one farsang, he erected a strong stockade with four gates, and to these he appointed vigilant guards, that no one without his authority and permission, and the signature or mark of the military governor should be permitted to pass in or out. By this restriction, therefore, the intercourse of foreign merchants and the commercial men of the country was entirey cut off; the reason of this was that the deceased Nawab had collected Muhammadans from all countries, and had filled his kingdom with them contrary to its former state (when it was full of Hindus) When these people, therefore, by the gifts, presents and liberality of the Nawab and of the kind-hearted Sultan became rich in gold and other valuables, they without leave or licence departed and returned to their own countries These restrictions were intended, therefore, to prevent their doing so in future. In addition to this, the Sultan stockaded the frontier between the limit of his dominions and the districts of the Karnatak Payanghat, from the boundaries of

Dindigul and Karur, to the Ghat or Mountains of Budweil, and the limits of Khumum, and twelve thousand foot soldiers, were stationed along this stockage, as a cordon, in order to prevent any one from entering his dominions from the Payanghat, or any one from quitting the Balu Ghat for that quarter.

The silver coins and rupees called Imami, having on one side the misra or line, "The religion of Ahmad enlightened the world from the victories of Hydar,"[78] and on the reverse the sentence, "He is the sole or only just King,"[79] were coined by his orders

The institution of the Muhammadi year which is thirteen years more than, or exceeding that of the Hijri, it being reckoned from the conclusion of the prophet's office, and the commencement of the duties of his mission (the office of prophet and that of a particular mission are considered distinct) being previously arranged and ready, was now made current throughout the whole extent of the Sultan's dominions. In this year Ghulam Ali Khan, Nuhnu Meah and others who in the year 1198, Hijri, were sent to the Sultan of Room (Constantinople), with presents, worthy of the two Sultans, such as new muskets, fabricated in the Sultan's arsenal, ten lakhs of rupees newly coined, valuable cloths, with gold jewels, of great value, seected from all the departments of the state ;[80] now returned from thence having fully obtained the objects of their mission, with a sword and shield, ornamented with jewels, and friendly and congratulatory letters from the Wazirs or ministers of the foot of the Musalman Throne, (the Sultan of Room is apparently considered the head of the Muhammadan powers or states)[81] and having presented themselves to the Sultan, they there detailed the circumstances of their mission, stating that the presents sent (to Constantinople) were all approved and accepted, but that among the warlike weapons none were so much esteemed and admired by the Sulan of Room as the rockets of which there were none in that country. The Sultan now, therefore, according to the suggestions of the Wazirs of Room, and the advice of his faithful Amirs, collected all the treasures of the state, or rather assumed the pomp and splendour of royalty,[82] and directed the formation of a throne of gold, ornamented with jewels, of great value in the shape of tiger, a figure from the first most approved by the Sultan English and French artisans, also of the greatest talents were assembled and constantly employed in

[78] *Din Ahmed dar jahan raushan az fateh haider ast*

[79] *hu' as Sultan at Wahid at 'adil'*

[80] Treasury, wardrobe and Zanana

[81] In the war against Tipu Sultan, in the Mysore, evidence has appeared of letters to the Ottoman Porte, claiming his aid as the "Head of the Moslem world," and Mahmood appears fully sensible of the hold which this rank invests him with over his most powerful vassals—Upham's *Ottoman Empire*, Vol I.

[82] It appears from this that Tipu wanted the sanction of the Sultan of Room, before he assumed the titles and distinctions of royalty

casting metal or brass guns[83] and the manufacture of muskets; they also made scissors, pen-knives, hour-glasses, pocket-knives with many bladxes &c. so that in the course of a month, one gun and five or six muskets of the best kinds were completed. The Sultan's manufactories were called Tara Mandal[84] and were established in four places, one in the Capital, another at Bangalore, the third at Chital Drug, and the fourth at Nagar; the chief part of the Sultan's time was, however, spent in collecting and enlisting men for his horse and foot, but notwithstanding this, the Amirs and Khans of old times, whom the late Nawab had allured to his service from all cities and countries, at the expense of hundreds of pounds, were now all at once cast down from rank and power, and the honour of the Sultan's confidence, and low bred, vulgar, young men were appointed in their places The Karwan Bashiaun, that is the chief merchants and horse-dealers, &c on account of now prices or the want of demand for their goods, abandoned trade and those persons who were willing to take up a musket and a pair of pistols were entered in the cavalry, and those who opposed this innovation were deprived of their rank and dismissed. As the confidence of the Sultan was chiefly placed in artillery and muskets, as the most efficient descriptions of arms, the brave men who excelled at[85] the handling of the sword and spear lost heart, and some cavalry officers were appointed and compelled to enlist men for the Jysh and Uskur horse and foot, who were ignorant of the rules and qualifications necessary for these divisions of the service, and consequently in a short time, confusion and ruin appeared in the fundamental regulations of the government and kingdom. About this time Kutubuddin Khan, Dowlat Zai, Ali Ruza, called Arkati, and Muhammad Ghius, companions and friends of the Sultan, and his Amirs were desptched as ambassadors to Hydarabad with valuable presents and friendly letters, the object of which was to strengthen the foundations of concord and amity, and that each should aid and support the other in all territorial and fiscal measures, and also to strengthen these relations by the ties of kindred and marriage, purely with regard to the interests if Islam. When the embassadors were admitted to the honour of an audience by Nizam Ali Khan, they presented the cloths and valuable jewels, and in private and in a friendly manner, represented, that, to the enlightened mind of the Nizam, it must be evident that rank and greatness in this world did not possess the quality of duration, and that its pleasures were always in a state of change, or evanescence,[86] that it was known to all that the whole of the countries

[83] *panj ras*

[84] Signifying a constellation

[85] Le maniement des armes blanches

[86] A verse is omitted here

of the Dekhan and Telingana, was formerly in the powerful grasp of a fortunate man of the Bahmani race, and that from the terror of the sword of that prince, the face of the territory of Islam was freed from the thorns and brambles of infidel opposition. At this time, therefore, that a Muhammadan Padishah or king should accord with and make friends of faithless infidels, and then cause them to lay violent hands on the territory and wealth of Musalmans, and the helpless inhabitants to be burned with the fire of persecution, would certainly meet reprobation both from God and man, and moreover that this dishonourable conduct would be the cause of shame and retribution at the last day—that it would be better, therefore, that the dust of enmity and revenge should be allayed by the pure water of peace and that the military and peaceable classes should not be disturbed, or their faith shaken for the enjoyment of pomp and state a few days ; at best a very short time—that for the sake, of their country, and religion they should fold up the carpet of enmity to each other, and strengthen the foundations of friendship and regard, by the rites of matrimonial connexion, that united in repelling and conquering the infidels, they might so use their best endeavours that the whole of the Muslim population, the poor, the peasantry, and strangers might repose on the couch of safety and confort, and pass their time in prayer for the long continuance of the reigns of the Kings of Islam. This address from the able and eloquent ambassador, although it made him (the Nizam) smile like the full blown rose, yet, as the sentences of the letter included the mention of matrimonial connexion, he, excited by his folly, became angry and gave these joy-dispensing words no place in his envious mind, and considering the term Naik which belonged to the Sultan's forefathers as discreditable, and relationship with him a disgrace according to the advice of his foolish women, he turned his face aside from the true path and dismissed the Eelchi, or ambassador, without the attainment of his object. A detail of the disputes and quarrels which occured at the time when Kutbuddin Khan returned is not entered in this book.

It is not to be omitted here,, that the Nizam entertained this vain and absurd opinion, that except himself, no one of the princes of the Dekhan was of noble lineage, and on his own nobility and greatness he gave himself these airs—did he not know that the term Naik in the language of the Rajas of Hindusthan, signifies a chief of courage and renown ? and even omitting this, the Naikwar tribe is not distinct from the four tribes[87]—that they should be considered low and vulgar. In truth in his birth the Sultan was not in any wise inferior to the others, (that is the Nizam and his family,) he was not born of a low woman, and as for

[87] Does he mean the Muslim, Shaikh, Syyad, Mughal, Pathan, or is it the Hindu divisions of caste ?

his claim to consideration on the score of wealth, grandeur, state and power, he had a long and powerful arm, and in courage and ability he was unequalled. Some ignorant men who deny the respectability of the surname of his ancestors, have fallen into a great error Do they not know that the power of the Almighty, the truly and only powerful, is infinite? that he can select any one he pleases and make him great in both worlds, and in this lower world can exalt him to the highest pinnacle of rank and station. It appears as if they knew nothing of the History of Timur Gorkan Sahib Kiran (Tamerlane), from whom the powerful dynasty of the emperors of Hindusthan is derived; what was his origin, and what did he become!—It appears also, as if they had never heard of Husain Kangu (Gangu) the first of the Sultans of the Bhamania dynasty, and who was styled Husain Shah Bahmani, and of whom it is related, that after his death the blazing lightning passed round the enclosure or precinct, (or rather performed the Towwaf[88]) of his tomb, the marks of the passage of which still remain, and who he was? Good God is it possible that on the strength of worldly power and distinction, low fellows boast of their noble descent and men of the dregs of the people, falsely claim to be Shaikhs and Syyads, the (the noblest families or tribes among the Musalmans) and consider no one equal to themselves! Verse—"low birth is hidden by wealth and station"—"The golden veil conceals the ugliness of the old courtesan"

[88] *Tawaq*

CHAPTER XII

The march of the Sultan and his army towards Kalikote and an account of the attack of Kuchi Bandar (Cochin), and the dependencies of the Raja of Maliwar,[89] and the defeat and heavy loss sustained by the victorious army from the mistakes or errors of the guides, and the second attack and conquest of that port,—occurrences of the year 1205, Hijri. A.D 1790

The conquering Sultan, giving no attention to the tales of the envious and interested, had just completed some private arrangements, when his spies brought intelligence that the Naimars of Kalikote (Kozhikote), had placed the foot of insubordination in the path of presumption, and that they had determined to rebel; that Urshud Beg Khan, the Governor or Foujdar of that district, although he exerted himself to compose or pacify them, and by presents of turbans and shelahs,[90] (ornamental apparel) strove to gain their hearts—still the infidels were unsettled and restless The Sultan at hearing of these things ordered the immediate attendance of the Foujdar, and a certain number of the chiefs of the Naimars. The former, according to the Sultan's orders made himself ready to attend; but the Naimars under excuses of to-day and to-morrow refused. At this time a spy, an interested man and a dire enemy to the Foujdar before mentioned, represented to the Sultan, that he, the Naimars, and the Raja of Maliwar, had united in heart and hand, and that he was sacrificing the interests of the Sultan for his own emolument and advantage. In consequence of this, the Sultan with his Amirs and court, four Kushuns, three Mowkubs or regiments of horse, and his artillery, marched towards that quarter, secretly determined to extirpate the rebellious infidels They, therefore, at the march of the Sultan, being much alarmed and fearful of the destruction of themselves and families, dispersed among the woody and mountainous parts of the country The Foujdar, however, advanced immediately to meet the Sultan, and having presented himself, was addressed by the Sultan in the following angry words;—"You were appointed to the government or regulation of this district—what have you done? You were ordered, moreover, by every art and device to make the Poligar of Maliwar obedient and tributary, and having collected his Paishkush to despatch it to the presence,—this also has not been done." The Foujdar in reply represented, "Your slave was so entirely occupied in the subjection of, or keeping in order the Naimars of this quarter, that he had no leisure to employ

[89] Malabar.
[90] Clothes worn over the shoulders

himself in any thing else—that independently of this, the Poligar was tributary to the Suba of the Karnatak, and therefore, he was not likely to be deceived by any arts or devices of his, that, if the Sultan would give orders, he would proceed with a body of troops, and after reducing him compel him to pay tribute." The Sultan replied to this," that it was evident he, the Foujdar, could never keep the country in proper order and subjection," and he was accordingly dismissed from his office, and Mahtab Khan, Bakhshi, was appointed in his place. The Sultan then returned to his capital and took up his temporary residence in the Durya Dowlat Bagh, or garden. The displaced Foujdar or Kalikote (Kozhikote) took up his quarters in the Tukia, (the residence of religious men, probably from fear of his life) of Kadir Wali, Pir Zada, and after a short time resigned the loan of his life to the Creator who gave it in the same place, and agreeably to the orders of the Sultan was buried in the Lal Bagh. Mahtab Khan Bakhshi, notwithstanding that he treated the inhabitants of that country with great kindness, forwarded them assurances of safety and invited them to come to him, still the benighted heathens gave no credit to his professions, and the instigation of the people of Kuchi Bundar (Cochin) raised the head of rebellion in every quarter, and prepared themselves for their defence.

The Sultan, also, no sooner became acquainted with these circumstances than he marched with his army by the route of Suttigal (Satyamangalam ?) and Korical (Karikal) to Kalikote, (Calicut or Kozhikote), and appointed a detachment of his troops to ravage the country of his enemies, and they accordingly lighted up the fire of oppression in all the towns and villages in that neighbourhood—*Verses,*—"When they marched into that country, they committed many cruel acts," they lighted up such a fire of plunder, "that at once they burned up every thing it contained." "From the hoofs of their horses, the mountains and plains,"—"were all trodden to dust," "and even from the rocks, trees and stones," "deep sighs arose and wailing." After the whole country had been swept by the besom of devastation, and when a host of the refractory and rebellious had been carried away by the whirlwind of desolation, those who remained being subdued, placed the ring[91] of servitude in the ear of their lives, and with their hands tied together submitted During this time, a party of Kuzzaks had spread themselves over the districts of Maliwar and Trichinopoly (Tiruchirapalli), and had pillaged and burned many towns of those districts The collector of revenue at Trichinopoly (Tiruchirapalli), therefore, addressed a petition to the Sultan, stating that between the government of the English company Bahadur and that of the Khodadad, the foundations of peace, and amity, was firmly established—but, that at the present time certain

[91] See Deuteronomy, chap xv, v, 17

Kuzzaks, ignorant men, had plundered the towns depending on that Suba (Trichinopoly), and that it was their intention to pluck up the root of the tree of friendship planted in the hearts of the two governments, and that it was indispensable they should be punished. In the reply, the Sultan wrote him that *his* troops would never plunder in any country without his orders, and that it apparently must have been the Poligars of the Collector's own districts—that they (the Poligars) had been looking for an opportunity like the present, and they had presumed therefore, to do the mischief, that he, the Sultan, was occupied in the regulation of his own territory, and the punishment of the refractory. In short, a month after the subjection of the country had been effected, the Sultan having acquired sufficient information from his messengers and spies respecting the Port of Cochin, he with the whole of his army marched thither.

The people of Cochin being aware of the Sultan's approach and intention, raised three or four batteries, (seemingly those of Cranganore and Ayakotta) on the banks of the different rivers, and surrounded them with deep ditches, and remained ready for battle, occupying the road with a very strong body of arches and musketeers; at nightfall of the day[92] on which he arrived (apparently), the Sultan ordered his troops to assault and take the batteries, and they, with honourable emulation and the greatest bravery, took them, and the Sultan immediately moved on to a place where two rivers crossed the road, and where the enemy had built a wall across the road of the ford, and had stationed themselves to defend it. The passage of the tide also above and where the water of the sea flowed into the river, was blocked up by a mound, so that the water was stopped in its passage, and the bed of the river became dry. But, although several of the Sultan's confidential servants, such as Turbeut Ali Khan, and others, took the liberty to represent that in front the road was bad and intersected by the beds of deep rivers, and that a night expedition was not safe, and God forbid that the enemy should gain an advantage and the Ghazies be defeated; still their advice was disregarded and the representation of no one met with approval, and the Sultan getting into his Palki with two Risalas, and two thousand regular horse, proceeded onwards forthwith, dark as it was. The Sultan's faithful soldiers now at one assault with their swords and muskets, drove the enemy before them and by the help of ropes and ladders, scaled and took the first works, and as the enemy lost the power of resistance and fled before the Musalmans, towards the fort, the Sultan halted where he was, and ordered his Hurkuras (messengers) to bring up the Kushuns and artillery. As soon as these arrived, two Kushuns forming the advanced guard, being in all points prepared for action, were

[92] December 28, 1789.

ordered on, and the remainder of the Kushuns kept in reserve, when at about day-break all of a sudden the treacherous enemy finding this the critical moment for them to obtain the victory, cut down the mound, which (as before mentioned) they had raised above in order to stop out the sea, and the tide rushing in with great violence filled up the rivers to the brim, and the road of succour and assistance to the advanced division of the Sultan's troops was cut off.

In this time the enemy attacked the Sultan's troops on all sides with arrows and musketry and caused incalculable distress and confusion among them, and, however vigorously they strove to repel their infidel assailants it was of no avail, and they were overwhelmed with all kinds of evil and calamity but notwithstanding all this, three or four hundred brave horsemen, men of good families, gave substantial proofs of their valour, and were all killed and wounded in front of the Sultan At this time Kamaruddin Khan, who was present with the Sultan, by adjurations and entreaties falling at his feet, took him out of his Palki, and by the strong exertion of loyalty and fidelity, caused him to be carried through the water to the opposite side of the river, and then constrained him to turn his steps towards the camp. But of those present in that battle not one man ever returned safe to the presence The Sultan's Palki with its bed, the great seal of the exchequer and a dagger were taken by the infidels

Some report that the Sultan's turban was in the Palki, but it is a great mistake, for the Sultan's turban at that time was upon his fortunate[93] head and the coloured turban which fell into the hands of the enemy belonged to one of his footmen, who ran before the Palki, and who was accidentally killed by an arrow, or a musket ball, and his turban falling near the Palki the benighted infidels thought it was the Sultan's and placed it in the Palki In short the Sultan and Kamruddin Khan escaped out of the whirlpool of their fortunes, and the rest of the Khans, such as Turbeut Ali Khan, Muhammad Omar, Urzbegi, and, Sayyd Khan the Darogha of the treasury, &c were never after heard of.

The Sultan's anger at this untoward event was excessive, but having caused his drums to beat for victory (as if he had gained one) he directed bridges of wood, cut down from the Jungle to be made, and having by their means crossed the rivers, he brought upon his enemies a resemblance to the days of judgement small and great.

The Sipahdars and Mowkuhdars, now according to their orders, attacked the enemy from different points to the extent or along a front of three miles and with their keen swords, relieved the shoulders of all the infidels they met (man or boy) from the weight of their heads[94]

As the power of resistance had now quitted the heathens, they, fearing the might and greatness of the Sultan and his army, fled to Maliwar, abandoning both their country and wealth. The victorious Sultan, therefore, now entered the walls of the port of Cochin, and took possession of every particle of the property remaining therein, as the arms, stores, guns &c. A nutmeg tree also, which was growing in the fort, he took up with the roots, and having wrapped it in rice straw, despatched it with the greatest care to Seringapatam, and it was there planted in the Lal Bagh, or garden—it did not, however, thrive, but soon died.

CHAPTER XIII

An account of the advance of an army under the command of General Meadows to the aid of the Raja of Maliwar, and the battles fought between the English army and that of the Sultan—the death of Burhanuddin Sipahsalar, who was slain near the Fort of Sati Mangal (Satyamangalam), the march of the Royal Standard towards the Payanghat, and an account of the different victories gained about that time, 1205, Hijri A D 1790.

When the conquering Sultan had completed the conquest of this country (Cochin, or Travancore,) he demanded tribute from the Poligar of Maliwar, and despatched a body of Kuzzaks to plunder and take possession of that woody country. The Poligar, therefore, trembling like a reed from fear of the Sultan's sharp sword, now sought aid and redress from the Governor of Madras and General Meadows was appointed to oppose the Sultan, the destroyer of his enemies, and advanced to Nuthur Nagar (Trichinopoly).

From that place, however, with the aid of the Poligar of Maliwar, who had assembled his army and was ready for action, he next marched forward by the route of Karur to attack the Sultan. Accordingly, in the vicinity of Coimbatore and Satyamangalam, he fell in with the advanced guard of the conquering army, and a sharp action followed, and from the clangour of the drums and trumpets, and the roar of the discharges of musketry, rockets, and cannon, the clamour of the day of resurrection arose from both armies, and the Kuzzaks having surrounded the followers of the British army in the forest of Dindigul, after killing and wounding many, took prisoners some of the sodiers with their women, muskets and baggage, the latter tied in bundles on their heads. Among these were some Muhammadan women, who from want of shame and fear of an hereafter, had gone aside from their religion, and had given up their impure bodies to the lust of men of other religions, (this refers to Europeans, I believe,) and they according to the orders of the Sultan were impaled. On this day, however, the troops of both armies after repelling the charges made by each other remained on equal terms, and in the evening the General taking up ground at the foot of the mountains encamped there.

The army the Sultan, however, surrounded the General's troops closely, and harassed them continually, by driving in their foraging parties, and stopping their supplies The next day, the General marched on and took the small fort of Satyamangalam (from which the Sultan had previously withdrawn the garrison), and left two battlions there under the command of Major

(Chalmers, or) Chambers He halted at this place a short time, and then marched towards Coimbatore, at which place at that time the Sultan himself was encamped—at hearing this news the Sultan, at the presumption of the general, was much excited, and with the whole of his army marched to meet him, and having taken up his ground for a regular field engagement, remained ready for action. On that day, however, the general did not advance, but encamped on the banks of the river Bhowani;[95] during this a body of English troops, which had been assembled at Seoram at first under the command of Colonel Kelly, lost its commanding officer, who died, and Colonel Maxwell, who had lately arrived from Bengal with five battalions of Native infantry, and a thousand Europeans, was appointed to command in his place, and with the subsidiary troops of the Poligars, that is the Poligars of Kalistri, Venkatagiri, &c. advanced by the route of Rai Vellore, and Ambur Garh, towards Coimbatore, and on the route leaving small garrisons in Wanumbari and Tirupattur (Tripatore), marched to the Ghat, or pass of Tuppur. The Sultan on being made acquainted with this movement, detached Syyad Sahib, Sipahsalar to arrest the progress of that body of troops, and he himself followed with the same intention, and marched in the direction of Dharompuri. The aforesaid Sipahsalar, however, had no sooner made a forced march with his division, than the Colonel (Maxwell), who was marching on the road to Dharampuri, suddenly countermarched and retired towards Gugungarh Syyad Ghaffar, therefore, with his Kuzzaks preceding the army moved on, and near that place fell in with and attacked the advanced guard of the English force, and cut them off, taking prisoners one hundred and fifty troopers and two hundred infantry.

The Colonel, therefore, on that day, kept the woody and hilly ground, and on the next marched towards Kaveri Pattan; when, however, he saw the Sultan's troops surrounding him on all sides, he kept close to the hilly country and marched in the direction of the Ghat of Tipur, and General Meadows proceeding by forced marches to join him, the two officers met at the foot of the Ghat near Kaveripur. At the period, however, of the junction of these officers, the faithful servants of the Sultan brought up their Kushuns between them, and displaying great bravery, obtained many advantages The English officers also with their troops charged the victorious army and fought desperately until the Sultan himself, with his Asad Illahi Kushuns, (or brigades) and artillery, vigorously attacked their rear and reduced them to such straights as left them no means or mode of escape.

The General, therefore, formed his army into a square, and taking his cattle and followers into the centre, marched by the

[95] One copy says, the Sultan did not advance.

route of Marpaich again towards Satyamangalam : in short, after the space of two or three months, in which the two armies had been continually doing all they could to distress and destroy each other, the supplies and provisions of the English army were exhausted, and the days of scarcity shewed their faces—the hope of further convoys of provisions or stores from any quarter now having vanished, the general with all his troops marched towards Trichinopoly (Tiruchirapalli). The victorious army, however, stopped his progress in the plain of Suttimangal, and so surrounded and so vigorously attacked him, that most of the officers (apparently the English), the lovers of justice and candour, expressed their astonishment at their valour. The keen sword and musket of the brave Musalmans destroyed many of the infidels, and it went very near that a total defeat and dispersion had fallen upon that army, when night came on and the veil of darkness fell before the faces of the fearless combatants, and both armies drew back their hands from the fight, and the General conceiving that day's march had been as difficult as if it had been on the tail of a serpent (alluding seemingly to the name of the road Marpaich, but there is some difference in the MSS here) halted where he was for the night.

When the Turk, or king of day, (the sun) marched with his army of light from the plains of the east towards the west, (in allusion apparently to the original country of the Turks), the General marched forward—he, however, left all his heavy baggage on the ground, and the Kuzzak horse and the Kushuns again were put in motion, and they surrounded him, and commenced the action like true and faithful soldiers, when, as fate decreed, Burhanuddin the Sipahsalar, who commanded the advanced guard of the victorious army, proceeded in front of the whole on horseback to examine the face of the field of battle, and to find ground qualified, or convenient for a cavalry charge It happened, that in front of him was a dry bed of a river, in which some English soldiers were stationed in ambush, and these seeing horsemen near them, fired a volley at them, and a ball from one of their unlucky muskets entered his valiant forehead, and he died and his soul sped to its eternal abode The troops with him now retired, and laying his body in a *palki*, and proceeding to the presence, reported the circumstances of his death. The Sultan, who had a tender heart, at the death of that strong arm of his prosperity, was much grieved, nay, so afflicted, that he shed many tears, and therefore, on that day he restrained his troops from fighting any more, and however much the Sipahdars and other officers desired that they might receive orders to attack and charge, and by that means decide the fortune of the day, still, no orders came, and they rubbed the hands of grief one upon the other. In this time the General (Meadows) perceiving that his enemies were timid and slow, marched on without delay, and entered the Fort of

Trichinopoly. The Sultan now consigned the troops of Burhanuddin Khan to Kamruddin Khan, and detached him to take the Fort of Satyamangalam, while he himself turned the direction of his standards towards the Payanghat and encamped in the neighbourhood of Turwur Paleh, and from thence detached his cavalry to plunder and destroy the towns (dependencies) of Trichinopoly (Tiruchirapalli) and those of Tanjore. The General now halted where he was for sometime, and then by the route of the sea-shore retired with his troops to Madras The Sultan, the destroyer of his enemies, now followed this army and arrived at Jingee and Purmokul Garh. In the meantime Kamruddin Khan, as soon as he had taken leave of the Sultan, immediately commenced the siege of the little fort of Satyamangalam, attacking it on all sides (it should be Coimbatore, according to Colonel Marriott) and after battering and destroying the walls prepared for the assault. Before, however, the victorious troops could take the fort by that mode of attack, the officer in command there, who was much distressed for want of ammunition, provisions, and water, despatched a messenger to the Khan, and made terms of peace, and after the sanction of agreements and covenants the fort was delivered up to the agents of the Sultan, and the Khan, having made over the fort to the charge of the Asaf of Sulaumabad, himself with his prisoners, returned to the presence. In result, orders were issued that the officers with Major Chalmers should be placed in confinement and sent to Seringapatam and that his Sipahees should be incorporated in the Sultan's Kushuns, and this was accordingly done

As soon as the General had arrived at Madras, the Sultan detached several large bodies of troops from his army to plunder and take possession of different parts of the country, and accordingly Kumruddin Khan was sent to take the Hill Fort of Purmokul Garh, the walls of which had formerly been battered down, but had lately been replaced by fortifications of earth, and an officer who had in former time been taken prisoner by the late Nawab with two hundred men, was appointed to command there. Kumruddin, therefore, according to orders with his own division of troops marched thither, and thousands of the poor inhabitants and peasantry of the neighbourhood, relying on the strength of the English garrison, having sought refuge on the hill were plundred and destroyed The cause was this, that immediately on the arrival of the Sultan's troops, the officer commanding in the fort frightened at their great numbers, and recollecting his former perils and hardships under pretence of violent headache, took to his chamber and left the defence of the fort to the Subadars and other officers, and they seeing from the want of order and arrangement in the store and provision departments, that there was no chance of successfully defending the fort, agreeably to the wishes of their officer peaceably surrendered it. The whole of the people, therefore, who had sought refuge there were placed in confinement, and at that time Kishan Rao, the Mutsuddi, or clerk of the Sultan's treasury, arriving, he exacted the sum of ten thousand rupees from these poor people, and then released them. The officer and garrison of Purmokul were also allowed to proceed to Madras.

CHAPTER XIV

An account of the arrival from Bengal of the Governor-General, Earl Cornwallis, Bahadur—the Commander-in-Chief of the English army and his confederacy with Nizam Ali Khan, and the Mahrattas Also, the march of the confederates to attack on all sides, and root up the power of the Khodadad (the Kingdom of Mysore) and the conquest of the Forts and Towns of the Balaghat Also, the Battles fought between the army of the Sultan and those of the confederates with other events of the year, 1206 Hijri—A D. 1791.

The maritime intelligence department of the English government now reported to the Commander-in-Chief of their army, the march of the Sultan to the country of the Karnatak Payanghat, that the whole of the province had been swept by the tempest of desolation—that the troops of the victorious army had occupied it on all sides, and that General Meadows, after some exertions, from the want of provisions, and other stores, being without resource, had returned to Madras—that if the enemy were not soon expelled, there was great danger of a general rebellion in that country, and that it would then quickly pass out of the hands of the English government

About this time, also, Abu Kasim Khan, called also Mir-i-Alam, the ambassador of Nizam Ali Khan, who had been sent to Bengal previously, by the policy of Mushir-ul-Mulk,[96] the Prime Minister of the chief of Hydarabad, to stimulate and incite the Commander-in-chief of the English army to the destruction of the Khodadad state, finding every thing favourable to his views, exerted himself to the utmost, and the Commander-in-chief, or rather the Governor-general wrote to the Nizam of Hydarabad, and the Chief of Puna (the Paishwa) recommending their conquering, and then dividing amongst them, the whole of the Balaghat provinces, and then despatched orders to prepare military equipment, and collect troops to the Governor, &c. of Madras—he himself making preparations at the same time.

The Nizam and Mahrattas who were looking out for an invitation to seize and plunder the wealth and territory of those who had no friends to assist them, in conformity to the suggestion of the Governor-general, with one accord assembled their troops and made all necessary preparations for war. The English officers too, in collecting their stores and munitions of war, each being separately appointed to his work, made all things ready with great labour, and Colonel Read, the Darogha of the intelligence department, who was appointed to the command of Ambur Garh, with great address, and by the liberal distribution of money, sweet

[96] *'alim kharab.*

words, and kind actions, brought over to his side the whole of the Poligars of the Balaghat, who from the oppression and cruelty of the late Nawab, and the tyrannical character of the Sultan had abandoned their own country, and had sought refuge in the towns of the Karnatak Payanghat; such as the Poligar of Gungundi Pala, the sons of Bhyreh Koor, the Poligar of Chak Balapur, Pud Nair, the Poligar of Venkatagiri Kote, who was residing at Charkul; Shunk Rayel, or Rawul, the Chief of Punganur, and besides these, the Poligars of Khut Kumnir, Madanapalli, Anikul, Onkus Giri, Cheel Naik, &c all being dispossessed of their lands, received written assurances of protection, and were despatched to their own districts on condition they should collect and forward supplies of forage and provisions to the English army; and they also received authority to retake or recover (by any means) their own districts and Taluks, and, notwithstanding the severe restrictions in the Balaghat, where without passes from the heads of districts, a man was not permitted to go from one town to another, he, Colonel Read, obtained maps of the whole of the country, by sending clever spies and able munshis at great expense, dressed as merchants into that country, and by their agency or mediation, also, several chiefs and officers of the Sirkar Khodadad, having been brought over to his interest, he sat waiting the arrival of the Governor-general, and although a certain Syyad Imam previously private intelligencer to Colonel Read, who was residing at the capital (Pattan) had obtained employment in the Sultan's service; still, he wrote and despatched correct intelligence on all subjects, continually to Colonel Read, and he also had assembled a number of traitors to his aid; when all at once the dish of his detection and shame appeared from beneath the blanket, (in allusion to some Persian custom, or game, apparently) for his treachery by reason of some correction he had given to a boy, his servant, or slave, was published to the world; and at length certain of the Sultan's faithful servants seized him and his boy and brought them before the presence, and detailed all the circumstances of his treachery; this doomed man, therefore, fell under the heavy displeasure of the Sultan, and he was asked by him, what have you been doing? "If you tell the truth you may by that means save your life for a time." In these difficulties this foolish man made up a story with truth and falsehood intermixed, and wrote the names of several officers who had leagued with him in his treachery, and presented them to the Sultan, and according to this list of names, fifteen persons, such as Lall Khan Bakhshi of Punganore; Mir Nazar Ali, Mokubdar and his brother, and Ismael Khan Risaldar, &c were seized and given over in-charge to the executioner, and after the proof or establishment of the secret intelligence writer's guilt (Islam Khan's) the Sultan asked him "how he who had eaten his salt could have acted so treacherously, and what punishment he thought such conduct deserved?"

The culprit however, returned no answer, and the Sultan then said, "send this gentlemen[97] with the rest of his companions"; and he was also put to death.

Another person also, named Imam-uddin, a news writer, who had been employed in the same work and who resided at Kolar and Nandi Garh, hearing this news at night, fled from that place to Kurumpaut, depending on Sautgurh Still, however, notwithstanding the disclosure of all this treachery, and the execution of his hired dependants, Colonel Read did not abstain from his intrigues and projects As soon as intelligence, that the troops, provisions, and stores were all ready, reached the Governor-General, he immediately with five thousand Bengal Sipahis, and two thousand Europeans, embarked on board ship and sailed to Madras, and after remaining there a month, he marched, accompanied by twenty-four regiments of Native Infantry; six thousand Europeans, and three thousand regular cavalry and with great discipline and order, arrived at Rai Vellore, en route to the conquest of the Balaghat.

In the meantime, the Sultan while he remained encamped near Turwadi, had entered into some negotiation with the French of Pondicherry for aid and support when his spies brought him intelligence of the march of the Governor-General In consequence, therefore, of this report, Muhammad Khan Bakshi was detached with a large body of troops, and marched by the route of the Chunguma Ghat to Tripatur—the fort of which was garrisoned by one hundred English Sipahis, commanded by an European Officer, and three hundred foot, belonging to the Poligar of Kalistri, under the command of Ankupa Nair. This fort, therefore, Muhammad Khan closely surrounded, and thus endeavoured to block up the road of escape to the garrison. The officer in the fort and the Nair, however, after counting the stars all night, before sunrise next morning, evacuated the fort and took the road to Ambur Garh. Muhammad Khan's horse, however, followed them close, and fell in with them near the foot of the hills of Jowadi Pala and at one charge defeated them.

The officer and the Nair were taken prisoners, and the horse returned. At this time, Nizam Ali Khan with forty thousand horse and twenty thousand foot, accompanied by his most trusty Amirs, and his sons Alijah, and Sekundar Jah, marched from Hydarabad, and encamped at Pankul, and he thence despatched his Amirs with a large force in advance to conquer the possessions of the Sultan Tht Commander-in-chief of the English army had effected the passage of his army by the Ghat, or pass of Mogli-evinkut Giri, and had posted detachments in the towns of More-wakul,[98] Kolar and Hoskote, and marching on had arrived at

[97] *buzurg zadeh.*

[98] Called by Colonel Marriott, Malwaggle

Kishan Rajpur, which is three kos from Bangalore; when the Sultan receiving intelligence of his progress, made a forced march to stop him.

It is not to be omitted here, that when the French heard of the movements of the English army and the plunder and ravage of the Payanghat, from their extreme regard and friendship for the Sultan, they were very unwilling that any injury should be sustained by his army—they, therefore, determined to send him a thousand men of their nation to assist him, that in all his measures they might be ready to serve under his orders—some, however, of the Sultan's servants, upon whose advice he placed the greatest reliance, with the view of manifesting their loyalty, represented that the throne and crown of that sun of the constellation of kingly power and greatness, (*i.e.* the Sultan) would rise and culminate without the countenance or assistance of others, and that the conquering Sultan did not in any way require the aid of French troops[99]—that, moreover, it was proper to consider to whom these troops had ever been faithful, and what prince with their assistance had been supported and established? By these specious arguments, they so effectually influenced the Sultan, that he rejected the offer of assistance from the French, and with his own troops only, marched to repel his powerful enemies, and the same night detached his Kuzzaks and rocketeers to surround and fire into the camp of the English army, while he himself proceeded to Bangalore. The Kuzzaks, therefore, remained all night attacking, or sniping and throwing rockets into the English camp, until the morning when the English Commander-in-chief (Lord Cornwallis), without taking much notice of them, marched on and left a place full of fear and danger, and that day encamped at Hosur, and the next day again marched to the north eastward and encamped at the distance of one fursung from the town of Bangalore

The Sultan now, therefore, appointed Syyad Hamid Sipahdar with his Kushun to the charge of the second or lower fort, and Muhammad Khan Bakhshi before mentioned, and a certain Bahadur Khan, who had previously been Foujdar of Kishingiri was appointed governor of the upper fort or citadel and Shaikh Onsar was sent with him.

The Sultan then marched on to the vicinity of Tunkri, where he determined to encamp, and directed his victorious standards to be planted there, neither the Sultan's tents nor those of any others, however, were yet pitched, most of the horse were scattered in search of forage, and only three or four Kushuns of the Jysh and Usad Illahi infantry, and two or three thousand stable horse (household troops) remained with the Sultan, when Colonel Floy

[99] It appears clear the author thinks he had better have accepted them.

(Floyd) with the whole of the English regular cavalry advanced and charged into the Sultan's camp, and all at once arrived in front of the Tope Khana or park of artillery. The artillery and the officers of the Kushuns, however, now immediately formed up and arrested their progress, and with their guns and muskets soon quelled their pride and insolence, and compelled them to retreat quickly.

It happened also that the colonel above-mentioned was struck with a musket ball in the throat and the wound depriving him of the power of speech,[100] the other officers commanding regiments, not being able to continue the engagement, turned their faces from the field of battle. The brave horse now pursued and attacked them, with the greatest vigour with sword and spear, and four hundred English troopers with their horses were taken prisoners—the remainder spared by the sword, fled, rising and falling to the main body of the army The next day Colonel Moorhouse[101] and General Meadows with a strong body of troops attacked the town (the Pettah of Bangalore) and after the sacrifice of thousands of men on both sides, and after an attack of six hours, the town was with great gallantry taken, and so large a quantity of spoil such as gold, jewels, &c., fell into the hands of the captors, that penury and want were thenceforward discharged or struck off from the muster roll of the English army. The colonel before mentioned (Moorhouse) was killed by wounds from musket balls during the storm. After this, the English collected the materials for their operations such as fascines, stockades, &c round the town and commenced raising batteries, and for fourteen days they battered the fort continually.

During this time, however, Kamruddin Khan, agreeably to the Sultan's orders, with his own division of troops, remained in the vicinity of Busoon Gori to render all the assistance he could to the besieged. When, however, the walls of the fort were battered down, the Sultan became very anxious and fearful for the result, and therefore gave orders that the fort should be evacuated , Kishan Rao accordingly was sent there and he brought away all the property of the state, such as the guns, the money, &c with the store and other departments; and they were despatched to Seringapatam, leaving only one Kushun and two thousand irregular troops, (Ahsham) with their artillery in the fort. It was, therefore, determined by the advice of certain of the Sultan's counsellors, that the defence of the fort, should be left to Monsieur Lally and that Kamruddin Khan and Syyad Sahib with a strong force should be appointed to make a demonstration against the English army, while the Sultan himself should march to arrest the progress of the Mughals (the Nizam's troops)

[100] See Colonel Welsh's Journal or Reminiscences Vol I, p 9.
[101] *moors muras*

and the Mahrattas. In pursuance of this arrangement the French Officer (Lally) actually marched and had arrived at the tank or reservoir[102] of the canal, when Kishan Rao, and some other traitors becoming acquainted with this plan gave a hint to the English Hurkaras, who were always about them habited as their own servants, and they immediately apprised the guards in the trenches that now the time had arrived to make an assault and take the fort. Kishan Rao after this left the fort, and at the bank of the tank above mentioned, meeting Monsieur Lally, took him by the hand and kept him in conversation about trifles, while the officers in the trenches as soon as they received the information before mentioned, immediately got their troops in readiness and a little after midnight all at once made their attack. Syyad Hamid the Sipahdar and the Killadars (commanders of the garrison) according to the directions of the traitor Kishan Rao, had allowed their men who were all prepared to defend the fort, to go to their quarters and cook their victuals, and therefore, except a few, sentinels, no one remained at their posts, but notwithstanding their helpless condition they boldly advanced to repel their assailants, and drove them back from the chain of the gate. The Europeans, however, having been quickly supplied with the wine (or rather spirituous liquor), which inspires courage, returned to the charge, and by the time the brave garrison had assembled, they had stormed and mounted the walls and towers. The Syyad being without his men and seeing he could not maintain his ground, escaped and joined the army The two Killadars with forty or fifty of their men planting their feet manfully at the gate, were there slain, as was Shaikh Budhan Risaldar, after giving manifold proofs of his courage and fidelity. Shaikh Onsar Sipahdar and the Naikwars (the Nairs or Hindu chiefs) and soldiers of the fort were taken prisoners. The fort, therefore, was captured and the garrison with their women and children, and their money and property of all kinds fell into the possession of the English soldiers, and the women were given up to violation.[103] Although at the time of the assault the Sultan mounted his horse, and with his troops stood ready to engage the enemy; still, he restrained his hand from shedding the blood of God's people, and although the Khan above mentioned (Kamruddin) and Syyad Sahib often requested orders to charge the English troops, the Sultan replied that the time would come by and by, for that the favourable opportunity had passed, and that they were on no accountn to allow their men to fall into disorder. The next morning the Sultan marched on, and placing the jungul or forest of Makri in his rear, encamped there. In short, after three or four days, the Commander-in-Chief of the English army appointed a garrison of two

[102] *kariz.*
[103] *namusha taraj dadnalah*

or three thousand native infantry and six hundred Europeans to the charge of the fort, and leaving there part of the stores of his army, marched by the route of Yulunka to cover and take into his possession the supplies of provisions and cattle, which the Poligars of the north, such as the chiefs of Chak-Balapur, Punganur (Punganuru), Khut Komnere and Maddan Palli had collected according to their engagements, and who with great gallantry had dispossessed the Sultan's officers some by fair, and some by foul means of the forts, towns, and villages, which had been previously their hereditary possessions, and were now enjoying themselves in their success without fear or restraint. Although in the neighbourhood of the place above-mentioned, Kamruddin Khan with a large force had possession, or command of the roads, and laboured hard to obstruct and defeat the English, and that the Kuzzaks also constantly hung on the rear of their army, and put to confusion and dispersed their followers, and cattle, plundering them of property to a great amount, and also, that the troops in general, in repelling their enemies used every exertion ; still, the days of conquest did not come to the Sultan's aid, but hid themselves from his sight

The commander-in-chief of the English army that day halted on the same ground ; the next day he moved on to the neighbourhood of Yusufabad, otherwise called Devanhalli, where he encamped, and having despatched an officer with a party of men to the fort, and having brought over the officer commanding there to surrender without resistance, he took possession of the fort, and divided the stores of grain and other articles among his own men. After the lapse of two days the Commander-in-Chief again marched and encamped near Balapur Khurd, but the officer in charge of the fort there, agreeably to the Sultan's orders evacuated the fort before the arrival of the English army and with all the infantry, Naikwars, and stores, retired to the Hill Fort of Nandi and consequently the advanced guard of the English took possession of the fort without opposition, and the stores and provisions that were lying about fell into their hands. The Commander-in-Chief here taking pity on the misfortunes of Ramaswamy Koor, to whom the possession of that district belonged in hereditary right, made it over to him with the fort, and its dependencies, on condition that he paid yearly a tribute of one lakh of rupees. He then marched on towards Ambajee Drug and as after a very long time his (Ramaswamy's) good fortune had favoured him and the capital of his district fell into his hands, at a fortunate moment he entered the fort, and after repairing and making arrangements for its security, he left there six hundred foot under his own followers and strengthening it with stores and artillery proceeded to Tulkai Gonda, a town or fort seated in the midst of a dense jungle The conquering Sultan now ordered Ancupa Nair and the English officers, who had been taken prisoners at the fort of Tripatur (Tirupattur), to be delivered over to the executioners, and Yogi Pundit the nephew of Achna Pandit the Naib of the Suba of Arkat, who during the reign of the Sultan, had been advanced to high dignity and had received the title of Raja Ramchandar, and was also appointed Serishtadar of the whole of the Taluks of Bangalore, but who from his evil destiny, had not acted in conformity to the orders of the Sultan, but had leagued with the enemy, was put to death in company with the Poligars of Harpanhalli, and Rai Drug, who had been imprisoned and were executed because for some days the fire of the Sultan's wrath burned fiercely, at the bare mention of the names of the Poligars. Kishan Rao was at this time sent to take charge of the capital (Seringapatam), and to despatch money for the payment of the troops, while the Sultan himself with the army and its departments marched in pursuit of the English army to Balapur Khurd. The splendour of the Sultan's standard, however, no sooner shone on that fort, than the garrison with great folly beat to arms and sounded their trumpets on the ramparts, at the same time howling and barking like a pack of hounds The Sultan, therefore, determined to punish them, and ordered his brave troops to assault, and they with ladders and ropes soon escaladed the walls and conquered their enemies, for although the garrison with one heart and hand giving up all care for their lives, fought so desperately that two thousand Ghazies bit the dust, they were at length subdued, and gave their heads and breasts as an oblation to the sword and spear, and three hundred foot soldiers who were taken alive, according to the orders of the Sultan for an example to others, had their hands and feet cut off, or broken with saws and hatchets by his executioners and they were then left on the ground. In a moment, therefore, the clamour of the day of judgement arose from these unfortunate men, and after this (most unjust and cruel act) the Sultan marched from that place and encamped in the neighbourhood of Sulket.

The Commander-in-Chief of the English army, Lord Cornwallis, in the mean time had taken the fort of Ambaji Drug from the Killadar Muhammad Khan Burka, and had razed the works to the ground, and after that encamped there two or three days. The Poligars who have been before mentioned in this period. forwarded provisions and cattle to the English camp, and received great praise and reward for their service The Sipahsalar or Commander-in-Chief of the English, then marched on and encamped near the fort of Murg Mulla, when Asad Ali Khan and Bhar Mal, the Dewan of Mushir-ul-Mulk, with five thousand horse, entered the English camp, and the next day they marched from that place by the road of Chintumani and Morwakul to Vinkat Giri Pala The brave and powerful Sultan with his victorious army had at this time turned the head of his generous steed towards the English army with the intention to attack it, when a jasoos, or spy dressed in a suit of mouring arrived, sent by his mother from Seringapatam, and this man in private informed the Sultan that the villain Kishan Rao conspiring with some other traitors, had so concerted and arranged that probably by this time a sedition had broken out in the capital, or would soon break out, the repression of which it would not be very easy to accomplish,—he having followed the path of the rejected[104] Khundi Rao, and had sent for a large body of English troops from Bombay and that the Queen (the Sultan's wife) had given up all hope or care of her life—at hearing this intelligence the Sultan despatched Syyad Sahib with a body of troops to provide for the security and order of his capital.

[104] *mardud*

CHAPTER XV

An account of the reduction to order and obedience of the Capital, and the merited punishment of the Traitor Kishan Rao, with the arrival of the Sultan there. Also, the Invasion and ravage of the Musalman Territory (Mysore) by the Mughals and Mahrattas, with other events of the same year 1206, Hijri—A D 1791

When Syyad Sahib received orders to depart, he proceeded forthwith by the route of the Makri Jangal and Rai Drug, and arrived at the capital of the Sultan, Seringapatam, at mid-night, and placed his encampment on this side the river, while he himself with a few friends, and four or five hundred horse advanced to the gate of the fort, and before the appearance of the first light of the morning, called out to the guard at the gate to open it. As it happened, that Asad Khan Risaldar and other loyal subjects of the Sultan had been appointed to the charge of this gate, they pleased at the arrival of the Syyad, opened the wickets, and he entered, and having stationed parties of his horse over different departments of the state, he proceeded to pay his respects to the Sultan's mother, and she seated herself in the Hall of audience. At this time the commander of the troops at the capital, who was deeply implicated in the treason of the Brahmin, finding his secret disclosed to the world immediately repaired to the Syyad, and boasting of his own fidelity and loyalty, and condemning the folly and treason of the Brahmin, persisted in demanding that he should be imprisoned. The Syyad, therefore, despatcher a Chobedar[105] to summon Kishan Rao, to the Hall of audience or Durbar, and as he, being aware of his danger, returned for answer, that it was unusual and unreasonable the Syyad should send him orders, that he had nothing to do with him—his answer confirming the suspicion before entertained of his treachery, the Syyad ordered the persons present to proceed to his house and seize him, and they forcing their way into his house and breaking open the door of his apartment, which he had bolted, or secured in the inside, they with their swords and muskets put him to death, and threw his body into the drain of the bazaar, and his house was plundered, and the property found in it carried to the treasury. During the last moments, however, of this fiend, he said—"I have lighted up a fire, which as long as the Sultan lives will not be extinguished ·" —this, alas, was but too true. His wife who was beautiful, faithful, and virtuous, of her own accord, despatched a message to the Queen, (*maleka zamana*) and sought refuge with her, and by the mediation of that veiled lady of the curtain of chastity and honour,

105 A man who carries a silver or gold-headed stick before chiefs in India and is employed as a messenger

she was placed in the Haram Serai of the Sultan. Another person has, however, told this story in a different way—he states that when the villain Brahmin, notwithstanding the favours and honours showered on him, was seeking the ruin of the Sultan; his virtuous wife becoming acquainted with his designs, and being disgusted at the base ingratitude and treachery of her husband, despatched a verbal message by her nurse to the Sultan's mother, informing her of his absurd and foolish machinations, and some, who say that the Sultan after the slaying of the traitor Brahmin, tyrannically forced his wife to enter his Seraglio, make a false charge and lying accusation, for at the time of the death of her husband, if she had not been willing to go to the Sultan, would she not under some pretence, or by some contrivance have put herself to death[106]—but omitting this, could she not have made away with herself when sent for to the Haram

But to return—the Sultan after the departure of Syyad Sahib, appointed Kamruddin Khan to command a body of ten thousand horse, that he should take every opportunity to attack and harass the army and baggage of the strangers, while he himself marched towards his capital to restore order there The General in Chief of the English in the course of three days, despatched all his Bunjaras and Lemauns,[107] and his hired cattle to Ambur Garh, and sending for all articles of necessity, such as stores of grain, bread, artillery and ammunition, he marched by the route of Bid Mangal, and Malur, to Bangalore The Sultan's Commander-in-Chief marching towards the English army, gave orders to his Kuzzaks to disguise themselves so as to appear like the troops of the Nizam, and attack the rear guard of the enemy, which was composed of the Mughal or Nizam's horse, and two regiments of English cavlary, and they like hungry lions among sleeping deer, fell on them and entirely defeated them, taking five thousand bullocks laden with grain, and two hundred Mughal horse. In short, every day the Sillahdars, Kuzzaks, Afghans, and Dekhanese, threw themselves like as the moth throws himself on the candle, on the pickets, and advanced parties of the two armies (the English and Mughal) and multitudes of men became the food of the unsparing sword, spear and musket, and the route of communication, and the passage of supplies to the enemy were completely shut and blocked up, so indeed that night or day, no one could quit their camp—and as during the course of this contention and warfare, by God's assistance, from the exceeding bravery of the soldiers of the victorious army, great fear fell on the minds of the enemy, the pride and insolence in which they had indulged, because the Sultan did not oppose them in person, was now

[106] The author supposes this mode of reasoning perfectly conclusive

[107] Men who carry grain about for sale on bullocks, the latter term, however, is not, I believe, used for Bunjaras in Hindusthan

changed to fear and trembling, and they became timid, doubtful and suspicious.

We have now arrived at the point where it is necessary to describe the movements of Nizam Ali Khan and the Mahrattas. The chief of Hydarabad selected the town of Pangul for his fixed encampment, and despatched his Amirs to conquer the Sultan's territory and accordingly Mallik Esau, Khan Miran, Yar Jung, with his division of troops marched, and after the labours of some months, took the forts of Ganji Kota, Tar Puttri, Tar Meeri &c., and Hafiz Farid-uddin Khan, entitled Moyud ud Dowla, with a large force marched towards Guti, and Kotab-uddin Khan Dowlat Zai, the Foujdar of that district with his body of troops opposed him; on the first day, however, fortune did not befriend him, and he was obliged to retreat. The second day he formed up his men in front of the enemy and displayed great courage, but at that very time he was ordered to attend the Sultan, and, therefore, he marched with his troops to Seringapatam. Hafiz, when he saw it was beyond the power of his followers to take the Hill Fort of Fyze Hissar, otherwise Guti (Gooty), levelled every thing in that district with the dust, and then returned and encamped at Kirpa, and after a short time, with little trouble took the town of Kirpa, and the fort of Sadhut, and next with four thousand horse and five thousand foot, and eight or nine guns, he commenced the siege of Guram Konda, and occupied himself day and night in endeavours to take the fort, but although he made several assaults and forwarded lying letters to (persons of) the garrison, still, the commanders of the hill and lower forts did not allow doubt or fear to enter their minds, but with different kinds of fire arms (shells, rockets, &c.) and the constant discharge of cannon and musketry, they blackened the face of the courage of their adversaries

The Chiefs of the Mahrattas, during this time having taken leave of the Paishwa, proceeded to take possession of the forts of the Mysore territory contiguous to their frontier, and accordingly Purusram, the Chief of Mirch, took some forts and towns in his neighbourhood—some by force and some intimidation and capitulation, and annexed them to his own district Budruzaman Khan the Sahib Subah of the fort of Dharwar, having strengthened that fort by the collection of stores of provisions, arms and ammunition, was besieged, and for eight or nine months did justice to his station (the Killadari) and his courage, but when his ammunition and provisions began to fail, he being without resource, made a regular capitulation and surrendering the fort to his enemies, he was made prisoner by the Mahrattas, with two thousand men,[108]—he, however, with his party was confined in

[108] A detachment of British troops, under Colonel Little, was employed in this siege.

one place, but at length his base enemy (the Paishwa) from the wickedness of his disposition, ordered his servants to put the Khan in irons, and send him to Puna, when the Khan heard of these orders he recited the Lahowl[109] on the violated faith of the agreements made by these scoundrels, and giving up all hopes of preserving his life, he bravely with his campanions retired fighting as he went towards Nagar[110] The Mahrattas in the meantime, in number like ants and locusts, crowded round his party and attacked them on all sides with musket and sword, and notwithstanding all the brave soldiers of the Sultan could do in their defence, they were overpowered, and after destroying thousands of the infidels, the Khan being wounded, was made prisoner, and he was put in irons, and confined on the Hill of Nurgunda, and his followers were all trodden under the hoofs of the Mahratta horse The whole of the towns and the villages of that part of the country, therefore fell into the possession of the soldiers of the Mahratta army. Hari Pant Phurkia, also, after taking possession of different parts of the country, advancing by the route of Harpanahalli, placed a man, named Shoom Shunker, the Poligar of that district, (who was in attendance on him as an Omeidwar of Volunteer) on the Musnud of his hereditary possessions He next reduced the Suba of Sura under his authority. The Chief of Mirch Parasuram, after having captured and garrisoned the forts of Dharwar, Angola, Murjan, Sanore &c marched to Chitaldrug, and sending the terms of capitulation to Dowlat Khan, (the Killadar) engaged if he would join him and give up the fort, that no injury should be done to him or his property, and that a jageer of four lakhs of rupees should be conferred on him;—this faithful servant, however, being then occupied in planning how he should destroy his enemies, affected to accept these conditions, and in reply sent word that at night he himself would visit the Mahratta, and in his presence make the necessary arrangements according to his wishes. Parasuram was delighted with this answer and remained in expectation of the visit When night arrived, however, the Sultan's faithful servant with two risalas of the Asad Illahees and one thousand irregular foot, quitting the fort with a determination to penetrate to Parasuram's tent and there do the best he could, marched into their camp.

When he had arrived in the centre of the camp, one of the soldiers being drunk fired off his musket, but, although, Dowlat Khan in the first burst of his anger ordered him to be put to death, still the report of the musket roused the whole of the

[109] The form of an exorcism used by the Musalmans, the words being *la haula we la quwatu illa billahi*

[110] It does not appear from this that he was in confinement as beforestated.

Mahrattas and they got themselves in readiness to receive their enemy, Dowlat Khan, now, therefore, stretched forth the arm of courage, and with his keen sword, cut and slashed the garment of life off the bravest of the Hindu soldiers, and prostrated multitudes of them on the field of death, and at length the whole of the enemy's troops were scattered and dispersed, and they with their officers took the road to Sura, and the brave Dowlat Khan by his enterprize and valour thus conquered his enemies, and with all the baggage of their army, the tents, arms, accoutrements and some horses with saddles and trappings returned victorious to his quarters. The chief of Mirch now marched from Sura and arrived at Mudgiri, and appointed a certain Mahdu, his sister's son to take the fort of Mudgiri, while he himself with supplies of provisions and cattle marched to join the English army—during this time the Commander-in-Chief of the English, in the space of fifteen or twenty days, having put his army in order (restored their material) marched towards Seringapattam by the route of Burdi and Chen Pattan, but the infantry of the Commander-in-Chief of the Sultan's army who were posted in ambush in the forest of Makri, during the dark nights gained many signal advantages over the army of the enemy, and every night captured five or six hundred Bunjaras, (men who carry corn about for sale), with their bullocks laden with corn, and returned after cutting off the noses and ears of the men, and whoever brought in a nose received a hoon or a pagoda (as a reward), any one who brought in an ear, received a purtab (or half a pagoda), for every horse two hoons were given. Every day, therefore, the Kuzzaks attacked the enemy in front and in rear, and exceedingly harassed and distressed their soldiers, often threw the followers into confusion, and almost all their bullocks laden with grain and stores were driven off and taken by them, and to that height was this harassing warfare carried on, that when the English army arrived in the neighbourhood of Kurri Khet, (or as it is usually written Karighat), there were no provisions or stores left in that army. It happened also that this was the rainy season and the water of the River Kaveri rushed down its bed with the greatest violence,—before the arrival of the English army, however, the Sultan had raised four or five batteries in front to oppose their passage and had armed them with musketry and guns, and the brave Sipahdars according to orders with their men, took up their stations in each to defend them.

This was no sooner done than the Commander-in-Chief of the English (Lord Cornwallis) before daybreak in the morning advanced and attacked the batteries, and took two of them in the most gallant manner. General Meadows also with a large body of troops made a fierce assault on the Hill of Karighat. The Sipahdar commanding there, however, whose name was Syyad Hamid, poured forth from the top of the hill such vollies of musketry and such a fire from his guns, that from the shock, the assailants were completely scattered and notwithstanding the exertions they made to take the hill, obtained no advantage, and after the destruction of thousands of their men they were obliged to retire—at this period two regiments of Europeans marched to attack the encampment of Husain Khan Khulil Sipahdar, which was pitched between the hill and the fort (of Seringapatam). The brave Husain Khan kept up a heavy fire from his guns until they arrived near, when he left his guns in the rear and formed line in front of the enemy, planting his feet firmly on the ground of his honour and duty, and in fighting and repelling his enemies he nobly distinguished himself: *verses*, "Behold on each side men keen for the fight,"—"their talons sharp for bloodshed" —"With the blood spilled, so much life passed into the earth," (from the bodies of the slain) "that the earth itself received life"—"On both sides the battle was long sustained,"—"the knots of contention were not unravelled." In short with the fiery musket, the bayonet, spear and sword, he did justice to his courage and character, and the Khan Khalil being wounded was at length taken prisoner by the enemy.

His men also, with the pride and devotion of Islam, after fighting bravely, one after another drank the cup of martyrdom. But to return; for fifteen or twenty days the Commander-in-Chief of the English army was sedulously occupied in watering the river bed of his labour,[111] and schemed and devised numberless modes of taking the Fort of Seringapatam, but it was all in vain, and he became more and more involved in difficulties, and to increase them still further, ensured the total want of provisions, the cries of famine, arising from all parts of his camp, and in addition, to the total deficiency of wood and forage, a seer (a measure weighing a little more than a pound) of rice, was sold nominally at the price of four rupees, but no one ever saw a grain, and three rupees was the price of a seer of flour of Khush Khushi-Soorkh, that is Raggee, (a small grain growing in the south of India). The rice of a seer of clarified butter was eight rupees, and a hoon was also paid for a chicken, but even at that price they were not procurable. The Europeans could not support this scarcity of food, and therefore, according to the orders of their officers the gun bullocks were killed and their flesh served to sustain their strength for some time—when, however, the Commander-in-Chief saw the signs of impending ruin in his army, and heard of the plunder of a large convoy coming from Malabar under a strong escort and which was captured by the Kuzzaks of Ghazi Khan Bede, and the Sillahdars of Syyad Sahib; the escort put to the sword and the stores, &c. all converted to the service of the Sultan; he fell into deep thought and reflection, and after the

111 Uselessly I suppose from what follows.

assembly and sanction of a council of war, he determined to take care of himself and his army, and to that end buried all his guns in the earth, and burned their carriages, and next shot all his weak and useless horses, and then marched on his return by the route of Kurri Koort

The Sultan when he became aware of this movement, determined to pass a joke on the Commander-in-Chief, and therefore, despatched five or six benghis or baskets of fruit under the escort of a party of rocket men, addressed to the Governor-General's[112] Persian Secretary : some of the officers of the English army understanding the joke, or the inference to be drawn therefrom, sent the fruit bearers back with a present and an answer to the effect that their Persian writer was not then present with the army. In short the Commander-in-Chief marched with the greatest difficulty, and the light guns which were indispensable to the army, were dragged along the road by the soldiers, and every day from day-light to the evening, they marched only about four miles, and although at witnessing the miserable state of their army, some of the Sultan's faithful Amirs and Khans represented to him that this was the time to attack them, and that if he would give orders they would pursue the English army, and cast the stone of dispersion and defeat among them, and by their prowess bring them with their hands and feet bound before him, still, his foresight and intelligence did not perceive any advantages in separating his brave army from himself, and therefore, he would not consent to it. The Sipahsalar of the English, therefore, moved on gently without molestation or fear towards Otridrug, the Killadar of which hill fort, seeing the multitudes of troops brought against him, suffered his courage to ooze out at his fingers' ends, and with the keys of the fort went to meet the Commander-in-Chief, who received him with great favour, and found a large quantity of stores and a great number of cattle there, of which having taken possession, he gave some relief to his suffering army. In fact three goats might be purchased for one rupee in their bazaar, and the famished people of the camp, being unable to support the pangs of hunger oppressing them, subsisted entirely on the flesh of goats and bullocks, and this diet gave them a flux or dysentry and many died—they could not, however, obtain any kind of grain—the Sipahsalar, or General, therefore, after encamping there two days and procuring some bullocks to draw his guns, marched towards Sondah Kupeh, where he arrived after a month's march,[113] (a mistake here apparently) and where Parasuram joined him with stores and provisions, and the English army was relieved by him from the miseries of famine, for the Mahratta sent his own Bunjaras to the English camp, and they

112 That is to the Commander-in-Chief

113 See Thornton, Vol II p 434

opening their stores of grain by his orders, in one day caused such a change in the state of affairs, that two seers of rice were sold to all for one rupee and four or five seers of jowar[114] for the same amount, and consequently half the scarcity was removed when Colonel Read, who had arrived at Bangalore with an immense supply of stores and provisions, despatched thence abundance of grain of all kinds, carts of arrack and bread, with fowls, ducks, geese, sheep and cattle, and for this he was highly complimented by the Commander-in-Chief, who in reward for his good and faithful service, appointed him to the collectorship of the revenue at Bangalore, Huskote, Kolar, Murwakul and Hosur, with the political agency of the Poligars of that part of the country.

The Commander-in-Chief after this, commmissioned and despatched several officers with strong bodies of troops to take the forts of Makri Drug, and Nandi Garh, and in consequence Colonel Gowdie with three battalions of native infantry and one regiment of Europeans, besieged Nandi Garh, and battered it on all sides. Colonel Read also marched from Kolar with six hundred Sipahis to attack the same fort, and he doubtless used the utmost exertion in its capture, for notwithstanding he received a musket ball in his thigh, he took it in eighteen days On the night of the assault, however, General Meadows went down to the trenches or breaching battery and promised the Europeans that all the plunder they took should be free , and likewise all the women who fell into their hands—(for by the mis-management of Lutf Ali Beg, the Bakhshi there, a great number of men and women were allowed to shut up in the fort), the General then gave orders for the assault. The storming party immediately moved off, and at one attack mounted and covered the hill, and took the fort, and fearlessly possessed themselves of the property and women of the garrison—thousands of women, therefore, were violated,[115] some of them to preserve their virtue and religion threw themselves from the top of the hill down a precipice to the bottom, and thus sacrificed their lives to preserve their honour. The Bakhshi before mentioned and Sultan Khan, the Killadar of the fort, were made prisoners. The fort of Makri Drug was also taken by capitulation after a siege of three days.

[114] A kind of grain grown in India

[115] A gross exaggeration I do not doubt.

CHAPTER XVI

An account of the arrival of Sikandar Jah and Foulad Jung the son of Nizam Ali Khan with Mushir-ul-Mulk, and a large army from the vicinity of Pankul in the camp of the English Commander-in-Chief, and the defeat of the troops besieging Mudgiri by the eldest son of Tipu, Prince Fattah Hydar; also, the death of Hafiz Furid-uddin Khan, styled Moyud-ud-dowla who was slain in the vicinity of Gurramkonda—the advance also, a second time of the Commander-Chief of the English army to Seringapatam, the arrival of the Mahratta Chief with his army, and the conclusion of peace between the English and the Sultan according to the views or instructions of the two confederates, (the Mahrattas and the Nizam) with other events of the year 1207, Hijri—A.D. 1792.

After the return of the English Sipahsalar (Lord Cornwallis) unsuccessful from Seringapatam, the Sultan with his usual prudence and foresight, as soon as the River Kaveri became fordable, despatched his eldest son Prince Futteh Hydar[116] with a large body of troops, and pay for one year, to the besieged garrison of Gurramkonda, who had to that period manfully resisted their enemies. As soon, therefore, as the prince received his orders from the Sultan, he marched by the route of Turri Gira towards the Suba of Sura, and keeping his troops under cover of the jungles or forests of Gulwari and Bukapattan, encamped his troops there, while he himself, with a small detachment (that is the Janbaz horse) selected from the whole army and taking with him the money, marched lightly equipped towards Gurramkonda. Hafiz Farid-uddin, the commander of the besieging party, being aware of Futteh Hydar's advance, prepared for action and left his batteries to meet him, when all at once the brave young prince with his Janbaz horse, fell in with and charged him so vigorously and effectually, that after but little fighting he separated the head of Hafiz from his body and it was stuck on a spear's head, and the whole of his followers, being totally defeated and dispersed, fled to Kirpa. The troops manning the batteries and the trenches now abandoning their property, with their lives only, took the road to the desert of annihilation.

The conquering prince, therefore, took possession of the baggage of the defeated party, with their tents and standards and sent them into the fort,—he next burned the materials of the batteries, and then having made over the money for the payment of the garrison to the commanding officer in the fort, and exhorted him to defend himself strenuously, took his receipt and

116 In all the MSS he is called in the heading of the Chapter the youngest son, and in the Chapter itself the eldest son—by a mistake I suppose.

marched towards the fort of Mudgiri. Sekundur Jah and Mushir (-ul-Mulk) with twenty-five thousand horse and thirty thousand foot had about this time encamped at Mursun Pally and Ulumbari, which towns are about sixteen or seventeen kos from Gurramkonda, but on hearing this intelligence, being in some alarm, they sought the cover of the hills and jungle of Sankul Pala. The brave prince, therefore, marched by night from his encampment to attack the besiegers of Mudgiri, who were Mahratta troops, and on his arrival there, raised the confusion of the day of judgment among them, and cutting off the head of the Mahratta officer who commanded there, returned victorious to the presence.

At this time also, Kamruddin Khan was commissioned to collect grain, cattle and other necessaries, and was sent to Nagar. After the lapse of about a week, the Hydarabad or Mughal chiefs, with their army marching by the route of Bangalore, joined the English Commander-in-Chief, at or near Khan-Khan Hulli. During this time also, General Meadows after the capture of the hill fort of Nundi Gurh, with a strong force marched towards the Barh Mahl district, with an intention to take the fort of Kishnagiri, and assaulting the town at night, captured it, and gave it up to plunder. The troops then ascending the mountain, reached the gate of the fort, when the garrison being aroused, came forward to repel them, and crowding to the walls poured forth such a fire of guns, musketry, rockets and shells that they put them to flight, and not satisfied with that, courageously pursued them and put the greater part to the sword. The General, therefore, marched back and joined the grand army. Colonel Gowdie, with his division of troops after the capture of Nandi Garh, marching by the route of Bangalore and Hosur, first subdued the hearts of the Killadars of Rai Kote with but little trouble, and by shewing them a sum of money and firing a few shots as the fort, it was surrendered, and having left a garrison in it he turned. But to proceed,—as soon as the rainy season was over, the Sipahsalar (Lord Cornwallis) with the army of the army of the Nizam of Hydarabad again marched to attempt the capture of the City of Seringapatam, and by long stages by the route of Chinapatam and Ootridrug arrived there, and encamped near Kurri Gooreh one day, and then leaving the Hydarabad army in the rear and placing some infantry in charge of the small fort of Kurri Gooreh, the General passed through the defile of the hills of Hurrur and still moving on at midnight fell on the batteries, which by the treachery of the Sultan's imbecile ministers had been left without defenders, and took possession of them and keeping up a heavy cannonade advanced towards the Sultan's camp. The Sultan, who with his army had encamped on this side of the river (Kaveri), and whose spies, scouts, and intelligencers had given him no information of the advance of the enemy, was completely deceived and as he had no time or opportunity to oppose them, ordered his musketeers and archers to file off to the rear, and retire to the city and place it in the best order of defence, while he himself mounted his horse and with a few faithful servants turned his face to the field of battle. From the darkness of the night, however, the troops fell into disorder and not being able to distinguish friend from foe, fought among themselves.

In this confusion Imam Khan and Mir Muhammad, Sipahdars, with their regiments arrested the advance of the enemy and performed their duty right manfully, and to the extent of their means drove the dark vapours of pride out of the heads of their opponents, but they were at length both slain.

During this time, General Meadows with the greatest gallantry advanced, and at one assault took possession of the walls of the city, or rather suburb of Ganjam, and the Lal Bagh, which were defended by a deep ditch and strong towers. The loss of these by the neglect of Mehdi Khan, the Sahib Dewan, left a great chasm in the foundations of the kingdom, for it happened on that night that the whole of the garrison of the fort above-mentioned, without the orders of the Sultan, were sent for under pretence of distributing their pay, and stationed before the gate of the fort of Seringapatam, and the walls and towers being left entirely bare of defenders, the General was victorious.

As soon as this intelligence reached the Sultan, he, with the whole of his army, retired into the city, and appointed two Risalas, or regiments of Asad Illahi Infantry,[117] (himself asking or entreating their aid) to recover the batteries which had been taken that night by the English.

As soon, therefore, as the morning dawned, these regiments marched to attack the batteries and advanced to the foot of the ramparts. It happened, however, that the Sipahsalar of the English army, was himself present in the battery, and his men consequently remained firm and drove back the storming party and although they repeated their assaults again and again, victory refused to shew them her lovely face and most of the Janbaz,[118] or bravest men sacrificied their lives in these unavailing attacks.

The Sultan's troops (the Asad Illahis), therefore, returned to the city. The valiant Sultan, now strengthened all sides of the fort of Seringapatam with guns, mortars and every description of fire-arms, and stationed his brave troops in all parts of the works, and with exceeding confidence and a truly royal spirit gave orders that his tents and canopies made of European velvet, the silk's of Khotan and China, and the embroidered or brocaded

[117] The Lions of God.

[118] The Janbaz, are men who devote themselves, or care nothing for their lives

cloth of Constantinople, should be raised on every one of the towers of Seringapatam, and the most beautiful Bayaderes, or dancing women, and the best singers,[119] and musicians being assembled were employed day and night in dancing, singing, and all kinds of pleasure and merriment The whole of the cavalry was sent towards Mysore, and two days after this Parasuram and Hari Pant, with their troops arrived and encamped in the neighbourhood of Char Kuli and Foulad Jung, and Mushir, also with their army encamped on the Moti Talao or great Tank.

No sooner did it become evident to all present, that the siege was likely to be protracted to a great length, and the war not likely to be easily brought to a close, except by the sacrifice of multitudes of lives, the fortitude and courage of the Sultan being well known to all, than the three confederated powers each separately in his own place sought the means of making peace. The Sipahsalar of the English army, in the meantime, raised a battery south of the fort, on the side of Ganjam, and another to the east of the fort on this side the river, and held all in readiness for the attack. At this period, however, the Sultan also unwilling to continue at enmity and war with the three powerful states, by the advice, or at the instance of some of his wise and faithful servants, despatched Vakils or ambassadors to the English Commander-in-Chief and to the Mahrattas, with valuable presents, and they shaking the chain of friendship and union[120] fulfilled their office, and made known their commission. The Sipahsalar (Lord Cornwallis) was delighted with the friendly propositions of the Sultan and determined to accept them. General Meadows was, however, of a different opinion, and did not give them a willing ear, and, after much dispute and contention, he received permission from the Commander-in-Chief to attack the battery at Somar-Peth, which might indeed be called the nose of the fort of Seringapatam, and of which the intrepid Syyad Ghaffar, the Sipahdar, had charge. He accordingly attacked it, and that brave man Syud Ghuffar, planting his feet firmly in the field of manhood, immediately grappled with his adversaries; for he advanced and met them in the field, and with the sword, musket, and bayonet, so vigorously repulsed them, that he drove the ball of victory before him with the Chowkan of valour,[121] and the storming party not having power to stand against him retired.

After about two hours, however, while the Sultan's troops were occupied in cooking their dinners, and had discharged all

[119] *Kalawantan.*

[120] Alluding to the fable of the Golden Chain, suspended before the Gate of Anoushirwan, the just, and which was shaken, whenever any one had to complain of injustice

[121] A Kind of cricket bat or golf.

fear of their enemies from their minds, the brave English, finding an opportunity again, all at once made a furious assault, and with but little trouble dispersed the Sultan's troops and took possession of the place.[122] This was, however, no sooner known, than Syyad Hamid and Fazil Khan, Sipahdars, with their troops, arrived to the aid of the defeated Sipahdar (Syyad Ghaffar) and together attacking the battery vigorously, they by main force retook it, and again occupied their station in it—but by this time two thousand English soldiers had measured their length on the field of blood, and those who escaped the sword returned to their army On this day, General Meadows on returning to his tent, loaded a pistol and fired it off on himself :—the ball, however, did not wound him mortally, but passed through the skin of his abdomen, and he had taken up another pistol (to put an end to himself), when Colonel Malcolm, the Adjutant-General, hearing the report, rushed into the tent, seized the pistol and despatched an account of what had happened to the Commander-in-Chief. Lord Cornwallis immediately visited the General in his tent, and taking him by the hand, returned thanks to God, that he was safe, and after consoling and comforting him with kind words said—"at this precise period, peace is our best policy, for although taking the fort and making the Sultan a prisoner be easy, and allowing both the Sultan and fort fell into our hands, still, I am not satisfied respecting our confederates, who are sharers with us in all things ; for in such a case what good will result to the Company's Government?[123] Indeed, after mature reflection, I am convinced this is the proper time to make peace," and the General now agreed to the truth of these words.

But to proceed, by the council and unanimous opinion of these confederated powers, the terms of agreement were arranged on the following basis, viz—that the Sultan should cede territory to the amount of three krores of rupees and pay a similar amount in money ;—that until the payment of the aforesaid money, one of the gates of Seringapatam should be given up and remain in charge of the English troops, or otherwise, that the Sultan should send certain of his sons, as hostages for the satisfaction of the three confederated powers, to the Sipahsalar of the English army. The prudent and clear-sighted Sultan, seeing the affairs of his kingdom ruined by the villany and neglect of his ungrateful and traitorous Amirs and Chiefs, of necessity was obliged to accept these terms, and the countries of the Barh Mahal, Suleem (Salem) Aturantgiri, Sankli Drug, Dindigul, Kalikote (Kozhikode), &c., were surrendered to the English ; and the whole of the districts of Kirpa, Tar Puttri, Tar Muri, and Bullari (Bellary), were given up to Nizam Ali Khan, and all the country on the other side of

[122] He calls it the place, but means the battery

[123] He, perhaps, does not mean this interrogatively, but affirmatively, that his proposition was the best for the interests of the Company.

the river Tungabhadra, was consigned to the Mahrattas, and one krore of rupees in money, with presents and dresses of honour was sent out to the confederates, and agreeably to the request of the English Commander-in-Chief, Mazuddin Sultan and Abd-ul Khalik Sultan, the sons of the Sultan, under the guardianship[124] of Ghulam Ali Khan, and Muhamad Raza Khutib, Arkati, were appointed ambassadors, (hostages) and sent off to the General, and these wise and learned envoys, by fair and specious speeches and words of apology, cleared the royal roads of friendship and peace from the dirt and rubbish of suspicion and enmity, and, having pleased the confederates with presents and offerings, caused their removal from the city of Seringapatam.

The confederated Chiefs having, therefore, divided the before-mentioned sum of money between them, returned to their own countries. The Commander-in-Chief of the English army, also, with his princely ambassadors, soon arrived at Madras, his attention and kindness to them continually increasing, and Colonel Doveton was appointed Mir Samani, that is, to conduct their household affairs and provide them with whatever might be required : (this office in Persian is called Mahmandari ; it is here Mir Samani), and he entertained them with the respect and attention due to their rank. The English infantry now, therefore, were withdrawn from all parts, depending on the Sirkar Khodadad, and marched to take possession of the Barh Mahal, &c ;—and proclamations of peace were made in all regions.

When the Sipahsalar before mentioned arrived at Madras, a palace in the fort was cleared for the reception of the ambassadors, and they were lodged there, and all necessary things prepared for their accommodation ; and their friends, servants, and teachers, had permission to go and come as they pleased, particularly Muhammud Khan Surajadowla (who had often written to the world-conquering Sultan, desiring to make peace with him, and join him), in this matter, (attention to the princes) was most earnest and persevering, and in kindness and courtesy, treated the princely ambassadors of the Sultan with more respect than he did his own children, and was continually sending them dainties for the table, fruit of the rarest kinds &c.

[124] *qataliq*

CHAPTER XVII

An account of the march of the Sultan's troops to punish the refractory Poligars of the frontier, and of the internal regulation of the kingdom and departments, which had fallen into disorder and decay, also, the rebuilding or reconstruction of the Fort of Seringapatam, events of the year 1207, Hijri. A D 1792

From the day that the three confederated chiefs returned successful to their own countries, the Sultan used his utmost endeavours to understand rightly the condition of his kindom and to ascertain the loyalty, and disloyalty of his chief civil and military servants, bankers &c. and he, therefore, demanded from each of his collectors, Foujdars, &c, an account of their receipts and disbursements, and from the context and connexion of these reports he became well informed, and assured that Mehdi Khan, his chief minister, in concert with several bankers of the Karnatak and other traitors, had placed his steps in the path of disloyalty and treason, and had desired that the fame and honour of his master and benefactor should be thrown to the winds of peculation and plunder, and that of this, the disordered condition of the finances and different departments of the State was an evident proof; as for instance, during the heat of an engagement, several guns by the direction of these villains had their muzzles stopped up with sand or clay. Accordingly, one by one, these wretches received the punishment due to their crimes. Their houses were plundered and the money obtained from them was forwarded to the ambassadors to pay the instalments of the amount demanded by the confederates. The displaced Amir, however, that is to say Sadik,[125] the false and faithless, was restored to the Musnud of the Dewani, or to the office of Secretary of State.—"Ah! the wolf was entrusted with the care of the sheep,"—that old wolf, therefore, whose heart, from the time at which he had been removed from office, was filled with the vapours of rancour and malice, seizing on this opportunity, accused most of the most faithful Amirs and Khans of neglect and disaffection, and by arguments without reason, and proof without foundation, (as he well knew that as long as the Sultan had faithful servants his evil purposes and intentions could not be accomplished), turned the Sultan's mind against them and in conformity to his orders they were put to death.

During this period, certain asofs, and spies, reported to the Sultan, that to the northward of Seringaputam, from every corner and every bush, rebels, and robbers raised the head of pride and

[125] A play on the word Sadik, which signifies true

insolence, and had advanced the foot of rebellion towards the conquest of towns depending on Mysore, and without cause or consideration had bound up their loins to injure and distress God's people, the subjects of that state : as for instance, one of the Chiefs of the infidels, named Vinkati Kureh, had strengthened the hill fort of Kureh Bundah, and as is customary gave himself out as one of the children of the Poligar of Murkeisi, and had seized and held possession of the fort of Mudgiri, and also, that of Ratan Giri, and that he was in readiness to defend himself About this time also, Muhammad Khan the Asof of Chitaldrug, and Dowlat Khan the Foujdar of that place, despatched an urzee (a letter) to the presence, representing that a strange man, whom some said was a connexion or reletion of the Poligar Chiefs of Harapanahalli, had made himself known by the name of Buspa Naik, a man who had been formerly put to death —that he gave himself the airs of a chief of rank, and had collected four thousand foot of the Bedur tribe, and had strengthened Hochungi Drug and the fort of Kuttur, depending on the Suba of Harapanahally and sought aid from all quarters, (even as the writer of these lines has detailed in the *Tuzkirut ul Bilad wul Ahkam* in the eighth Ourung or Chapter)

But to proceed ; at this the fire of the Sultan's wrath flamed violently, and Syyad Sahib was appointed with a large force to punish the chiefs of the infidels in the vicinity of G[illegible]ri Bandar, Mudgiri, &c. and Kumr-uddin Khan was also despatched with a large division of troops to chastise the infidel of Harpanahally.

The Khan had no sooner received his appointment from the Sultan than he departed, and by forced marches reached and surrounded the fort above mentioned, and with his guns and musketry threw the stone of defeat and dispersion among the garrison, and having stormed the fort took it by force of arms, and placing a detachment in that small fort marched towards Hochungi Drug. The chief before mentioned (Buspa Naik) with two thousand Bedurs (mountaineers apparently) was ready to meet him, having filled the hill fort with arms, ammunition and provisions, and indeed he exerted himself strenuously in repelling the attacks of the Sultan's troops.

For seven months, therefore, he maintained his ground and opposed them valiantly ; at length, however, the Khan's anger being much excited by the brave and obstinate defence of the infidels, he ordered his troops to assault the fort, himself mounting his horse to direct the attack and his victorious soldiers without giving any attention to the numbers of their enemies, (they were only two thousand he says a little before) advanced steadily to take revenge on them, and with the greatest intrepidity mounted the ramparts and towers, and soon sounded their trumpets and beat their drums in token of victory. The infidels also, advanced to meet them like men devoting themselves to death, and fought with such intrepidity that the Khan himself was wounded. But at length the besieged could no longer resist the blood-drinking swords of the Ghazies and they were dispersed in the desert of defeat[126] and the infidel chief with four hundred men was taken prisoner. Sham Shankar the nephew of the slain Naik, Buspa, who by the assistance of the Mahrattas had seized a portion of the dependencies of Harpanahally and resided at Narayan Gir, hearing this news fled to the other or Mahratta side of the River Tungabhadra. The Khan, therefore, according to the orders of the Sultan for the sake of example, cut off the hands and feet of some of the prisoners and the virile members of others, and then let them go. The walls of the mountain and fort, &c. which had been the aid and refuge of he rebel infidels were razed to the foundations and he then returned. Babar Jung, the Subadar of that Suba, (Harpanahally) who in the defection and contention of the troops had sought refuge in Chitaldrug, after the disturbances were quelled returned to that country. and with his own troops recovered the towns of Anigunda, and Kanakgiri, and having sent assurances of safety to Hari Naik, the Poligar of Kanakgiri, invited him to meet him, and on his arrival gave him the sanad sanctioning his continuance in the Government of that Taluk, with an honorary dress, and an elephant, and thereby gained his heart; for the Poligar, now having his mind at ease, professed himself one of the slaves or rather servants of the Sultan, and became tributary and obedient.

Syyad Sahib in the course of two or three months, after some opposition recovered Guri Bundah, Mudgiri and Ratan Giri, from the hands of the rebels and, having cut off the noses and ears of some of the abject infidels, returned.

Syyad Hamid, the Sipahdar, from his faithful and good services was honoured by the present of kettle drums, an elephant and howda, and also ennobled by the title of Nawab, and he was then appointed to the Government of Nagar.

In a very short time, however, his fortune declined, for he was taken sick and departed to the mansions of eternity. About this period also, the wife of the Sultan who on the arrival of the Allied Powers at Seringapatam, by the concussion and shock of the battering guns[127] was seized with a palpitation of the heart, her delicate frame being much shaken, in a few days departed to enjoy the gardens of Paradise, (the age of Mohi-uddin Sultan being then five or six years), the daughter of Syyad Sahib, therefore, according to the desire of the Queen Mother, the young lady being approved by the Sultan, was now selected to supply her place and was accordingly affianced to him.

It is not to be omitted here, that Kamr-uddin Khan in the

[126] *idbar.*

[127] *Khafqan*

hope of obtaining in marriage the bright star of the constellation of royalty; that is to say, the sister of Fatteh Hydar Sultan, had frequently in every service in which he had been engaged, nobly perilled his life, but as he was not a man of that rank or character to qualify him for such an honour, the Sultan united him in marriage with one of the daughters of the Nayut, (name not mentioned) and he Kamr-uddin Khan being on all accounts hopeless, now become careless and indifferent in all matters of duty, and more than that, he secretly adopted the language of these chiefs envious of the prosperity of the Sultan, and was anxiously desiring and waiting the downfall of the State. But to return; in a very short time by the exertions of the Sultan's troops the heads of the rebels of that quarter were brought low, and some of the Poligars, when they saw and were convinced that opposition to the Sultan was like voluntarily placing the foot of ill luck into the net of destruction, being ashamed of their misconduct, apologised and asked forgiveness and became tributary and obedient. The Poligar of Punganur, through the mediation of the English Commander-in-Chief, by the payment of a lakh of rupees yearly, as horse-shoe money, obtained the sannads or grants of his own Taluk from the Sultan, and was allowed to remain in peace.

From this period the Sultan renouncing all punishment, such as beating, flogging, or displacing the officers of his Government, after much deliberation determined on exacting an oath from each of them, and, therefore, in the month of Zi Huj, the Asafs of the Taluks and Parganas with the Governors and accountants were assembled in presence of the Sultan, and after prayers and reading the Khutba of the Eediddoha, all of them before the mimbur, or reading desk of the Mosque, each having the Koran on head, took that oath he would not fail in his duty to the government, nor make any false charge nor embezzle the money collected and forwarded by him on account of the revenue; that he would not allow the poor or the peasantry to be oppressed in word or deed—also, that they should pass their time in prayer, their regular and daily duties, and abstain from forbidden things. After the imposition of these oaths and engagements, every one received the presents given on dismissal; but notwithstanding all this, these faithless men after taking the oath as soon as they arrived at their own Parganas, discharged all care of it from their minds, and committed crimes the bare mention of which must be avoided, and whatever unlawful things their wicked minds conceived or desired, those they accomplished

Ah! these fools did not know to what degradation and misery the evil influence of these wicked actions, after breaking their oaths would reduce them—God protect us from the like. As the Sultan had a great aversion to Brahmins, Hindus and other tribes, he did not consider any but the people of Islam his friends, and, therefore, on all accounts his chief object was to promote and provide for them. He accordingly selected a number of Masalmans who could scarcely read and write, and appointed them Mirzas of the treasury departments and placed one over each of the other accountants, to the end that the accounts might be submitted by them to him in the Persian language, and in the exent of his Dominions in every Pargana by his orders was placed an Asof,[128] and in the towns yielding a revenue of five thousand[129] hoons or pagodas one Amil, (or collector) one Serishtadar, one Ameen, and one Majmudar, all Musalmans, but, although the Sultan's plans involved the displacement and ruin of the Brahmins, such as the Deshmukh,[130] Deshpandeh and the Kanungo, and all of that tribe were at once thrown out of office—still, these people by sycophancy and their knowledge of business, and by intriguing with the Amils and Asofs were continued in their employment in revenue affairs as usual, without the knowledge of the Sultan, and the Asofs and Amils, relying on the ability of these Brammins in revenue arrangements, abandoned the duties of their offices and without fear or apprehension gave themselves up to pleasure and passed their days and nights in witnessing dances and singing and enjoying themselves in all ways, and the rapacious Brahmins,[131] in the meantime plundered all the Taluks at their discretion, giving half to the Asofs while they retained the other half for their private use. Although the Sultan heard all this from without (from his spies, I suppose), yet still keeping in view the oaths of these faithless men, he neither punished the offenders nor did he manifest anger at their misconduct.

The Sultan also built a Masjid in every town and appointed a Muezzin, a Mulla and Kazi to each, and promoted the education and learning of the Musalmans to the utmost of his power. He himself also spent his time in prayer, reading the Koran and counting the beads of his rosary—as in a Kasidah written in his praise, some one said, "Even as he gained the stars and the heavens by the help or the blessing of his rosary" "So by his sword, he conquered the world and the people of the world." The man, however, who neglected his appointed prayers and the adulterer, he considered his personal enemies. When, therefore, for the sake of his religion, the Sultan withheld his hand from the duties of government, and conquest, and ceased to inquire into the actions and conduct of his agents and servants, every one in his place did as he pleased fearlessly, and without restraint The old Khans and faithful servants of the state were now cast down

[128] Meaning in other words a Foujdar or Magistrate
[129] In some copies ten thousand.
[130] Officers employed in the collection of the revenue
[131] *bi ha laq.*

from confidence and power, and low men, and men without abilities were raised to high offices and dignities, men of rank, also, who had always been employed in highest duties and services, were reduced to the lowest and humblest offices, for this reason, that it was the wish of the Sultan that every Musalman should derive benefit, or reap all advantages from his kindness alone, in order that the lower classes of people should not despair of obtaining rank and office [132] From this cause, however, it was that disorder and disaffection forced their way into the very foundations of the state, and at once the nobles and Khans being alarmed and suspicious, became the instigators of treachery and rebellion, and the before-mentioned Amir (Mir Sadik), covered with kingly benefits, opened wide the doors of deceit and fraud on the highest and lowest servants of the state, until at length the reins of the government and the supreme direction of affairs, all fell into his hands, and his duties and rank rose higher and higher, pride, however, now found its way into his empty head, and most of the questions relative to government and revenue he took into his own hands, and decided on them without asking the consent or pleasure of the Sultan. He also by his oppression and violence filled all parts of the kingdom with tumult and sedition, and regulated matters of the highest importance at his mere fancy and caprice, he also, by reading charms, incantations, and by prayers for domination[133] (for his necromancers burned half a maund of black pepper every day),[134] he so subjected the mind of the Sultan, that when he heard complaints against this villain from the mouths of his Amirs, he listened to them, but extinguishing the fire of his royal anger with the pure water of clemency and forbearance, he did not in any way discountenance or punish him, but on the contrary, still strove to raise him to the highest dignities, and threw the mantle of mercy and kindness over his crimes The Mir, therefore, by the Sultan's daily increasing favour, gained authority and power over all the forts and castles of Mysore, and treating the chief men of the kingdom with neglect and insolence, he allowed no one any share in the conduct or administration of public affairs, he also, dispatched misplaced or unnecessary firmans and orders to the different dependencies of the state, and neglected to report to the Sultan the state of the different departments, the condition of the people, and the occurrences in the kingdom

When some of the Sultan's faithful officers saw this state of things they withdrew their tongues and hands from his service;

[132] Or, that the people of Islam should derive all benefits and advantages from the table of the Sultan's beneficence alone

[133] *wa ba'imliyat 'azimat khwani wa da'ut taskhirat*

[134] I do not know the precise use or intention of this, but the people of India burn black pepper as a charm to drive away evil spirits.

but, to proceed, the Sultan now determined to rebuild the fort of Seringapatam, after a new plan, and threw down the old walls and built towards the river two stone walls of great strength, with a deep ditch, towers, and curtain ; and to the south, four or five strong walls, so that the Darya Bagh, became included in the fourth fort. To the west also, he laid the foundations of four walls, or ramparts, of which two very strongly built were finished.

CHAPTER XVIII

An account of the return of the Illustrious Ambassadors (the Sultan's sons) in the year 1208 Hijri, and the naming of the Kutcheries, or Brigades of Infantry, after the great and glorious names,[135]—also, the distinction and honours conferred on the Sultan's Amirs, by the title of Mir Miran. The preparation or formation of the throne of the kingdom, and the arrival of one of the Princes of Iran or Persia, the cause of his coming being the enmity of the Amirs and Chief personages at his (Father's) court. An account also, of the marriage of the Sultan, and a detail of the events or occurrences in the kingdom, from the beginning of 1208, to the year 1212, Hijri, A D 1793-1797

After the ambassador princes had remained at Cheenapatam or Madras a year and some months, and on both sides, that is, both on the part of the Sultan and British Government, the conditions of peace and friendship had been fully established and the amount agreed on, paid, they returned, aad the Sultan then made a hunting and pleasure excursion to the environs of Devanhalli, and there on an extensive plain he received the ambassadors, his sons, and their enlightened tutors or guardians, and now entertained hopes of victory and success. Ghulam Ali Khan and Ali Raza Khutib, however, from suspicion of disaffection, were placed in arrest, and the escort of the princes was dismissed with honours and royal presents

A banquet was also given by the Sultan, at which every thing which could promote festivity and joy was provided, and every one of the Sultan's Amirs, and his brave officers received his favours with increase of rank and pay. *Verses*, "He increased their rank and dignity"—"His soldiers were delighted with his liberality."—"They were all well pleased and satisfied"—"and from the weight of his favours and benefits they were all bent down to the earth." It was also in this expedition that the most distinguished of his officers were honoured with the title of Mir Miran, and the Kutcheries[136] (brigades, or divisions) were named or numbered after the Ismail Hussena, the names of the most high, which are ninety-nine in number; as, for instance, the Ilahi Kutcheri was named the Rehman Kutcheri, the Ghaffar Kutcheri, the Ghaffur, and so on, and the Sultan having made this new regulation, returned to his capital and appointed three or four Sipahees to each Kutcheri, and abolished the name of Jysh,[137] calling them all Uskur.[137] It is not to be omitted here

[135] *asmaul Husna.*

[136] These according to Kirkpatrick each contained several Kushuns or brigades

[137] These words are synonymous.

that Syyad Ghaffar, the faithful servant of the Sultan, was the first person distinguished by the title of Mir Miran, and Muhammad Raza, the son of Ibrahim Sahib, the maternal uncle of the deceased Nawab and the grandfather of Tipu Sultan,[138] also, raised the standard of Mir Miran, and was also styled the Binky Nawab. The cause of his being so named, was this—on some former occasion, the Sultan had deputed him with a body of troops to quell disturbances raised by certain rebel Naimars, and by his bravery and good conduct, he having brought the signs of the last day on these misguided people, and having taken many of them prisoners, he shut them with their wives and children up in a house, and burned them alive (with the fire of example, or as a warning to others). He was, therefore, called by his name.[139] Khan Jehan Khan, and Purnia, the Brahmin, and some other persons of the Nayut tribe, and some the sons of religious men, who neither possessed courage nor a knowledge of the military art, but who were acceptable to the Sultan; the patron of all Musalmans, were raised to the rank of Mir Miran and dignified by being allowed the use of kettle drums, &c.

To the whole of the Mir Mirans were also presented dresses of gold embroidery, and tassels, with jewels arranged in a certain order, and jewelled gorgets. About this time the Sultan changed the names of the different arms (fire arms), as for instance, a banduk or matchlock, was called Tofung, a tope, or cannon, Duruksh,[140] and a ban, or rocket, Shuhab &c[141] The throne of the kingdom was also at a fortunate period finished as was desired, but as according to the customs of kings of Delhi, first introduced by Sultan Jalal-uddin Muhammad Akbar; for they previously demanded the daughters of the family of Jaswant,[142] (that is, I conclude, the daughters of the Rajput Princes of Hindusthan), previous to the Sultan's ascension, a certain ceremony remained unperformed, the Sultan having despatched hundred of thousands of pounds to the Raja of Kutch; by his presents and favours made him obedient and willing to send his daughter to him in marriage. At that period, however, fortune being employed in endeavours to ruin those professing the true

[138] The following is in parenthesis, but I have thought it best to put it in a note The eldest son of the said Ibrahim that is, the eldest brother of Muhammad Raza, who was called Amin Sahib, and who was the Bukhshi of the whole of the Silladar horse, was killed in full Kutcheri, for some trifling offence, by a Sipahi named Syyad Miian

[139] Which in the Kanarese language, means the Burning Nawab

[140] Persian, lightning.

[141] Arabic, a falling or shooting star.

[142] Jaswant signifies possessed of courage or enterprize, but there is some fault in the MSS here, the word Doli, or Dukhtur being omitted, as persons acquainted with the customs of Hindusthan will perceive.

religion, and the defender of God's people; this happy result was not attained. About this time the Prince of Iran (Iraun), on account of the opposition and enmity of Aka Baba, an eunuch (of his father's court), was obliged to quit his own country, and after suffering many hardships, arrived at Seringapatam.

The liberal Sultan visited him, and lodged him in the suburb of Ganjam, and treated him with princely courtesy and kindness, and besides rich dresses, carpets, &c other necessary articles, such as provisions, &c., allowed him two thousand rupees a month for the payment of his servants. As the Sultan's aim was to join and act in concert with the kings of Islam, for this reason and from friendship and good intention, he despatched ambassadors with valuable presents, elephants and friendly letters to Zuman Shah, the son of Timur Shah, the son of Ahmad Shah Durani, the Chief of Kabul and Sultan of the Sher Abdali tribe, to propose and arrange the modes of affording each other aid and assistance and that powerful sovereign accorded all the requests of the Sultan, and honoured the envoys with many presents of great value. When the terms of peace and amity were confirmed between the two kings by oaths and treaties, the ambassadors returned to the Sultan with rarities and presents of that country, and letters in reply, signifying the establishment of friendship and the laying of the strong foundations of amity between the two states. After some time had been passed in pleasure in the year 1210, Hijri,[143] the Sultan espoused a lady, previously betrothed to him, who was entitled Khodija-i-Zuman, or the Lady of the Age, (the daughter of Syyad Sahib), and the marriage banquets and entertainments were prepared, and for a certain number of days the Khans and Amirs who were appointed to the office of Mir Samani, (a kind of stewardship) arranged all things conducive to pleasure and enjoyment, and all the officers and men of the army received gifts from the treasury of that fortunate prince, and from his delicious feasts, the tongue and palates of both high and low were sweetened and gratified. By his royal munificence also, the musicians and singers, or Bayaderes, with their magic glances, were placed beyond wages or want.

The kind and friendly Sultan next sat at one table with all his Amirs and soldiers, and with the greatest condescension ate his dinner of rice and milk with them; and during the repast said that he and they were all brethren in religion, that being of one tribe it was indispensable all jealousy and enmity should be cast aside from their minds, and that they should unite in heart and relying on God alone, bind up their loins strongly to make war on the infidels, with a firm determination to devote

[143] A.D. 1795. The Prophet Muhammad's first wife was named Khadija.

themselves to Martyrdom in the cause. After saying this, the Sultan with his own generous hands distributed among his officers and soldiers honorary dresses of a red colour, and he then again said that they must consider these red dresses as the dresses in which they were to devote themselves in his service. Ah! notwithstanding all this conciliation and these favours from the Sultan, these hard hearted men, still refused to follow the path of loyalty and good fortune.

The next year, the Sultan determined that the marriages of the royal princes[144] should be solemnized, and orders to that effect were issued. The Mir Samanan or stewards of the ceremonies according to these orders, superintended the marriage of Mihi uddin Sultan with the daughter of Muhammad Ali, otherwise called Haju Mean, and the prince was introduced to the Moon of the Heavens of purity and virtue, and according to the rules and customs of the royal marriages they were placed in conjunction on the nuptial throne.

In the course of the third year, the wife of the Sultan gave birth to a daughter and died about a month after, and the child soon after drank the milk of Paradise, or died also

About this time, the Prince of Iran agreeably to the request of the Amirs of his own country received permission to depart, and as the Sultan entertained a great regard for this prince, he honoured him with many valuable presents of money and jewels, and at parting said, "after you have made your arrangements regarding the Capital for the Sultanat of Persia, it is my wish that you and I in concert with Zaman Shah should endeavour to regulate and put in order, (divide between them seemingly) the countries of Hindusthan, and the Dekhan." The prince agreed and pledged himself to this proposition. Previous to this, the Sahib Dewan,[145] (one of the Devil's children) who was styled the Mir Asof, had frequently represented to the Sultan the wickedness, faithlessness and disloyalty of the Sect of the Mehdivies, who are called Ahl-i-Daira, while to all appearance they were true men and faithful servants; the Sahib Dewan being afraid of this tribe. The Sultan, therefore, merely to gratify him, expelled the whole of them with their women and children from his dominions.[146]

After this, from motives of prudence and foresight, the Sultan selected ten thousand men from the soldiers in his army, Shaikhs and Syyads, inhabitants of Seringapatam, Kolar, Hoskote, Devanhalli, Suba Sura, great Balapur and Tanjore, and called them his Zumrai Khas, that is his own division or body guard,

[144] They are called princes, although one only appears to have been married

[145] Mir Sadik

[146] See the *Transactions of the Bombay Literary Society* for an account of this Sect, vol 2 page 281.

the sign or object of their incorporation being derived from the sentence, *"dur Zumrai Ma Ghumm Nubashud,"*[147] that is, "in our company sorrow shall find no entrance," the letter *ghayn* being the symbol of men of foreign nations, *mim* to denote Mughals and Mahrattas, *nun* for Nayut, *be* for Brahmin, *alif* for Afghan, *shin* for Shea and *dal* for the Ahili Daira, or Mehdivies, these, however, were not included in the Zumra or company. The men of this division of the army now became the most acceptable in the eyes of the Sultan, and all confidence was implicitly placed in them, to that degree indeed, that towards the end of the Sultan's reign, this (Zumra Gumra),[148] infidel battalion gained complete ascendancy over all the departments of the state, and entered boldly into all the measures of Government—as an instance of this, one of these men named Mir Nudim an inexperienced man was made Governor of the Fort of Seringapatam, and although the Sultan placed entire dependence on this worthless body of men, still, they were outwardly obedient only, for in their hearts they were all the devoted servants of the Sahib Dewan, for that traitor had laid a deep plan, for the ruin of his master's state and kingdom, and this plan consisted first, in breaking up or ruining the army, and the Khans and Amirs of rank by the reduction of their pay, and by degrading them from their offices and dignities; after this also, by sycophancy and studying the disposition or caprices of the Sultan, and by taking the most sacred oaths, (For God preserve us not a word passed his lips but it was accompanied by solemn oaths on the Koran) he having quieted the suspicions and doubts of the Sultan as to his intentions, he drew to his side all the Huzurian, (courtiers or servants of the Sultan) so effectually indeed that the Urz Begi (presenter of petitions), and others among the evil councillors, the running footmen, messengers, servants and spies, without the Dewan's permission and sanction, had not the courage to make any report whatever to the Sultan, and the letters regarding the government and revenue which arrived from different countries were opened by the Dewan with his own hands, and read without the knowledge of the Sultan, and the contents being altered or erased, other words dictated by his will and pleasure were substituted, and then the letters were sent to the Sultan; indeed, the dust in that part of the country (the court) did not rise except by his breath. Praise to God, the other Asof Miran Husain, was a low fellow and a debauchee, who never followed any path but that of pride and vanity, and who in different districts and towns was carried

[147] *dar zamrah-i ma gham nabashad* This is one of the verbal refinements of the Sultan; he seems latterly to have become childish in these matters

[148] *Zumrah Gumrah* (Persian)

in his *Palki* on the shoulders of dancing girls as ugly as demons to his Katcheri or hall of audience, and sometimes he assembled all the Telinga Kalavants (dancing or singing women) without veil or garment, and he himself stripping off his clothes joined them naked and thus shamelessly paraded about among them. It will be evident from this, what kind of order and regulation in the duties of the State could result from a man so debauched and abandoned as he was. The other Mir Asof was a man named Shir Khan Cholori, who was proverbially as stupid and silent as an ox In the hands of such foolish, incompetent men, the different departments of the State were so confounded and ruined, that of the revenue of the kingdom not one eighth part ever arrived at the treasury, and the regulations and orders of the Sultan reached no part of his dominions save the Capital. Notwithstanding all this, the mild and clement Sultan endeavoured to provide for his religious people, and he considered himself fortunate when they received their stipends.

About this time Dhondaji Wagh, a devoted servant of the Sultan (an account of whom is separately given in the *Tuzkirut il Belad, va ul Ahkam*, in the tenth Ourung, or Chapter) being a man of great courage and enterprise with three or four hundred well mounted horse (*Dc uspa*), roved about and plundered in the territories of the Mahrattas, Nizam Ali Khan and the Mysore The Sultan, therefore, sent a Kowl Namah, or assurance of safety, to him and allured him by promises of increase of rank to his service. When Dhondaji, therefore, placing confidence in the word of the Sultan came with his troops and dependents to the presence, the Sahib Dewan in his devilry and malice found out some cause of offence against him and with every artifice and pretence sought his ruin, and at length by false charges and suggestions to that end, he so stimulated the Sultan that having sent for him one day under pretence of speaking to him, he was seized at the gate of the Palace, put in irons, imprisoned and circumcised, and the honour of Islamism conferred on him, and his body of horse was then incorporated with the Sultan's army.[149] Nevertheless, the favour of the Sultan towards that worthy man still continued to increase, as for instance, he was allowed ten fanams Sultani a day, which sum amounts to three rupees, and a teacher was appointed to instruct him, (in the Muhammadan customs and religion) but, although after a time, a kutcheri or brigade was named after him, and orders were issued for his release it was to no purpose, for the Dewan, like a scorpion, still continued to strike at him with his venomous sting, making a representation to the Sultan to the following effect—"King of the World, find another man

[149] Dhoondia Wagh was a Mahratta, not a Pathan as supposed by some

equally insolent, enterprising and brave, as he (Dhondaji), and then let him go. For it is known to all that when he was weak and of no account, he then beat the troops of Hydarabad, Puna (Poona), and the servants of the Sultan, and therefore, after this to make him an officer of high rank in your army and independent, is far from good policy, for with his power and rank it is possible he might raise such a disturbance as the hand of redress might not be able to quell or remedy," the opinion of this fool was, therefore, accepted by the Sultan, and that faithful servant and well-wisher was left in prison. At first he was named Shaik Ahmad, but latterly at his own desire he was entitled Malik Jahan Khan,—but to proceed, the faithless Dewan seeing his power nearly absolute, in all matters followed the dictates of his own will and caprice, as for instance, Ghazi Khan, who might be said to constitute the strongest support of the Khodadad State, without the commission of any crime, but merely on suspicion of intrigue or collusion with Mashir-ul Mulk (of Hydarabad), was ordered to be imprisoned and was then subjected to very severe treatment.

During the latter part of the Sultan's reign by the advice of certain infidel or atheistical persons he used or adopted letters from the Koran of the characters of Osman, may God be pleased with him, which are not read, and which letters from the days of the prophet Adam to the days of the seal of the prophet (Muhammad), no one of the kings of Arabia, or Persia, had ever dared to use, and which no learned historical, or sacred writer had deemed it proper to employ.[150]

CHAPTER XIX

An account of the march of an Army under the command of General Harris, the Commander-in-Chief of the English forces, agreeably to the orders of Lord Mornington, Bahadur, and according to the advice of Abul Kasim Khan Shasteri, and Mashir-ul Mulk, (the Prime Minister of the Nizam of Hydarabad), to Seringapatam, and the battles fought between the Sultan and the Sipah Sirdar, or General before mentioned, the assault and capture of the Fort of Seringapatam, the Martyrdom of the Protector of the World, the Sultan, and the fall of his Kingdom and Government, all of which events occurred in the years, 1213 Hijri A.D. 1798-1799.

It may be proper to observe here, that the Sultan in certain matters frequently acted precipitately and without thought, and in these cases would attend to no representation, even from his most faithful servants. As an instance, at this time, he commissioned certain envoys and dispatched one with presents of great value, and friendly letters to Zaman Shah, to strengthen the foundations of peace and amity; and, another was sent to Kutch to bring thence the Tika;[151] another person was also sent with very rich presents to the Sultan of Room, or Constantinople. About this time, also several Frenchmen under the command of Monsieur Seepoo, or Seboo[152] arrived at the presence from the Port of Maurice (the Mauritius) and as in Europe, during seven years, the fire of war and slaughter had been lighted up daily between the English and French nations, and they had employed every scheme and artifice in the ruin and destruction of each other, now at the arrival of these French, and the permission given them (to visit Seringapatam), the horse-shoe of the English chiefs was placed in the Fire,[153] and they fearing that by the aid, and at the instigation of the French, the troops of the Sultan would proceed to the attack and pillage of the towns of the Karnatak and Hydarabad; in consultation and concert with their friends; they formed a plan for the destruction of the Khodadad state; and assuming the arrival of the French as the plea and ground of their hostilities, they with the advice of Mashir-ul Mulk and Mir Alam, wrote a detailed account of these occurrences to Lord Mornington Bahadur, then residing in Calcutta, and he who was looking out for such a contingency,

[151] This word signifies an ornament or mark on the forehead used by ladies It also signifies the installation or inauguration to an office, or of a Sovereign Prince; here apparently it signifies the Daughter of the Raja, who had been affianced to the Sultan, and whose presence was necessary, as before stated to his accession to the throne

[152] *Sibu* M Chapius.

[153] *n'al dar atash* A common simile.

and who was also well acquainted with the weakness and disorganization of the departments of the Mysore state; with the greatest promptitude and speed embarked with four thousand Sipahis on board ship, and arrived at Madras in the month of Shaban il Moaz-um, and having assembled the army there under General Harris, Commander-in-Chief, dispatched it in advance to the conquest of Seringapatam * From Hydarabad also, Colonels Roberts and Dalrymple, with four thousand of the Bandari, or coast Sipahis, (which force Mashir-ul Mulk had sent for to attack and break up the troops of Monsieur Peron, the Frenchman who had succeeded Monsieur Ramon,[154] the friend or servant of the Nizam of Hydarabad, and which service they had fully accomplished;) and with them also two thousand Bengal Sipahis, who formerly were stationed near Husain Sagar, agreeably to the orders of the Commander of the army, with their stores and guns, marched towards Madras. Mir Alam, also, with eight thousand horse, and Roshan Rao, with six thousand men disciplined by the late Monsieur Ramon, marching by the route of Pangal Ghat, and crossing the Ghat of Budweil (Badvel) and Vinkatagiri joined the English army in the vicinity of Goriatum. As soon as the army with its stores and artillery had assembled, Lord Mornington wrote and dispatched two or three letters to the Sultan, requiring him to deliver up into his hands the Frenchmen newly arrived at his capital; to receive and retain ambassadors or residents on his part, in the fort of Seringapatam, and also to surrender to the English the ports on the sea coast, such as Gorial Bandar, Mangalore, Honawar &c ports where ships arrive As the Sultan among these requisitions did not accept or agree to one, and as he sent no answer to any letter, the General according to the orders of the Lord before mentioned (Mornington), with General Floyd, commanding the cavalry, General Burgess, the Commander of the Europeans and other Generals, on the 2nd of the month of Ramzan, 1213, Hijri, marched on, and by successive stages passing by Ambur Garh, and Tripetur (Tirupattur), arrived in the neighbourhood of Rai Kote. At that time certain interested persons represented in studied, pompous language to the Sultan, that the English army with certain wry faced fellows (with a disease which draws the face to one side), from Hydarabad, were advancing to throw away their lives, but that altogether they did not amount to more than four or five thousand, and that the Chief of Puna (Poona) had refused to join or act in concert with them

The Sultan, therefore, at hearing this intelligence appointed Purnia, Mir Miran with a large body of troops and other Mir Mirans to punish the insolence of the invaders of his country

* In this part I have followed Colonel Marriott's copy of this work

[154] Raymond

while he himself gave orders to assemble his Amirs, and the remainder of his army. The Mir Miran above mentioned having taken leave marched towards the English army. About two *kos* to the westward of Rai Kote, his cavalry having the cover of the forest attacked the English army, but in a scattered and confused manner, and the regular regiments of cavalry of the enemy advanced and formed their lines for action. The Sultan's horse surrounded this body on all sides, and after the Kuzzaki mode vigorously attacked them[155] The General halted four days before the Ghat, and on the 2nd Showal-ul-Mukurrim, moved on and encamped near Anikul, when the Kuzzaks, or light cavalry, charged the advanced guard of the English and put a considerable body of them to the sword, but, in place of praise and eulogy they received from the accursed Mir Miran, in reward nothing but abuse and blame, he demanding of them with oaths and imprecations, why they attacked so rashly

It appeared, therefore, to every one, after this that the intention of their officers was to avoid fighting and consequently they displayed no more zeal or enterprise, and more like an escort or safeguard quietly preceded and followed the troops of the enemy as they marched along. As soon as the whole of the troops and their officers and departments were assembed under the shade of the Sultan's standard, and the Sultan became fully aware of the invasion of the enemy, he marched from Seringapatam with the whole of his Amirs and army, and pitched his tents in the plain of Chenaputtun, on the very road which his treacherous servants had pointed out for the advance of the enemy. The General, however, turned aside from that road, and according to the advice of his scounts and guides advanced to Khan Khanhully As soon as this intelligence reached the Sultan, he expressed great anger at his spies. and made a forced march in that direction, and in the neighbourhood of Gulshanabad, otherwise called Maruli, stoped the further progress of the enemy, he being perfectly ready for action.[156] The troops of the enemy also advanced and formed their lines for battle—*Verses*—"The sound of the soldiers tramp came up from the field of battle," "and fear struck the hearts of the bravest of the brave" "The dust rose so thick that the passage to the Heavens was blocked up" "The reins of safety fell from Men's hands" "The shouts and clamour of the sodiers warmed the soul." "The neck was taken in the noose of the Kumund," "(a lasso, or running knot, formerly used in battle by the Persians, and other eastern nations), "when on both sides the armies were formed" "The champions began to look out for their bravest competitors" "Punishment commenced her duty of cutting off heads." "And

[155] It does not say with what result

[156] March 27, 1799

light quitted the eyes of the world." "From the quantity of blood that flowed into the low ground," "the earth assumed the fiery colour of red brimstone." "The two armies charged and met in numbers like ants and locusts." "By their shock they threw the world into confusion."

Although from the battle of that day, it appeared evident how the war would end, still, the faithful troops of the Sultan performed many worthy and gallant actions, and fought with the artillery of the enemy hand to hand, and shoulder to shoulder, and raised the tumult of the last day among them, and some of the bravest men closing with them with their muskets and pitiless swords sent many of them to eternity—the brave men of the enemy's army also, planting their feet firmly on the ground, like men devoting themselves, threw themselves bravely on the Musalman troops. Certain also of the brave and faithful officers of the Sultan, with their regiments came forward, and manfully withstood the fearful charge and shock[157] of the English, and like lions attacking a herd of deer, or wild asses, fell upon their assailants, and broke their ranks, and scattered them like the daughters of the Bier.[158] The false Kamruddin Khan, however, when he received orders to charge the enemy with his cavalry, alas, most shamefully neglected his duty; for having put his body of horse to a canter, he like a blind man (instead of charging the enemy), fell upon a division of the Sultan's brave troops, and put them all into disorder and as good fortune, and prosperity, had turned their backs on the Sultan's army, and as the signs of mischance and bad fortune every day manifested themselves more and more, many of the unfortunate soldiers gave up their lives gratuitously and the rest regularly and with slow steps retired from the field. This undoubtedly was all predestined and under the power and control of no one. The English army, therefore, gained the victory and were much elated.

At this time news arrived that a body of English troops from Bombay commanded by General Stuart, bringing a very large convoy of stores and provisions was advancing by the route of Coorg, straight towards Seringapatam. The Sultan, therefore, immediately with the whole of his troops and artillery, leaving some of his chief officers to make head against the enemy (General Harris) marched off to attack that body,[159] and in one day and two nights arrived in front of them, and gave orders for the attack. The faithful Syyad Ghuffar, who in bravery and loyalty had no equal, grappled[160] with the enemy on one flank,

[157] *Koh shikoh*

[158] A constellation so called, this appears to refer to the gallant resistance made by Tipu's Infantry in this action

[159] Battle of Sedaseer. [160] *aurkht.*

while Husain Ali Khan, the son of Nawab Kutubuddin Khan carried death and destruction among them on the other, raising the flames of war to the skies—the other Mir Miran, (General Officers) also, in charging and defeating the enemy used their most strenuous endeavours, and with their swords, musketry, and artillery, put the infidels to flight, and they giving way to the necessities of the time, and having no power to withstand the shock of the Sultan's blood-drinking lions, leaving part of their baggage behind them, slank into the Jungle, and occupying its outets remained there. The troops of the Sultan, however, still followed them, and vigorously attacking them again, strained every nerve to rout and destroy them. At this critical period Muhammad Raza, Mir Miran, haying by much entreaty obtained from the presence leave to charge, proceeded with his division like a raging lion towards the enemy, and stretching forth the arm of valour, it went near that the whole of the enemy's army was cut up and destroyed The ambush of fate, however, having girded their loins to accomplish the defeat of the Musalmans, a musket shot from the enemy accidently struck the head of Muhammad Raza, and he fell mortally wounded. His victorious soldiers took up his corpse and carried it to the Sultan, who directed it to be forwarded to the capital, while he occupied himself in the defeat and dispersion of this force; when spies brought intelligence that the Bombay army had retired from further opposition, and had marched by the route of the Jungul to Kalicote (Khozicote). The Sultan, therefore, returned to Seringapatam, where he had scarcely arrived, when General Harris having crossed the river by the Ford of Hosilly, and passing Sultan Peenth, encamped to the westword of the fort, and the next day the English regiments made an attack on several strong outworks which covered the fort, and were occupied by the Sultan's troops, and after a sharp contest and the slaughter of most of their defender took them On the same day, Husain Ali Khan, the son of Nawab Kutubddin Khan, a very brave man, with the greatest gallantry threw himself into the ranks of the enemy, and there drank of the Sharbat of martyrdom. The English troops now according to the orders of their commander, collected the materials for their batteries from the gardens of that vicinity, and one battery was thrown up to the westward of the fort, and another to the north west,[161] and these having been completed they began to batter and breach the walls, and to set fire to the city by throwing shells into it.

The illustrious Sultan when he saw his fortunes in this melancholy position, and that the storm at length had burst around the walls of his capital, with the native firmness and hardihood of his character still determined neither to quit the

[161] *bayab.*

fort and retire to some other place, nor offer conditions of peace He resigned himself, therefore, to the will of God, and having committed the defence of the fortification of his capital to the Zumra (or his choice troops) he determined to fight to the last. Kamruddin Khan who was an excellent partisan was detached with a large body of troops to cut off the supplies and reinforcements of the English and their confederates, and Fatteh Hydar, with the whole of the cavalry and Sillahdar horse with Purnia the Mir Miran and others were detached from the Sultan, and encamped in the plain of the Kanghat, still at times the Sultan's horse paraded round about the English army, but as their officers gave them no orders to engage the enemy, mortified and distressed they rubbed the hands of sorrow on each other. In short the army of Bombay also arrived, and encamped in the vicinity of Bahadur Pur When the Ghazies of the Faith saw they had no choice but to light up the flames of war, they every day well armed and appointed threw themselves on the troops of the enemy, as the moth flies at the lamp, and is destroyed by it, and to repeal and put to flight the authors of this tumult and disorder, they most manfully exerted themselves. Fortune, however, was adverse to giving aid or success to the Sultan's troops, and they lost or neglected the proper modes of prosecuting the war successfully ; as for instance, the case of the Mehtab Bagh , where the faithful Syyad Ghaffar was stationed, and which he long defended against the assault of the enemy, and after the loss of thousand of lives did not allow it to fall into their hands At length, however, the enemies of the Sultan by their advice procured him to be recalled and stationed in the fort, and another person was sent to replace him. The English troops, therefore, immediately attacked the Mehtab Bagh, and at one assault took it, and filled it with artillery and musketeers, and thence ran on their approaches towards the fort. About that time the mild and humane Sultan, sent for Monsieur Seeboo (Chapuis), the French Officer, and asked him what plans or measure he could recommend ? The Frenchman replied, "that his faithful servant's advice was this, that the Sultan with his cavalry, infantry, treasure, women &c. should quit the fort and retire to Sura, or Chitaldrug, and detach a body of his troops to oppose the infidels, or if he thought best he might deliver him (Monsieur Chapuis) and the rest of the French up to the English, and then an accommodation might be made between the contending parties, or if he chose he could give up the breached walls of the fort to the charge of Monsieur Lalli, for defence, without, however, allowing Lalli to be subject to the interference or control of the Sultan's Indian officers." The Sultan in reply respecting the surrender of the Frenchmen, said, "if on your account, you being strangers from a distant land, the whole of our kingdom should be plundered and laid waste, well and good , but you shall not be delivered up , "but for an answer to the remainder of Monsieur Chapuis's excellent advice, the Sultan sought counsel from the Dewan, and he in furtherance of his own views and projects said—"It must be well-known to your highness that this people (the French) never kept faith with any one and your highness may be well assured, and if you give up the fort to their care and defence, that at that very moment it will fall into the possession of the English, for both these people (the English and French) consider themselves originally of the same tribe, and they are one in heart and language."

After this villain (the Dewan) by such misrepresentations had turned the mind of the Sultan from the right path, the walls of the city being much battered and breached, the Sultan with an intention to quit the city had his treasure, valuables and Zenana (Seraglio) and also all his elephants, camels, carriages, &c. kept in readiness to move at the shortest warning, and held a consultation on the subject of his departure with his Amirs. In this council Budruzaman Khan Nayut, inconsiderately said to the Sultan, "may it please your highness from the circumstance of your departure and that of the ladies, princes, treasury &c. the courage of your faithful servants will fail, and the bonds of union in the garrison of the capital will be broken asunder." The Sultan at hearing this looked up towards the heavens, and sighing deeply said, "I am entirely resigned to the will of God, whatever it may be," and forthwith abandoned his intention of quitting the capital. The articles packed, however, still remained ready for removal in the treasury The unfortunate Ghazi Khan[162] about this time was put to death in prison by the hands of the Sultan's executioners at the instigation of the same traitor (the Dewan); in fact, though the walls of the fort was battered down, still, the information was withheld from the Sultan. At length, however, on the twenty-seventh of Zi Kad, from some secret source, he became acquainted with the treachery of certain of his servants, and the next morning he wrote with his own hand a list of some of their names, and having folded it up, gave it to Mir Moyinuddin, with instructions to put his orders therein contained into execution that night (that is to put those named to death) in order to strengthen his government.

The Mir, ignorant, or unaware of the tricks played by fortune, and the changeable heavens, opened this paper and persued it in full Durbar. It happened, however, while he was reading it, that a sweeper, or menial servant of the palace, who could read and write, cast his unlucky eye upon the paper and saw the name of the lying Dewan the first in the list. This ill-omened wretch, therefore, immediately reported the circumstance

[162] The celebrated Commander of Hydar's irregular infantry and cavalry, called Bede and Pindaras.

to him and said this night will be your last (or the night of your burial). At hearing this intelligence, he, the Dewan[163] kept on the alert at his own quarters, and at about mid-day sent for the troops stationed in the works near the breach under pretence of distributing their pay among them, and having collected them near the Ali Masjid, remained looking out for what ill-luck might bring forth.

The Sultan on that day, which was the 28th of the month[164] (*tahatu 'shu'a'a*) mounted his horse, and after inspecting the breaches in the wall or defences, ordered a party of pioneers to rebuild and repair them, and having directed his gold embroidered pavilion to be raised on the walls for his reception, returned to the palace, and then retired to the hummum or bath. As the astrologers according to their calculations of the stars had determined that day to be unlucky, they represented to the Sultan, that to mid-day and for seven Gharies (or near two hours) after, was a time extremely unpropitious to him, and also that a dark cloud overshadowed the fort during that period; that it would be advisable, therefore, that the Sultan should remain with the army until the evening,[165] and give alms in the name of God. This prediction of the astrologers did not please the Sultan, still, however, in respect to the charitable donations which repel and dissipate misfortune, whether it be earthly or heavenly, he gave orders all should be made ready and after he had bathed and had left the bath, he presented an elephant with a black Jhool, or caparison, and a quantity of pearls, gold, and silver tied up in each of the corners of the caparison to a Brahman, and a number of poor men and women being assembled, rupees and cloth were distributed among them. The Sultan then having ordered his dinner to be brought, ate a morsel, and was about to take more, but he was not so fated, for all at once the sound of weeping and wailing reached his ears. He, therefore, inquired of those present what was the cause of the outcry, and it was then made known to him that the faithful and devoted Syyad Ghaffar was slain. The Sultan, therefore, immediately left off eating and washed his hands, saying[166] "we also shall soon depart," and then mounted his horse and proceeded by the road of the Postern on the river, which is called in the Kanarese language, Holi Vuddi, towards the flag or western battery. The Sultan's enemies, however, who were looking out for opportunities to betray him, as soon as the worthy Syyad was slain, made

[163]This man evidently supposes some secret correspondence or intelligence between the Dewan Mir Sadik and the English General, or some of his staff. [164] Lunar month

[165] One copy says, seven hours of the day, that is to one, or half-past one o'clock

[166] These words appear to be understood as a prophetic intimation of his death

a signal from the fort by holding out white handkerchiefs to the English soldiers, who were assembled in the river ready for the assault, informing them of that event, and accordingly at about twenty minutes after mid-day, the European and other regiments mounted the walls by the breach, and before the Sultan's troops could be collected to man the walls and bastions of that flank of the works, they with but little labour took the fort. The garrison, although they quickly came to the rescue and the repulse of their enemies, and with sword and musket, steadfastly resisted them, still, as on all sides so much disorder and confusion reigned, that remedy was hopeless, they mostly threw away their shields and dispersed and left their women and wealth to the soldiers of the enemy, covering their shameless heads with the dust of cowardice and disgrace. It was about the time that the Sultan's horse and followers arrived near the flag battery, that the lying Dewan followed in the rear and shut up the Postern before mentioned, blocking it up securely, and thereby closing the road of safety to the pious Sultan, and then under pretence of bringing aid, he mounted his horse and went forth from the fort and arrived at the third gate (of the suburb) of Ganjam, where he desired the gate-keepers to shut the gate as soon as he had passed through; while, however, he was speaking, a man came forward and began to abuse and revile him, saying, "Thou accursed wretch, thou hast delivered a righteous prince up to his enemies, and art thou now saving thyself by flight? I will place the punishment of thy offence by thy side;" this man then with one cut of his sword struck the Dewan off his horse on the ground, and certain other persons present crowding round him soon despatched him, and his impure body was dragged into a place of filth and uncleaness and left there. Mir Moyinuddin being wounded fell into the ditch and died there. Sher Khan Mir Asof, also, was lost in the assault and was never after heard of,—when the Sultan, the refuge of the world saw that the opportunity of a gallant push was lost, (some copies say lost and some not) and that his servants had evidently betrayed him, he returned to the Postern or sally port, but notwithstanding he gave repeated orders to the guards to open the gate, no one paid the slightest attention to him; nay, more, Mir Nudim, the Killadar himself, with a number of foot soldiers, was standing at this time on the roof of the gate, but he also abandoned his faith and allegiance, and placing his foot in the path of disloyalty (took no notice of his master).

To be concise, when the storming party firing furiously as they advanced, arrived near the Sultan he, courageous as a lion, attacked them with the greatest bravery, and although the place[167] where he stood was very narrow and confined, he still

[167] Said to have been a gateway.

with his matchlock and his sword killed two or three of the enemy, but at length having received several mortal wounds in the face, he drank of the cup of Martyrdom

After this, therefore, what followed in the slaughter of the Musulmans, the plunder of their property and the violation of their women had better be left untold. The French troops in the Sultan's service during this time wrung their hands in grief, and having assembled at the gate of the palace, they fired a few vollies at the storming party and then desisted from further resistance. The whole of the treasuies, wealth, and property of all kinds belonging to the Khodadad state, therefore, which was great in amount beyond conception, fell into the plundering hands of the English soldiers, and they who had been reduced to death's door by the want of supplies and the dearness of provisions, who had been obliged to pay two rupees for a seer (a measure of little more than two pounds) of rice in the Hydarabad camp, when they could get it there, three rupees for a leg of mutton; and two rupees for a bundle of the roots of grass; now all at once became well provided and rich in all things. The princes with all their property, the Zenana or women of the Sultan and Karim Sahib his brother were all taken prisoners Fatteh Hydar the Mir Lashkar or Commander-in-Chief, however, who with the infantry, cavalry, elephants, artillery and stores, the strength of the kingdom, was encamped near the Kurighat Hill, at hearing this dreadful intelligence, marched and took the road to Chenraipatan.

The English officers now after great search, having found the body of the injured and oppressed Sultan, it was placed in a Palki and left for the night in the treasury, and the next morning the whole of his children, servants and friends having seen it for the last time and established its identity, the General gave leave for its interment, and it was deposited in the earth in Lal Bagh, in the Mausoleum of the deceased Nawab, on the right side of his tomb, and there rested from the treachery and malice of faithless servants and cruel enemies. Alas! this great accumulation of state and grandeur, pomp and splendour, at single revolution of the faithless and ever changing heavens, was so lost, that no one knew what had become of it Truly,—*verse*—"what garden of prosperity ever raised its head to the skies?"—"that in the end, the cold withering blast of desolation did not tear up by the roots?"—"Upon whose head did fortune ever place a kingly crown"—"upon whose hands and feet death (fate) did not ultimately cast its bonds." The following are elegiac verses written in commemoration of this event.

"Tipu Sultan was slain unexpectedly." "He shed his blood for the sake of the religion of the true God," on Saturday the 28th Zi Kad, "The day of judgment manifested itself," "At the seventh hour, from the morning, blood flowed from every wall and door, in the streets of Seringapatam." "Tipu lived in honour fifty years and reigned seventeen."—"His heart was ever bent on religious warfare," "and at length he obtained the crown of martyrdom, even as he desired." "Ah! at the destruction of this prince and his kingdom," "Let the world shed tears of blood." "For him the sun and moon shared equally in grief" "The heavens were turned upside down and the earth darkened." "When I (the poet) saw that sorrow for him pervaded all." "I asked grief for the year of his death" "An angel (Hatif) replied, let us mourn his loss with burning sighs and tears"—"For the light of the religion of Islam has departed from the world," *nuru'l islam din az dunya raft.*[168]

In short the agents of fate and destiny did what they willed, or what was in their power. All the elephants, and camels, the treasures, jewels, valuables, and property of every description, belonging to the Sultan, fell into the hads of the English. The new throne was broken up, and the diamonds, jewels, with chests full of jewelled gorgets and pearl necklaces were sold by auction (*harraj*) and all the arms and stores were plundered, and the library of the deceased Sultan sent to Europe.

After about a week, Kumruddin Khan, who anxiously prayed for such a day, came with great pleasure, to offer his services to the General commanding the army, and having negotiated with him respecting his Jagir, Gurum Koonda, and after receiving the Sanad, entitling him to retain that district, he marched thither with his drums beating to take possession.

Fatteh Hydar Sultan also, when he saw the symptoms of fear, distress and despair, prevailing among his followers, and at the same time heard the consolatory and conciliatory language used by the English General and other of his officers; included in which were hints or hopes held out of his being placed on the throne; abandoned all intention of fighting or further opposition, although several of his bravest officers, such as Malik Jehan Khan,[169] who after the death of the Sultan had been released (by the British troops) and had presented himself to the service of Fatteh Hydar Sultan, also Syyad Nasir Ali Mir Miran and other Asofs dissuaded him from peace and strenuously urged him to continue the war. They represented to him that the

[168] This last verse gives the date, 1213 Hijri, or A.D. 1798-9 Another person found the date in the words *nan beweh shikashta shud*—the bread of the widows and orphans has failed—another *ah nasl-i Haidar shahid Akbar shud* Alas! the Son of Hydar is a Martyr.

[169] That is to say, Dhundia the partisan chief, whose force was so effectually dispersed and destroyed by the British troops under the command of the Colonel Arthur Wellesley, at Konahgul, or according to the Persian account, Kotal Behnawer See Thornton's History, Vol. III. p. 93, 115 &c

Sultan had devoted his life only to the will of God, but that his dominions, his strong cities and forts were still in the possession of his servants, and that his army with all its artillery and stores was present That if there were any intention to reconquer the country, or if any spirit or courage remained, now was the time (for exertion), and that they were ready and willing to devote their lives to his service. This descendant of Hydar, however, notwithstanding his constitutional or hereditary bravery, at the suggestion Purnia, the Brahmin (who in promoting the ruin and destruction of the Khodadad state had employed his utmost endeavours) and the advice also of other traitors of the Sultan's court, (every one of whom thinking of his wife and family, abandoned his duty and loyalty), was deceived, and acted in conformity to their wishes, at once rejected the prayers of well wishers, and consequently washing his hands of kingly power and dominion, he proceeded to meet and confer with General Harris.

After this was arranged, according to the advice and desire of the (Governor-General) council, a boy of five years of age, one of the lineal descendants of the former Rajahs of Mysore, was seated nominally on the Masnad of his hereditary claim to that territory in Mysore; and a country, the revenue of which amounted to thirty lakhs of pagodas,[170] was assigned to him under the prime ministry or guardianship of Purnia, and all the children and relations of the deceased Sultan, (many of whose ladies remained,) with Karim Sahib and his family were sent to Rai Vellore, and a liberal salary was allowed to each of the princes, and to the present time they still reside in the fort of Vellore.

The following is the list of the princes :

Mohi-uddin Sultan ; Hydar Ali Sultan, known by the name of Fatteh Hydar, this is the eldest of all the brethren ; Abdul Khalik Sultan ; Moiz-uddin Sultan, Subhan Sahib Sultan ; Shukurullah Sultan ; Ghulam Ahmud Sultan ; Ghulam Muhammad Sultan ; Surwur-uddin Sultan and Yasin Sahib Sultan ; with his two brothers, Jama-uddin Sultan,[171] and Monir-uddin Sultan. These with their women, families and followers, all reside together.

The mind of the General (Harris) being now perfectly at ease, he proceeded to Chital Drug and took possession of all the hill forts and strongholds in that part of the country, and placing garrisons in some of them, he returned to Madras, and thence sailed for Europe, accompanied by Colonel Read, General Floyd, &c.

170 3,000,000

171 This prince was residing in London two or three years ago, but died lately at Paris,

The countries of Guty, Ratna Giri, Murkeisi, Harpanahalli, Ani Gundi, Punukund, Murgsura and other places were added to the territorits of the Nizam of Hydarabad for a time. After this, however, in the year 1215, Hijri, (A.D. 1800) they were given back in Tunkhwah to the English Government. (To defray the charges of a subsidiary forces apparently.)

Malik Jehan Khan (Dhundia) who had escaped with only one horse, in a short time, by his own vigorous exertions increased in strength and reputation so much, that he collected together a body of twenty-five or thirty thousand horse and foot, and raised a great tumult in the country, situate between the Kishna and Tungabhadra Rivers, and Babar Jung, and others joined him. By the aid also of the chief of Kolapur, during a sharp engagement, he in a furious charge killed Gokla the Mahratta and Parasuram the chief of Mirch, and having struck off their heads stuck them on the points of spears.

At length, however, it fell to his lot to be opposed to the English troops, and after much hard marching and fighting day and night, during which time no decisive action was fought, (although in this period his successes were great and he obtained much spoil,) still as he had no fort or stronghold in his possession to which he could retire and deposit his stores and followers, and by that means compete with the English on fair ground: after a hard struggle for two years from the treachery of the Afghans of Kirpa and Kurnole, (Kurnool) he received such a defeat from the English troops (under the command of the Colonel Sir Aurthur Wellesley in the neighbourhood of Kotal Bhanawur,[172] (called Konahgull by Thornton) that with the exception of his name and fame, no memorial of him whatever has remained.

Kamruddin Khan for a time exerted himself in vain desire to obtain a government, but at length a fatal disease, too terrible to be described, seized him and he died in great agonies. Many of the Sultan's Sirdars or officers, however, such as Budruzaman Khan, Ghulam Ali Khan the elchee or convey; Muhammad Raza Khutib; certain of the Mir Miran and Sipahdars; the brethren of Burhanuddin, that is the sons of Lala Mian; Ghulam Ali Bakshi, Gundahchar, &c. receive liberal salaries from the English East India Company according to their respective claims. A thousand praises are due to their courage and constancy.[173]

In the year 1215, Hijri, Hydar Ali the son of Karim Sahib (the son of Nawab Hydar Ali) made his escape from the English and joined the Mahrattas.

[172] Otherwise Hunur

[173] I think the Author here speaks ironically.

CHAPTER XX

A description of the amiable personal qualities, the disposition, manner and usages of that ornament of the throne of silence, (death) Tipu Sultan [174] These, notwithstanding from the abundance of evidence and proof they require no detail, or amplification, still agreeably to custom, a concise account of them is here given.

In his courts the splendour of kingly magnificence and majesty were well sustained. He had profited to a considerable extent in all the sciences. He wrote and composed with ease and elegance, and indeed had a genius[175] for literary acquirement, and a great talent for business; and, therefore, he was not obliged to rely on the aid or guidance of others in the management of public affairs He had a pleasing address and manner, was very discriminating in his estimation of the character of men of learning, and laboured sedulously in the encouragement and instruction of the people of Islam. He had, however, a great dislike to, or rather an abhorrence of, the people of other religions. He never saluted (or returned a salute to) any one. He held his Durbars from the morning until midnight, and after the morning prayers, he was used to employ some time in reading the Koran, and he was to be seen at all times with his Tusbih or rosary in his hand, having performed his ablutionary duties He made only two meals a day, and all his Amirs and the princes dined with him But from the day on which peace was made between him and Lord Cornwallis, Bahadur, (to the day of his death) he abandoned[176] his bed and bedstead and selpt or took a few hours rest on certain pieces of a coarse kind of canvas called Khaddi, (used for making tents) spread upon the ground. He was accustomed on most occasions to speak Persian, and while he was eating his dinner, two hours were devoted by him to the perusal (from standard historical works) of the actions of the Kings of Persia and Arabia, religious works, traditions and biography. He also heard appropriate stories and anecdotes related by his courtiers. Jests and ribaldry, however, from the repetition of which the religion of Islam might suffer disparagement, or injury, were never allowed in the courts or assemblies of that most religious prince. For the sake of recreation

[174] See the 115 Psalm, 17 verse, for a similar expression The Dukhmas or Sepulchres in which the Parsis deposit their dead, are called by them "Towers of Silence."

[175] *saliqat*

[176] Apparently from having made a vow to that effect, a custom very common in the East.

(*tafnan*)[177], as is the custom of men of high rank, he sometimes witnessed dancing (or was present at the performance of Bayaderes) He was not, however, lavish or expensive in any of his habits or amusements, not even in his dress, and contrary to his former custom he latterly avoided the use of coloured garments. On his journeys and expeditions, however, he wore a coat of cloth of gold, or of the red tiger stripe embroidered with gold. He was also accustomed to tie a white handerchief over his turban and under his chin, and no one was allowed to tie on, or wear, a white handkerchief in that manner, except himself.

Towards the end of his reign he wore a green turban Shumlehdar (twisted apparently) after the fashion of the Arabs, having one embroidered end pendant[178]. on the side of his head. He conferred honours on all professors of the Arts, and in the observance of his prayers, fasts and other religious duties, he was very strict, and in that respect the instructor,[179] or example of the people of Islam. Contrary to the custom of the deceased Nawab, he the Sultan retained the hair of his eyebrows, eyelashes, and moustaches. His beard, however, which was chiefly on his chin, he shaved thinking it not becoming to him. In delicacy or modesty of feeling he was the most particular man in the world, so much so that from the days of his childhood to that of his death, no one ever saw any part of his person except his ancle and wrist, and even in the bath he always covered himself from head to foot.

In the whole of the territories of the Balaghat, most of the Hindu women go about with their breasts and their heads uncovered like animals. He, therefore, gave orders that no one of these women should go out of her house without a robe and a veil or covering for the head This immodest custom was, therefore, abolished in that country. In his strict sense and keen perception of propriety and right he was unequalled. It happened that on some festival or day of rejoicing, he went to his father's private apartments to present his congratulations to his mother, and after the performance of this duty, and presenting dresses to her and her servants, he laid himself down to sleep a short time. During this period two ladies of the deceased Nawab's family, both of them young and handsome, (God knows with what intention good or bad) came forth from their apartments, and began to rub his feet While, however, they were doing this, he awoke, and when he saw they were the widows of the late Nawab, (or in the place of his mother), he became exceedingly angry at their presumption, and trembling with rage, said, "you are both of you my mothers, what insolence is this of which you have been guilty

[177] To see or patronize the skill and accomplishments of the Bayaderes

[178] *turra*

[179] *'allam.*

and by which you have blackened my face, what answer shall I give tomorrow to my father?" (meaning at the day of judgement); after this expostulation he sent for one of the eunuchs of the Serai and directed him to punish these women, so that they might be an example to others.

In courage and hardihood the Sultan took precedence of all his contemporaries, and in the management of a horse and the use of the spear in the world he had no equal, as will appear after an attentive perusal of this work. He was fond of introducing novelty and invention in all matters, (and in all departments), as for instance, the year called Muhammadi, an account of which has been before given, also the names of the solar months. For although these months are in usage among the Hindus, still as they became necessary in the computation of the revenue accounts, he gave them names from the Persian according to the Abjud, Howuz, Hutti[180] system of numeration as Ahmadi Bihari, Julwi, Darai, Hashimi, Wasai, Zuburjudi, Hydari, Tului, Yazdani, Eezudi, Bunai. &c.

Towards the conclusion of his reign he abolished these names[181] and called the months by others; such as Ahmadi, Bihari, Tukki, Sumri, Jafari, Hydari, Khasrovi, Deeni, Zakuri, Rahmani, Razi, and Rubbani. In the same manner also, the names of the cycle of sixty years, as for instance, Ahud, Ahmud, Ab, Ja, Bab, Buja, Abud, Jad, Jah, Ouj, &c. He also altered the impression on the hoon, or pagoda and rupee to a different form, as has been before related in the account of his coinage.

The Siduki was an ashrafi or gold mohur, with the same impression, as the rupee.

The Faruki was a pagoda, having on one side the name (Faruki) and on the other the letter *Jim*.

The Imami rupee also was of the weight and value of two rupees, this is now current.

The Bakuri, a half rupee.

The Jafari, a quarter of a rupee.

The Kazimi, two annas.

The Fulum or Fanam was called Rahuti and the Anna, Ayuh.

The terms employed in the measurement of grain were as follows. The Seer (a weight a little more than a pound) was called Duk, and weighed twenty-four fuloos or half-pence.

The Mun was called Atul, which is about four seers or pounds.

The Dhurra which is a quarter of a Mun was called Hoob

The Kurro which was sixteen Asur or Seers, was called Bede, and the Khundi which is twenty Kurras, Ahya.

[180] *abiad hauuaz hutte*. (Persian). [181] *Tarah*

Besides these inventions, his workmen cast guns of a very wonderful description, lion mouthed . also, muskets with two or three barrels, scissors, pen-knives, clocks, daggers called sufdura, also, a kind of shield woven and formed so as to resist a musket ball.

Besides these he also instituted manufactories for the fabrication or imitation of the cloths of all countries, such as shawls, velvet, Kimkhab, (cloth of gold), broad cloth (European), and he expended thousands of pounds in these undertakings.

His chief aim and object was, however, the encouragement and protection of the Muhammadan religion, and the religious maxims or rules of the Sunni sect, and he not only himself abstained from all forbidden practices, but he strictly prohibited his servants from their commission.

He also formed regulations on every subjtct and for every department depending on his government, every article of which was separately written with his own hand. If, however, he dismissed any one from his office for any fault, or neglect, he after correction and punishment, was accustomed to re-appoint him to the same office again, and from this cause it was that during his reign, treachery gained head so far as to cast his kingdom and power gratuitously to the winds

On the top of his farmans or public papers, he was accustomed to write the words,—"In the name of God"—in the Toghra Character in his own hand, and at the end his signature was in this form so

THE CONCLUSION OF THIS WORK

Praise and Thanksgiving to God[182] (*ve·se*)—"that what I asked has been granted by him"

When the commands obeyed by the world, briliant as the light of the sun, exalted as the Heavens, of that great personage (the name of this great personage is not given, it being in the opinion of the author sufficiently known) whose heart is the abode of purity and sincerity, were issued to this gatherer of crumbs from the table of the wise and learned, that he should reduce to writing in a plain easy style the History of the Kingdom of Mysore, and with his pen describe faithfully the whole of the wars and conquests, (made by the rulers of that country), notwithstanding certain contingencies and worldly troubles (*'awuiq*)[183] and the scanty means and mean abilities of this ruined man; the difficulties which beset him in obtaining the means of subsistence and the fatigue of a long journey; all strongly operated to prevent his attempting so great an undertaking and threw the stone of indecision at the glass of the firmness of his determination; and his mind the finder or inventor of signs, or symbols,[184] with the tongue of humility in detailing such high and praiseworthy qualities and actions, said "what power has a speechless ant that he should be able to move a mountain? or what strength has a fly that he should take such a burden on his shoulders?" being, still, however, obedient to the commands and bound to the orders of the great personage before mentioned, without attempting the difficult task of composing flowery and ornamented periods, a few lines have been written describing the conquests and other events of the reign (of Tipu Sultan), his excellent qualities and singularly good disposition. Stories of his liberality, and relation of occurrences displaying his kind and forgiving temper, his generosity to his friends, his zeal for the propagation of the religion of Islam, and for the destruction of infidels and infidelity—In writing these details the purity of the author's pearl-stringing pen, has not been sullied by the dirt of misrepresentation or falsehood, such being the practice of hired sycophants of low character, or of foolish rhapsodical writers only. (The Author after using the third person, now speaks in the first—but to continue as he began).

[182] *alhamdu lillahi wa al minnat*

[183] Some variation in the MS here I have followed Colonel Marriot's copy.

[184] *khatir nukteh yab ramuz afrin.*

The hope and trust of the Author, therefore, from the princely sons and dependants of the Sultan is, that they will look on his book with the eyes of impartiality and approbation, and give him the meed of praise in proportion to his claims and merits, which (meed) is the harvest of the life, and the chief source of gratification and delight to the poor and needy scholar. And as the History of the Nawab Hydar Ali Khan Bahadur, and a commentary on the reign and actions of Tipu Sultan, are both included in this work, for that reason the Author has sought and found the year of its completion in the word (Persian : *tawarikh*). Towarikh (which is the plural of *tarikh*[185] a date of a month or or year, and a term generally applied to History,) that is to say, it was the year 1217, Hijri, (A.D. 1802), and it was on the 9th of the month of Rajab ul Morujub, that he turned the reins of the horse-like pen from his career on the race-course of the paper to the end, that his soul might be released from the toils of anxiety, hard study, and deep reflection, and that at length the object of his desires (rest, or the completion of the work) might show him her lovely face.

min hunna ushr'u fi'l maqsud birabbi'l maujud.

From this commences the accomplishment of the Author's desires, by the aid of the Lord of all existence

SERINGAPATAM : THE CAPITAL OF TIPU

(*By G. B. Malleson*)

Just seventy-eight miles from the British cantonment of Bangalore, and nine from the Hindu capital of Mysore, on an island formed by the winding of the river Kaveri, may be yet seen and visited the once famous fortress of Seringapatam To the man who gazes at this fortress from the outside its battlements still present the appearance they offered to the besieging army of General Harris on the morning of the 4th May 1799. The breach through which his troops effected an entrance on that memorable day is preserved, unrepaired, a monument of British prowess; the ramparts remain now as they were then, the only exception being that the embrasures are empty of guns. The fortress resembles, in fact, a disarmed and blinded giant, in his youth and middle age the terror of the southern peninsula, but who now lies, the helpless and powerless slave of his conqueror, testifying to the living generation that neither strong walls, powerful artillery, nor that courage which is the offspring of love of supremacy and hate to the foe, can withstand the assault of the daring children of the islands of the West

Thus lies this fortress, still an object of deep, even of passionate, interest to the numbers who flock to visit it. It has known strange vicissitudes. In a certain point of view its history presents a nearly accurate type of the history of Hindusthan. Originally Hindu, threatened then by the Muhamadans, then by the Marhattas, converted subsequently into the Muhamadan capital of Southern India, the strong fortress finally succumbed to the power which had subdued all three. The history of each period is full of interest; of that relating to British occupation particularly so, for not a century has elapsed since the leader who ruled the country of which it was the representative capital dictated peace to the English under the walls of Madras, and seventy-seven years ago its final subjugation was regarded by the greatest of Indian Governors-General as the crowning act which settled for ever the question of British supremacy in Southern India.

The island on which Seringapatam stands is formed by the divergence of two arms of the river Kaveri. It is about three and a half miles in length, and one mile and a half in breadth across its centre, which is its broadest part. The natural lay of the land on the island falls and narrows from its centre towards its extremities. But at its lowest point it is still considerably above the river level at its greatest height. The west end of the island, on which the fortress is built, slopes more especially towards the north, in such a way that the rising ground on the opposite side of the river commands a distinct view of the interior.[1]

The fortress covers a space of about two thousand[2] square yards. Its northern and western fronts are covered by the river, which thus forms an enormous wet ditch, neither fordable nor navigable between the months of June and November.

Prior to the years 1792 the great strength of Seringapatam lay, indeed, in the development of the natural strength of the soil. Thus, excepting the north-west bastion, the entire revetment was formed of natural blocks of granite of an enormous side. The ditches were excavated from the rock itself; whilst, on the northern side, a glacis had been cut in the living rock, though, from the fact of the counterscarp having been left incomplete in two places, a continous covering was not afforded to the rampart On the eastern and western sides it was surrounded by double walls, each wall covered by a double ditch, the gates were covered by exterior works; the north-west angle, that assaulted in 1799, was defended by a strong interior work, whilst, in the centre of the fortress and on the southern rampart were strong cavaliers

But in 1792 it was greatly strengthened On the east of the place a covered way was built *en cremaillere* in order to defend that face from an enfilading fire from the northern bank of the river. Works of a similar character were added to the parapet of the northern rampart, where also cavaliers and traverses *en gazon* were built To the north eastern angle of the fortress a bastion on the latest European system was then added; whilst, just before the siege of 1799 a second interior rampart, covered by a deep ditch, was hastily erected along the whole length of the northern face.

About this period, likewise, several sluices were constructed for the purpose of admitting and retaining the river water in the ditches. From the north-eastern angle of the fortress likewise, the river bank was scarped and covered by a parapet extending as far as the Daryadaolat, the summer palace of Tipu Sultan. The eastern face of the garden in which this palace is situated was defended by a rampart and ditch, and, starting from this point, a good intrenchment traversed the island right up to the bridge which separated it from the mainland.

As it stood in 1792, the fortress and its environs are thus described by Major Dirom, who was present as Deputy Adjutant-General at the siege of 1792 :—

"The fort and outworks occupy about a mile of the west end

[1] Dirom's Narrative
[2] See page 148

of the island, and the Lal Bagh[3] about the same portion of the east end."

"The whole space between the Fort and the Lal Bagh, except a small enclosure, called the Daolat Bagh, on the north bank near the fort, was filled, before the war, with houses, and formed an extensive suburb, of which the village of Ganjam is the only remaining part, the rest having been destroyed by Tipu to make room for batteries to defend the island and to form an esplanade to the fort.

"The town, of modern structure, built on the middle and highest part of the island, is about half a mile square, divided into regular cross streets, all wide, and shaded on each side by trees, and full of good houses. It is surrounded by a strong mud wall, and seemed to have been preserved for the accommodation of the bazar people and merchants, and for the convenience of the troops stationed on that part of the island for its defence.

"A little way to the eastward of the town is the entrance into the Lal Bagh. It was laid out in regular shady walks of large cypress trees, and full of fruit trees, flowers, and vegetables of every description."

"The fort thus situated on the west end of the island is distinguished by its white walls, regular outworks, magnificent buildings, and ancient Hindu pagodas (temples), contrasted with the more lofty and splendid monuments lately raised in honour of the Muhamedan faith. The Lal Bagh, which occupies the east end of the island, possessing all the beauty and convenience of a country retirement, is dignified by the mausoleum of Haidar and a superb new palace built by Tipu To these add the idea of an extensive suburb or town, which filled the middle space between the fort and the garden, full of wealthy industrious inhabitants, and it will readily be allowed that this insulated metropolis must have been the richest, most convenient, and beautiful spot possessed in the present age by any native prince in India."

Such indeed it may have been prior to 1792, but it is so no longer. The dismantled fort, the open breach, the towering minarets, the village of Ganjam, the garden and country house of Tipu, the mausoleum of Haidar and his son, still indeed remain; but the white walls, the Hindu temples, the magnificent buildings, the spendid palace in the Lal Bagh, the good houses, and the wealthy inhabitants have long since been things of the past. The fortunes of the town have followed the fortunes of the fortress, and the decay of the one has supervened on the dismantlement of the other! But it is not with the Seringapatam of the present that I have to do. With but one solitary

[3] Where now rest the remains of Haidar Ali and of Tipu.

exception, which I shall notice in its place, all its romance is concentrated in the period prior to and ending in 1799. To that period, which might not inappropriately be styled the rise and fall of Seringapatam, I propose now to refer.

The earliest mention in history of Seringapatam goes back as far as 1133. In that year, it is stated, Raja Vishnu Verdana, of the Ballal dynasty, converted from the Jain to the Vishnuvite form of faith by a Brahman named Ramana Charlu, conferred on that apostle and his followers the tract of country on either side of the river at Seringapatam, and known, then as now, by the general name of Ashtagram or the eight townships.

This tract of land would appear to have remained in the possession of the descendants of those settlers for more than three hundred years, during which time they were subject to the Hindu dynasty reigning in Vijaynagar. Nor was it until 1454 that one of them, named Timmana, asked and obtained permission to erect there a fort and temple. The fort, built in honour of the god Ranga, he called Sri-ranga-patan or the city of the holy Ranga. The temple was dedicated to the same patron; its dimensions at first were small, but were subsequently greatly enlarged by their founder, he having obtained materials by demolishing 101 Jain temples at Kalaswari, a village, still existing, modway between Seringapatam and Mysore

For some years the town and fort of Seringapatam continued to be governed by the descendants of Timmana but the time at last arrived when the rising importance of the place required that it should be ruled by a Viceroy appointed from Vijayanagar. The exact date when the transfer was made I have not been able accurately to ascertain, but it is scarcely material to the narrative. It probably occurred before the close of the fifteenth century. But in the year 1564 the kingdom of Vijayanagar succumbed itself to a coalition of the Muhamedan kings of the Dekhan. Seringapatam, however, was not affected by this overthrow. The Vijayanagar Viceroy, Trimal Raj, still reigned there unassailed, at least by the Muhamedans. The enemy he most dreaded, and with whom he had had constant differences, was the ruler of a rising power whose capital lay within ten miles of his own fortress—the Raja of Mysore. Till 1610, however, Trimal Raj maintained this last dependency of his royal house. But in that year, "worn down with age and disease," foreseeing that his power, long undermined, must inevitably succumb sooner or later to his ambitious neighbour, he determined to retire from the cares of Government. He entered then, into a compromise with Raj Wadiar, Raja of Mysore, in virtue of which he retired to spend the remainder of his days at Talkad. Seringapatam was at once peaceably occupied by Raj Wadiar, who made it the seat of his Government.

Twenty-eight years later Seringapatam stood its first siege. The assailants were the troops of the Muhamedan king of Bijapur commanded by a General of repute, Rand Dhula Khan. The defenders, the Mysore army, were led by their youthful sovereign, Cantarava Narsa Raj, the third in descent from Raj Wadiar. Of this siege no minute details have reached us. It is only known that the Muhamedans having effected a practicable breach, made a general assault, but were not only repulsed with great slaughter, but followed up and severely harassed. The sovereign who had thus gallantly defended his fortress, took an early opportunity to augment its defences, and, noting the signs of the times, suppied it (1654) with provisions and military stores so as to enable it to offer a protracted resistance to any invader.

For twenty-four years after the failure of the Muhamedan invasion Seringapatam remained unassailed. But in 1662 a new enemy presented himself This was the Raja of Bednur, urged on by the fugitive descendant of the ancient royal family of Vijayanagar who had taken refuge at his court. Again, however, the besiegers were foiled. Again, too, minute details are wanting, this alone being certain that the besiegers retreated in confusion and dismay to Bednur.

But more stirring times were approaching. In 1697, the still maiden fortress was suddenly assailed by a Marhatta army, acting as auxiliary to Zulfikar Khan, General of the renowned Aurangzib. At that time the main army of the Mysoreans was befort Trichinapali, and Seringapatam had been left with a feeble garrison. But, learning of its danger, the Dalwai,[4] then before Trichinapali, despatched a force under his to its relief. On approaching the fortress the relieving army outwitted the enemy and completely defeated them.

The next danger, however, occurring in 1755, was greater. The assailants were the troops of the Subadar of the Dekhan, led by the renowned Bussy, and aided by 500 Frenchmen. Their object was to exact the tribute, acknowledged but never paid, by the Rajas of Mysore to the representative of the Mughal. At that time, too, the bulk of the Mysore army was at Trichinapali aiding the French in their contest against the English. The celerity of Bussy's march made it impossible for the Dalwai, Devaraj Urs, who commanded in Seringapatam, to hold out till that army should arrive to relieve him. Bussy lost not a moment in making regular approaches against the north-east angle of the fortress. In a few days an assault would have been delivered, the result of which had been scarcely doubtful, when Devaraj agreed to pay the demand of fifty-six lakhs of rupees. But the treasury was empty. One-third of the amount was raised by the

[4] Dalwai, the title of the holder of the hereditary office of Commander-in-Chief in Mysore.

plate and jewels of the Hindu temples and the immediate property and ornaments of the Raja, and bills were accepted for the remainder. But it was found impossible to meet the bills on maturity. They never were met, in fact, and of the gomashtas who had been taken off by the besiegers as personal securities for payment many died in prison.

Two years later the Peshwa, Balaji Rao, appeared before Seringapatam with an army. At that time the country was distracted by internal contentions. The Raja was a virtual prisoner within his palace : the Dalwai, Devaraj, was sulking in a corner of the province; his brother Nanjanraj, was Mayor of the palace; and Haidar Ali, who commanded a portion of the army, was already brooding over plans to secure that post for himself. The defence, however, was ably conducted by Nanjanraj, and had he ordered up his army from Dindigal, it would probably have succeeded. But, he did not do so, and before Haidar could arrive to aid him, Nanjanraj was forced to come to terms. He had to pay heavily for his defeat, and was forced to yield fourteen districts and to pay five lakhs of rupees before the Marhatas would depart.

The next attempt upon the fortress took place after Haidar Ali had succeeded in virtually supplanting the Hindu dynasty. It was made by the Marhatas under Trimbak Rao, who preceded it by inflicting upon the Mysore army led by Haidar and Tipu a defeat at Chirkuli, eleven miles to the west of Seringapatam. When this battle engaged Haidar was suffering from intoxication, and Tipu from the effects of a fearful beating administered to him by his father when in that state. The natural result was defeat. The beaten army, almost disarmed, hurried panic-stricken into Seringapatam that night, and had the Marhatas followed them up, the place would assuredly have fallen. But Trimbak Rao delayed his appearance for ten days, and then rather blockaded than besieged the fortress This blockade lasted for fifteen months, when it was terminated by the payment by Haidar of five lakhs of rupees and the renunciation of seven important districts on his northern frontier.

We now approach the time when our own countrymen first made acquaintance with this famous fortress. But to understand thoroughly how this acquaintanceship began it will be necessary to describe, in the briefest manner, the mode by which Haidar Ali dispossessed the ancient Hindu dynasty.

The curse of being born in the purple had been gradually falling upon the ruling family. Subsequently to the demise of Chick Deo Raj in 1704 the administration of the country had been virtually conducted by the Dalwai, or hereditary Commander-in-Chief The most famous of these, Devaraj, administered the affairs of the country with vigour, and, on the whole, with fair success, till the year 1756 when he was supplanted rather than succeeded by his brother, Nanjanraj. This nobleman, who had for some time virtually commanded the army, had previously engaged the services of Haidar Naik, a soldier of fortune, who had shewn soldierlike conduct as a volunteer at the siege of Devanahali. The reputation of Haidar increasing daily Nanjanraj called upon him in 1756 to aid him in restoring order in the ranks of the army, then mutinying for want of pay. Haidar responded and came to Seringapatam, but no money being forthcoming for the purpose, Nanjanraj resigned his office in disgust Haidar, aided by a confidential Hindu friend, Khande Rao, soon succeeded in settling the accounts of the army. Having effected this, Haidar, leaving Khande Rao to watch over his interests, and reappointing Nanjanraj as Minister, joined the army in the field. Very soon after this Nanjanraj was removed and was succeeded by Khande Rao, Haidar receiving as payment for his share in this transaction assignments of districts equal to more than half the territories of the State. Then very soon did the Hindu nobility discover the mistake they had committed in thus elevating Haider. A plot was set on foot by the Queen dowager, Nanjanraj Urs, and Khande Rao, to get rid of him. For a moment it seemed likely to succeed. Attacked in the garden of the Darya-daolat Haidar swam the river and fled for his life. But the triumph of the conspirators was short. Levying fresh troops, Haidar attacked and defeated the army of Khande Rao at Nanjangod, then, marching to Ganjam, thence dictated terms to the helpless Raja. From that time, June 1761, Haidar Ali was the real ruler, of Mysore, the nominal title only being left to the Raja and his successors, who remained under close surveillance in Seringapatam, till released by the events of the 4th May 1799.

Haidar's first war with the English shewed the abilities he possessed as a soldier. Though not always successful he generally knew when to strike a decisive blow. Thus it happened in 1769, that taking advantage of the distance from Madras of the two main hostile armies, he made a raid at the head of 6,000 chosen horse to that city, and dictated peace under its walls to the Governor (29th March 1769). Then followed the disastrous campaign with the Marhatas beginning with the defeat of Chirkuli and ending with the ransom of Seringapatam. After an interval, in the course of which he repulsed the troops of the Nizam and the Mahratas from his territories, Haider entered upon his last war, famous for his defeat of the detachments of Colonel Baillie and Colonel Braithwaite, and the sanguinary and not altogether unequal contests which he maintained against Sir Eyre Coote at Porto Novo, Pirambakam, and Arni.

Haidar died immediately after the last named engagement

(17th December 1781) but his death did not interrupt the war. It continued to linger under his son and successor, Tipu Sultan, till the month of March 1784.

But Tipu, though he then made peace with the English, did not cease to carry on warfare with his neighbours The Nizam, the Marhatas, and the Coorgs, in turn occupied his troops. At last, he ventured to attack a protected ally of the English, the Raja of Travancor. This was an insult which was not allowed to pass unnoticed, and a new coalition of the English, the Nizam, and the Marhatas was formed to punish the disturber of the public peace.

The early part of this war was characterised by varying successes, but it was brought to an issue by the determination expressed by Lord Cornwallis to strike at the heart of his enemy's dominions. These views he at once attempted to carry out. Bangalore was taken on the 7th March 1791; its fort on the 21st; Seringapatam itself was seen and threatened in May; but owing to the want of supplies, to sickness, and to the late season, it was not till the 5th February 1792 that the British army was able seriously to threaten the capital of the Sultan.

The story of the siege which then ensued has been told with perspicuity and force by one of the chief actors in the scene[5] from whose work I have already quoted. In many respects it was a memorable event, and though not conducted to the same forcible issue as that which followed it, it abounds with traits of gallantry and interest. Moreover it was successful.

Before however presenting an outline of this siege, it may be pertinent to glance for a moment at the position occupied by Tipu and his father in the estimation of the people of India, for it was that estimation which gave them half their strength, and which endowed Seringapatam with a prestige exceeding that of any other great fortress in Hindusthan.

At the time when Haidar Ali and Tipu flourished the leading powers of India south of the Satlaj were the Marhata confederacy, composed of the often disunited chiefs of Puna, of Baroda, of Indur, of Nagpur of the country ruled by Sindia, the Nizam, and Mysore. For all practical purposes the others did not count. Now, of those I have enumerated, Madhaji Sindia had shewn the greatest capacity and the most farsighted views. But Madhaji, though dealing to the English in the western Presidency some very severe blows, had in the end been beaten; and at the time of the siege of Seringapatam by Lord Cornwallis he was endeavouring to bring about a general confederacy against us, which would have tried our resources to the utmost. But he was working quietly, in the dark, and the prestige of victory did

[5] Major Dirom then Deputy Adjutant-General of His Majesty's Forces in India.

not then sit on his brow. The other Marhata powers, unprepared at the moment to follow the lead of Madhaji, were then quiescent. The Nizam was our ally. It was the ruler of Mysore alone who had shewn himself at all equal to the English on the field of battle. It was Haidar who had dictated peace to us under the walls of Madras ; it was Haidar who had fought a not unequal battle with the General who had been the right hand of Clive at Plassey, and, though Haidar was dead, his son lived, having inherited his love of power, his ambition, his lust of conquest. It was not yet known indeed how far inferior in ability, in judgment, in management of men, was Tipu to his sire. Men saw in him the ruler of the table-land which looked down upon the Carnatak, a land fruitful in warriors, strong in hill forts, well watered by its rivers, and whose island fortress dominated southern India Seringapatam under its later Hindu sovereigns had never been aggressive, but under his two Muhamedan rulers the English in Madras had learned to speak of it with respect, whilst in Trichinapali and in Madura, in Trevandrum and Cochin, its name was never mentioned but with awe Madhaji Sindia had not been blind to the vast prestige exercised by the ruler of Mysore, and he had secretly pressed alike upon Tipu and the Nizam the desirability of abstaining from isolated warfare, of nursing their resources until he should be able to bring to their aid the vast power of an united Marhata confederacy to combat the one enemy who would otherwise swallow them all up in detail—the English From what is known of Haidar's character it seems not improbable that he would have listened to the advice of the greatest of Indian Statesmen But Tipu, besides lacking judgment, laboured under a misfortune still common in the world, and to be seen in all religions—he was a bigot He hated all infidels, whether Christian or Hindus. He would take counsel of none of them. Thus it was that he foolishly precipitated the contest, not only isolated, but with his natural allies, the Nizam and the troops of the Peshwa, in league with his enemies. Tipu was beaten in the field ; but yet he had the satisfaction of witnessing the English retreat (May 1791) from Seringapatam. But when in February of the following year he saw them occupy the hill which crowns the opposite bank of the Kaveri, and learned that they had seized the French Rocks, when too he counted in their ranks the cavalry of the Marhatas and the trained contingent of the Nizam, it is more than probable that he thought, and thought with regret, of the rejected advice of the chief of the house of Sindia.

Although the fortifications were greatly strengthened subsequently to 1792, the intelligent traveller will have no difficulty in following Lord Cornwallis' plan of attack upon the fortress It must always be recollected that in the two sieges, those of

1792 and 1799, the main attack on Seringapatam was conducted each time from different sides. In the former year it was made from the north and east, in the latter from the west and north-west. Lord Cornwallis' first care was to clear the upper portion of the ground on the north bank of the river, where Tipu lay with his army computed to be 100,000 strong; then, to effect a lodgment on the island itself. This plan he determined to carry out on the night of the 6th February. On that night and during the following day, Tipu's intrenched camp was stormed, the passage of the river was effected, the Lal Bagh and the village of Ganjam were occupied. By this success the English gained a strong position on the island to the east of the fortress.

The position of both parties on the morning of the 8th February may thus be described. Tipu held the fortress, the Daolat Bagh, and the works connecting the one with the other. His communications with the south and west were likewise open. The English on their side had cut off their enemy on the north and on the east, had invested the fortress on those sides, and had effected a secure lodgment on the island. But that was not all. Whilst dismay and despair reigned in the camp of Tipu, whilst his forced levies were deserting and his foreign hirelings were submitting, the English were full of the confidence which deserved success always inspires.

Tipu himself was so overcome by the disaster that he made overtures for peace. With that object in view, he released two of his prisoners, Lieutenants Chalmers and Nash, and loading them with presents, sent them to the British camp with letters for Lord Cornwallis. The propositions contained in those letters were entertained; but the negotiations which followed did not interfere with the vigorous prosecution of hostilities.

I have stated that the fortress had been invested on its northern and eastern sides. It had been originally intended that the main attack should issue from Ganjam, by making a lodgment in the Daolat Bagh. From thence regular approaches were to be run against the north-eastern angle of the fort, which would also be subjected to a strong enfilading fire from batteries on the northern bank of the river. But Colonel Ross, the Chief Engineer, having been able to reconnoitre the northern face of the fortress very closely, and having ascertained that the curtain was very weak, extending close along the bank of the river, leaving no room for outworks; that the flank defences were few and of little consequence, having also received information corroborative of these views from some of the European deserters from Tipu, judged it more advisable to make the principal attack across the river against the northern face of the fort. Lord Cornwallis admitted the force of Colonel Ross's views. It may be interesting to record in this place the other advantages and the disadvantage which an attack on the northern face across the river offered to the view of Lord Cornwallis and his Chief Engineer. They are thus recorded by Major Dirom :

"The ditch," writes that officer, "excavated from the rock, was dry, and said to be inconsiderable; and it appeared to be so from what could be observed in looking into it from the pagoda hill. The stone glacis, which, built into the river, covers that face, was broken, or had been left incomplete, in two places, including several hundred yards of the curtain; the walls might therefore be breached to the bottom, and would probably fill up the greater part of the ditch[6] The fort, built on the declivity of the island on the north, was then exposed in its whole extent, and every shot fired from that quarter must take effect, while the slope of the island also to the west end exposed that part of the fort to a very powerful enfilade attack from the ground by which it is commanded on the south side of the river opposite to the south-west face of the fort.

"The north branch of the river, which would intervene between the main attack and the fort, was the only objection It seemed possible, by repairing an old dam or embankment, to throw the water entirely into the other branch; at all events, the channel, though rugged, was not deep or impassible, and the embarrassment of such an obstacle was in some measure compensated by the security it gave against sallies, and the cover it would afford in breaking ground at once within breaching distance of the fort The fire, too, from that side, could not be very considerable, and there was a certainty of carrying on the approaches rapidly, and breaching the place with little loss"

For these reasons it was determined to attack Seringapatam on its northern face The first preparations to carry out this plan were made on the 18th February. Two days prior to that date Lord Cornwallis' army was reinforced, on the northern bank of the Kaveri, by the Bombay force under General Abercromby, consisting of 2,000 European, and 4,000 Indian troops, fit for duty.

On the following day, the 19th, a diversion was made to beat up the Mysore horse encamped on the south side of the river. Whilst the enemy were engaged, ineffectually, in meeting this attack, a detachment from the main body attacked and occupied a redoubt on the north bank of the river nearly opposite the middle of the fort on that side, at a distance from it of about 1,500 yards. This having been effected the north-west side of the fort was invested by the Bombay force. This force took up a position on a rising ground, just beyond gun-shot of the fort.

[6] Many of these defects were remedied subsequently to 1792. Vide page 139.

Tipu's personal activity and vigour at this point of the siege is thus described by Major Dirom : "He was seen frequently every day on the ramparts, particularly at the north face, viewing our approaches, and giving directions to his own troops. He was constantly bringing guns to the works and cavaliers on that side, and had multitude of people at work, thickening the inner rampart, filling up the embrasures to strengthen the parapet where he could not have guns, and repairing such as had been blown and damaged by the firing of his cannon. He had at first employed his people in completing the glacis and strengthening the works on the east face of the fort towards the island ; but since the opening of our trenches towards the north side, all his attention and exertions were directed to that quarter. He was at work day and night, making every preparation possible for a vigorous defence."

But Tipu's affairs were drawing to a crisis. On the 22nd he attempted to dislodge the advanced picquets of the Bombay Army. The action, which lasted all day, was well fought on both sides, and it was only at nightfall that the Mysoreans gave up the contest. The ill success of this attack, added to the knowledge that 20,000 Marhatas, under Parseram Bhao, were advancing to invest the south side of his fortress, and thus to blockade him entirely, at last decided him. On the 23rd February he accepted in principle the terms offered him by Lord Cornwallis. Hostilities were then suspended, and though nearly breaking out again in consequence of the unwillingness of the defeated Sultan to resign Coorg, they came on that date actually to an end. The treaty, by which Tipu agreed to pay three crores and thirty lakhs of rupees and to cede about one-half of his territories, was signed on the 19th March.

Peace then came Tipu, but it was a peace dictated by despair. His whole soul was bent upon a renewal of the struggle under more favourable circumstances. With this object in view, and noting the reason which had prompted the allies to attack the north side of the fort, he greatly strengthened that face. In fact by the new works, by the double ramparts and double ditches which he added to the northern and western faces, he made of Seringapatam as it were a fortress within a fortress—a fact with which, strangely enough, the English only became acquainted on the day of the storm.

Nor did he neglect the eastern and southern faces. The double ramparts and double ditches he added on the sides may yet be easily traced. But he constructed, in addition, a new line of intrenchments from the Daolat Bagh to the Periapatam bridge (close to the village of Pakhshwan) within 6 or 700 yards of the fortress Whilst carrying on these military works he instituted quasi-reforms ; but these consisted mainly in the substitution of confiscation for a regular system of revenue. The titular Raja having died he plundered his palace, and appointed no successor.

But the chief end on which his aims were bent was to obtain allies. He could scarcely hope for these in India. The man who would have cemented a general alliance of the native powers against the English, Madhaji Sindia, died in 1794; and after his death the policy of isolated action became the policy of the native chiefs. Now, both the Peshwa and the Nizam had benefited so largely by the war of 1791/2 at Tipu's expense that he felt it was useless to try to gain them. Failing then the princess of India he had recourse to Afghanistan. In 1797 he despatched an embassy to Zeman Shah Abdali, ruler of that country, proposing an alliance between that prince and the Muhamedan powers of India to drive out the English and the Brahmins. Zeman Shah, however, perhaps could not, certainly did not, respond, and it seems possible that but for the rays of hope disseminated by the French Revolution, Tipu would, after this failure, have resigned himself to his fate.

Strange indeed in appearance, that that mighty upheaving of all the old ways in France, an upheaving which cast down thrones, and levelled its shafts specially at kings, should have found its first sympathiser in the sovereign of Seringapatam! Yet, after all, in reality, not so very strange It had been a favourite maxim of Haidar, familiar to Tipu from his earliest youth, that the Europeans could only be conquered by Europeans. In his eyes, then, the French Revolution was only an event which placed France in antagonism with combined Europe; which, as her armies gained strength, defeated coalition after coalition, and, finally, in 1797, triumphed over every country except the one he hated most, inspired him with the hope that by her aid he might yet realize the dream akin to that for which Dupleix had schemed, and Bussy and Lally had fought in vain.

Adventures fleeing to his court from Pondichery captured by the English fanned these visions; but it was an accident that ripened them to action. In the early part of 1797 a French privateer, commanded by an adventurer named Ripaud, was driven on the coast near Mangalore. This man, finding his way to Seringapatam, succeeded in persuading Tipu that he was an envoy to him from the French republic. He established in Seringapatam a branch of the Jacobin Club, composed mainly of the refugees from Pondichery; and this Club, constituting itself an integral portion of the French nation, and swearing hatred to all kings excepting to "Tipu Sultan the victorious" persuaded the infatuated Sovereign, against the advice of his ablest counsellors, to send an embassy to the Isle of France and to the Directory, to demand aid for the expulsion of the English from India.

Tipu's ambassadors reached indeed the Isle of France, but

the number of men whom they persuaded to embark in their perilous enterprise did not exceed[7] seventy-six Europeans and twenty-six Mulattos.

It happened, too, unfortunately for Tipu that the Governor of the Isle of France, General Malartic, had made no secret of the request which the Mysore ambassadors had preferred. He had even issued a proclamation, dated 30th January 1798, in which he invited the people of the island to rally to the Sultan's standard A copy of this proclamation found its way to Calcutta, was published in the newspapers, and attracted the attention of the Governor-General, Marquess Wellesley[8] (18th June 1798). The Governor-General was well acquainted with the previous endeavours of Tipu to obtain allies, with the fact that he had strengthened the fortifications of Seringapatam; and was only waiting opportunity to retrieve the misfortunes of 1792. The proclamation of General Malartic not only confirmed his information on these points, but gave him an opportunity for calling Tipu to account; nor was the necessity for such action lessened in the eyes of the English ruler by the interception of a letter addressed by General Bonaparte to Tipu from his Head Quarters in Cairo, informing the Mysore Sultan that he had arrived on the shores of the Red Sea with a numerous and invincible army, full of desire to free him from the English yoke, and desiring him to send to Suez an intelligent person in whom he had confidence to confer with him.[9]

The Governor-General remonstrated with Tipu. Tipu, (8th November 1798), as yet unprepared for war, tried to cajole the Governor-General. (25th Decembtr 1798). The Governor-General then unfolded to Tipu his knowledge of all his proceedings and asked him to furnish security for peaceable behaviour, giving him but one day to consider his reply, and warning him that delay would be dangerous. Tipu delayed not a day, but upwards of a month, and then gave a vague and unsatisfactory, and, as Marquess Wellesley deemed, a contemptuous reply. The Governor-General hesitated no longer, but at once directed the British Army, under Major-General Harris, to march into the territories of the Sultan to enforce the necessary security.

Thus began the last war with Tipu Sultan. The reader, while he cannot fail to see how entirely Tipu brought it on himself, cannot the less refuse his homage to the foresight and

[7] They were, One General, One Naval Captain, One Colonel, Two Artillery Officers, Six Naval Officers, Four Ship Carpenters, Twenty-six Officers, Sergeants and Interpreters, Thirty-six European soldiers, Twenty-six Mulatto soldiers MICHAUD, Vol I. *Annual Register*

[8] Then known as Earl of Mornington

[9] This letter, dated 7th Pluviose of the 7th year of the Republic, is attached as a piece justificative to Michaud's history of Mysore.

decision of the great Marquess, who thus gave evidence of a knowledge of the time to strike in politics, not less remarkable than that invariably displayed by his illustrious brother on the field of battle.

The plan of the English was to attack Mysore on two sides; viz, from Vellore by an army under the command of General Harris, aided by a contingent furnished by the Nizam, and from Cannanor under General Stuart, advancing by way of Coorg. To these two armies, numbering upwards of 43,000 men,[10] Tipu had to oppose an army as yet not assembled, and the uncertain hope of aid from France But though not confident, he did not despair. Hastily assembling his troops, he threw garrisons into the most important places, and then set out, at the end of February 1799, for Periapatam, at the head of about 60,000 men, with the hope of surprising and beating in detail the Bombay army which he was aware was marching by way of Coorg. Tipu's manoeuvres against the British army were skilful and seemed at first to promise success. Aided by a fog, he (5th March 1799) succeeded in cutting off their advanecd brigade from their main body, but the valour of the British supplied the deficiencies of their tactics, and after a conflict of several hours the Mysoreans were repulsed. Leaving then a small party to check if possible, or at least to harass, the Bombay Army, Tipu hastened from Periapatam with the main body of his troops to oppose General Harris, who, he was informed, had crossed the Mysore frontier. He found him on the 27th March taking up a position at Malavali, about forty miles from Seringapatam and fifteen from Madur He at once determined to attack him, and opening immediately upon his advanced posts, he followed up

[10] LORD HARRIS' ARMY

Europeans.		
Cavalry	884	
Artillery	608	
Infantry	4,381	
		5,873
Natives		
Cavalry	1,751	
Infantry	10,695	
Gun Lascars	1,483	
Pioneers	1,000	
		14,929
Subsidiary Force officered by British Officers furnished by the Nizam		10,157
Nizam's Native Force		6,000
		31,086
Bombay Army		6,420
	TOTAL	37,506

the fire by a charge of 15,000 horse. But the shock of the Mysore Cavalry, impetuous as it was, could not prevail against the steady discipline of European Infantry supported by a murderous fire of artillery After an hour's combat, in which they lost 1,000 men, the Mysoreans were finally repulsed Tipu retreated in all haste on Seringapatam, ravaging the country behind him, so as to render the advance of the English, who depended for their supplies on the country through which they marched, difficult if not impossible On the 30th March a portion of his infantry and artillery, including his French auxiliaries, and numbering altogether about 8,000 men, entered Seringapatam. His cavalry and the remaining infantry were left on the north bank of the Kaveri, as well to harass the English force, as to constitute a disposible army upon which to fall back in case of need

Meanwhile General Harris detecting the object of Tipu in ravaging the country, had resolved to outwit him, and by crossing the Kaveri at a point below Seringapatam, to march through a well cultivated tract, as yet undevastated. Instead of following Tipu in his retreat and of pursuing the route taken by Lord Cornwallis in 1791-2, he marched in a south-westerly direction to Sosilla, about a mile above the junction of the Kaveri and Kabani, crossed the former river there, and marching without interruption by the south bank, took up, on the 5th April, the positions to the west and north-west of the fortress, which had been partly occupied by the Bombay army under General Abercromby in 1792. Eleven days later he was joined by General Stewart, to whom he assigned a position to the north by west of the fortress.

The second siege of Seringapatam differed in this respect from the first in that in the interval which had elapsed between the two the British Government had discovered that Tipu was a man who would hold no engagement as sacred. In dealing with him, therefore, Marquess Wellesley was animated by feelings very similar to those which animated the counsels of the allied sovereigns when in 1813-14 they had to treat with Napoleon. Both alike felt that a treaty would have been but a truce, binding only so long as the enemy should not consider it to his advantage to break it The policy of humbling Tipu by depriving him of one-half of his territories had been tried. It had failed, because the outlying portions of his dominions having been lopped off, his power had become more concentrated, his hatred more intensified. In a crisis of the world's history, when no obstacle seemed able to bar the advance of daring genius, it was necessary for the safety of the British interests in India, that the one sovereign who hated those interests, and who had himself seen what his troops, led by his father, could accomplish, should be rendered, as far as possible, harmless for evil. Hence it was, that when in the course of the second siege, Tipu sued for peace, terms were designedly offered him, which he could not accept without signing at once the abdication of the position he had inherited and the renunciation of the power ever to recover it.[11]

General Harris, after consultation with his engineers, determined to attack the fortress on its north-western angle, breaching the western side. The fortress had indeed been here considerably strengthened, but it was still its weakest point. The curtain, nearly five hundred toises in length, was armed by only three pieces of cannon, the river besides, for five months of the year, was fordable the whole length of it. The plan being settled, the operations began at once. General Harris with the main body was to attack the place at the angle caused by the junction of the northern with the western face, whilst the Bombay division should take up a position in continuation of the line formed by Lord Harris which should bring it opposite the northern side of the angle with a view to direct an enfilading fire on the defences, and thus to diminish the opposition to the main attack.

On the 20th April the fire opened from the northern attack. This was followed up by successful dislodgment of the enemy from a position four hundred yards in advance of his other field works, a success which enabled the besiegers to establish, in the course of the night, a parallel at a distance of 780 yards from the fortress, and 440 from the enemy's intrenchments still remaining outside it.

Alarmed at this, and at indications which he noticed of erecting another battery on the northern bank, Tipu, on the 22nd, directed a vigorous sally to be made against our positions on that bank This sally was well planned, and the troops who conducted it, led by Tipu's corps of Frenchmen, behaved with great spirit, penetrating the English intrenchments, but it was finally repulsed with the loss of 700 men.

On the 23rd, the fire from both attacks silenced the enemy's guns, the enfilading fire from the northern bank rendering it impossible for the Mysoreans to defend the curtains.

On the 26th, the approaches meanwhile having steadily advanced, the English, led by Colonel Wellesley, dislodged the enemy from their last remaining intrenchment. This was 380 yards in front of the fort on its western face, covered on its right by a redoubt, and on the left by a small circular work open to the rear. The intrenchment was indeed carried, but as

[11] These terms were the cession of half of his dominions, the payment of the expenses of the war, the delivery of two of his sons as hostages, and the surrender of Seringapatam into the hands of the English till the conclusion of a definite peace. To these terms, to consider which only twenty-four hours were given him. Tipu did not deign a reply.

the enemy with great gallantry still held the circular work which enfiladed it, it was extremely difficult for the English to maintain their position. It became necessary then to drive the enemy from the circular work, and from some ruins near it. This was accomplished on the 27th, under a heavy fire from the walls of the fort.

The Sultan, now driven to depend on the defence offered by the fortress itself, again expressed a willingness to treat. But the conditions offered were such that he felt he could not accept without degradation Again there is forced upon us the similarity of his position to that of Napoleon in 1814, and again do we see the same passions bringing about similar results.[12] He resolved to resist to the bitter end.

Meanwhile day by day the parallels approached nearer, until on the 3rd May the breach on the western side of the angle was reported practicable. The previous night the river had ascertained that the descent into the ditch from the retaining wall of the counterscarp was only seven feet; that the ditch was fordable; that the rubbish of the rampart and fausse braye formed an irregular but continued slope from the ditch to the summit of the rampart, and that it would be only necessary to provide means to accompany the assault for the descent from the counterscarp into the ditch. It was determined then, the breach having been reported practicable on the 3rd, to assault on the morning of the 4th. Early on the morning of that day, Major-General Baird, who himself had been nearly four years a prisoner in Seringapatam, issued his orders for the assault. He directed Lieutenant-Colonel Dunlop with six companies of Bombay European flankers, supported by H. M.'s 12th and 33rd regiments, ten companies of Bengal Sepoy flankers and fifty artillery men, to assault the north rampart and to push on with the European flank companies until he should meet the south attack under Colonel Sherbrook consisting of the flank companies of the Scotch brigade and the regiment de Meuron, reinforced by the grenadier companies of H. M.'s 73rd and 74th regiments.[13]

It was not till 1 o'clock in the afternoon that General Baird stepping from the trenches sword in hand called upon his

[12] "If," says Alison, "sound political judgment may perhaps condemn the pride which made him so obstinately refuse the conditions offered to him at Chatillon, and throw all, even in that extremity, upon the hazard of war; yet it must be admitted that there was something magnanimous in his resolution to run every hazard rather than to sit down on a degraded throne."—*History of Europe*.

[13] The storming party consisted of 2,494 Europeans and 1,882 Indians, composed of H M.'s 12th, 33rd and 74th Regiments, ten Companies Bengal Sepoys, eight Companies Madras Sepoys, one hundred Artillery men and a proporton of gun Lancers—*Sir D Baird's Report.*

men to advance. In a moment the storming columns sprang up, dashed into the river, and crossed it under a heavy fire of musketry. In six minutes the forlorn hope, followed by the main body, had gained the summit of the breach and planted the British standard on the rampart. But the breach had scarcely been gained when they found themselves confronted by an inner rampart lined with troops, separated from them by a wide and deep ditch and defended at its angle by a high cavalier. Unable to storm this, yet determined to penetrate by some means into the interior, they ran along the ramparts, some to the left, some to the right. We will leave them thus running to follow the fortunes of Tipu Sultan on this eventful day.

Tipu, during the siege, had more than once shewn to his followers that he despaired of the result. Instead of striving to inspire them with courage, he, with the bigotry which had become habitual to him, had had constant recourse to astrologers and priests. On the day of the assault he was distinctly warned by his ablest General, Syyad Ghaffar, that he would be attacked that day. Not only did he refuse to believe it, but he permitted one of his youthful flatterers to summon the men from their positions in the traverses and on the ramparts to receive their pay at midday. They were in the act of receiving it when the assault was delivered. Syyad Ghaffar was hurrying to the Sultan to remonstrate against this act of folly, when, turning aside for a moment to issue orders for the severance of the slight connexion which did exist between the outer and the inner rampart, he was killed. Tipu was about to sit down to his midday meal when this intelligence reached him. Though greatly agitated, he still continued his meal, and was engaged at it, when he was informed that the assault was actually being made. He hastened at once along the northern rampart towards the breach, on nearing which he fired seven or eight shots at the stormers, killing two or three. Finding, however, that his people were falling about him, and that the stormers were advancing, he ran back along the rampart until, from the outside, he reached the sally-port whence the way was open to him to join his cavalry on the other side of the river. But he disdained to flee Believing that the inner fort was still secure, and that from its ramparts he might yet be able to drive back the foe, he mounted his horse and endeavoured to force his way through the sally-port, the direct road into the interior fortifications. But before he could reach that gateway it had became choked with fugitives fleeing from the English soldiers who had managed to penetrate the inner fort in the mode to be related immediately. The Sultan, however, who had already been twice slightly wounded, still endeavoured to press his way, when his horse was shot under him, and almost immediately afterwards he received a third wound, severe though not fatal. His attendants then placed him in a palanquin. But as it was impossible in the crowd and tumult to move this conveyance, Tipu would appear to have left it and to have crawled towards a gateway[14] at a little distance, leading into a garden. Here he was attacked by some English soldiers One of his attendants then proposed that he should save his life by disclosing his rank. But this Tipu refused to do, and when an English soldier attempted to seize his sword belt, Tipu though nearly fainting from his wounds, made a cut at him with his sword. The soldier at once shot him dead His body remained undiscovered for several hours

To account for the manner in which the English had succeeded in entering the inner fort it is necessary to retrace our steps. It would appear that a party of the stormers who had reached the outer rampart after those in advance had run along it to the right and left, finding that the enemy on the inner rampart had followed the movements of the assailants, deserting the position nearly opposite the breach, endeavoured to find some means by which they could penetrate into those inner fortifications. It happened fortunately for them that a temporary platform about one foot in width,[15] in the endeavour to remove which Syyad Ghaffar had been killed, still remained. Narrow, having a great depth below it, and of some length, the crossing it was so hazardous that the following day, in cold blood, not a man would venture to attempt it.[16] But in the excitement of that memorable 4th May there was no hesitation. In single file the men crossed over, and it was these men who, running across these inner lines, were able to meet on the other side the fugitives who, with Tipu amongst them, were endeavouring to enter the place which they deemed their last refuge.

From that moment the fighting was over. The carnage, though considerable, was much less than might have been expected in a city taken by storm, especially when the stormers knew, as many of the stormers on this occasion did know, that about ten days before, the English soldiers who had been taken prisoners in different actions before the siege had been put to death in the most barbarous manner, by having nails driven through their skulls.[17] The French contingent surrendered at discretion. The two elder sons present of Tipu, ignorant of their father's death, shewed a manly resignation to their fate. The houses of the chief Sirdars as well as those of the merchants and bakers were generally pillaged. But the palace was secured and the wealth it contained reserved as booty for the army at large.

14 This gateway was afterwards destroyed —*Lord Valentia*

15 Some call it a wall.

16 Valentia

17 General Baird's Report

Such was the capture of Seringapatam, carrying with it the fall of the dynasty of the Muhamedan adventurer Haidai Ali. How the old dynasty was restored, and how with that restoration the name of Mysore became connected with peace and industry instead of, as theretofore, with rapine and aggression, it is no part of my task to relate But I have not yet done with Seringapatam. The interest it had excited did not perish with Tipu. Indeed within the short space of ten years it was destined to revive in a manner more exciting, more startling, and more original than at any previous period.

But before I refer to that last exciting passage in the history of the fortress, I think I shall be justified in suggesting for the tourist of the present day, whilst the story of the storming is still fresh in his recollection, some hints which will enable him without the aid of a *cicerone* to recognize the most interesting points of the fortress.

I will suppose then that the traveller is starting from Mysore. Driving through the villages of Kalaswari, Sultanpet, and Pakshwan, he finds himself suddenly, at a turn of the road, facing the western side of the fortress, the breach distinctly visible at its northernmost end. Descending from his carriage he walks along the nullah which there joins on to the branch of the river known in olden days as 'the little Kaveri' until he finds himself nearly opposite the breach. Descending then towards the bed of the river, he sees two guns planted in the ground. These represent the advanced parallels from which General Baird issued on the memorable 4th May to storm the fortress.

The view from this point is striking and impressive. The traveller sees what General Harris, General Baird, and Colonel Wellesley saw on that famous morning. The fortress stands now, its guns and defenders excepted, as it stood then. There is the battered fausse-braye and the breached rampart; the ruined cavalier giving no signs of the second rampart below the level of, and separated by a deep ditch from, the rampart which was visible. To the left, the enfilading position taken up by the Bombay forces, a position which manifestly must paralyse the defence against the direct attack. All is unchanged. As I write these lines, 8th February 1876, the Kaveri is as fordable as it was on the 4th May 1799. There are the stage, the scenery, the foot-light : the actors only are absent.

The traveller returns to his carriage, and drives on till he finds himself in front of the southern face of tht fortress. Here he enters by a gateway made by the English.[18] The road he

[18] The road has been made to deviate from the old gateway, called the Elephant gateway, erected by Tipu Sultan in 1793 This still retains an inscription of which the following is the purport : "In the name of God the merciful and gracious In the year 1209, commencing from the

should take runs only through a part of the town, along the southern and western face of the palace of the Sultan. Passing these, he should leave the road and drive direct to the north-west angle. Alighting then from the carriage, he ascends the rampart, and walks about a hundred yards till he reaches the angle A turn to the left is then made, and, in a few moments he stands on the summit of the breach. From this point he views the scene as it presented itself to the defenders on the 4th May, 1799. In the distance he can see the village of Palhali, and by the aid of the French Plan, executed in 1801, the position of the English becomes clear to him.

At first there are many things to astonish, even to puzzle him. He can comprehend the weakness in one sense of the defensive position, attacked from the west, and that attack aided by a very heavy flanking fire from the north. He can comprehend how our men without difficulty climbed over the shattered faussebraye, and crossed the ditch, but how they clambered up the parapet surprises him It is true that a man, unencumbered, can now, though not easily, make the ascent; but carrying his musket and ammunition, it would not only be not an easy, but a very difficult task Yet the forlorn hope of the storming party stood upon that rampart six minutes after they had leaped out of the advanced trenches! The whole world does not present a nobler monument of pluck and daring than does that shattered parapet And though it may be urged that the enfilading fire from the north had cleared the angle of the rampart of its defenders, yet if the traveller turns round he will see the cavalier, *then* defended by a second rampart, and that rampart lined with troops, who, had they been but cool and steady, could have picked off our stormers, as almost singly and breathless, they mounted the breach. Well may the traveller be struck with awe! Well, may he draw in his breath with a feeling of pride and veneration for the race that preceded him! No more daring deed has been recorded in the

birth of Mahomed, on Tuesday the 9th Khusrave, the Emperor began the construction of the Fort, when the star Jupiter was in its influence.

"During the commencement of the construction the rainbow was shining over the air, whilst the stars Mercury (and others) were in good conjunction with each other The influence of these stars decide, by the grace of God, that this Fort will ever remain permanent, exempted from every kind of misfortune"

The date noted corresponds to our year 1793 when the fortress was greatly strengthened

I may observe that the traveller ought most certainly to alight from his carriage, and pass through this gateway One glance makes the situation clear to him On the other side of the gateway he sees the old Hindu fort of Seringapatam, with the gateway begin the enormous works which made it a fortress within a fortress

11

world's history than that the scene of which he then contemplates.

But he supposes our attacking soldiers now on the rampart. Let him imagine their surprise when they discovered on reaching the spot which, they had been led to believe, would place the fortress at their mercy, that they were as far from that result as before. Facing them was a second fortress, covered by a rampart and a deep ditch, protected at this point by a heavily armed cavalier It is true that of all these defences the ruined cavalier alone remains. But having read all that has been written on the subject, having made personal and repeated enquiries on the spot, having thoroughly examined the ground, and having had the good fortune to be assisted in my research by many capable officers in the active branch of the service, I shall be able, I trust, to make clear a matter which, in consequence of the alterations made in the fortress subsequent to the year 1799, has mystified many.

The traveller, when crossing the green plot which lies between the western wall of the Sultan's palace and the north-western angle of the fortress will have observed, all along the northern face several yards in rear of the rampart, a line of tamarind trees. Now I have ascertained that these tamarind trees were planted in the year 1800, on the alignment formed by the inner ditch and rampart. Lord Valentia who visited Seringapatam shortly after the siege (1802) writes then that the inner ditch and ramparts had been totally destroyed. He speaks of the young trees springing up behind the outer ramparts. A very old man, verging upon 100 years, interrogated by Captain Malet and myself in 1874, assured us of the fact of the planting of the tamarind trees in 1800, the English, he said, having first destroyed the rampart and filled in the ditch which previously existed along the alignment Granting this, the isolated position of our soldiers on their gaining the outer rampart becomes clear.[19] If the enemy had been cool and resolute, and if the slight communication between the two ramparts had been severed, as Syyad Ghaffar had intended, they had really gained nothing but certain destruction. We can understand now, what would have been difficult to comprehend before, why Tipu should have endeavoured to force his way into the inner fortress rather than to join his cavalry in the field For he deemed himself, once within its walls, to be doubly safe. He would have entered, and he would still have repulsed our men, but for that solitary wall or plank of communication between the two ramparts, a wall or plank so narrow that the same men who

[19] The soundness of the argument above is further proved by an inspection of the French Plan, executed in 1801, which has been referred to before.

crossed it on the 4th May, "were afraid, on the following day, when their blood was cool, to re-cross it."[20]

When the traveller has had time to take in the whole of the events of the few minutes which followed the storming of the outer rampart, he should drive towards the sallyport on the northern face of the fortress. It will be recollected that Tipu reached this sallyport before our troops reached it, and by it he might easily have escaped, as the river was fordable, and his cavalry were on the opposite bank All the English accounts[21] confirm this statement. He might have escaped had he wished to escape. This cannot fail to be clear to the traveller, who will recollect that Tipu reached that gate from the outside before our soldiers reached it from the inside, that the gate itself led into the inner fort. Instead, however, of escaping he tried to make his way within. But there he was met by the British soldiers, who, entering by the narrow wall, had traversed the chord, whilst he had been trying to penetrate by the outer arc, of the circle.

The arch to which Tipu dragged himself, after having been thrice wounded, only to meet his death, has been destroyed, but a wooden door leading into a garden, about a hundred yards to the right of the sally-port, is indicated as the spot where the unknown British soldier extorted blood for blood.

Retracing his steps, or possibly taking it *en route*, the traveller, coming from the famous north-west angle, is shewn an underground vault in the outer rampart which is stated to have served as one of the prisons in which some of the European soldiers were confined. Probably the story is true. The oldest Indians state it to have been so, and one man even asserted to me that in this place the prisoners were murdered ten days before the assault. The vault is bomb-proof, and there are many purposes for which it might have been used. When I first visited Seringapatam, and subsequently, this vault was always indicated as the prison in which Sir David Baird had been confined. But this is certainly not the case. In his memoirs[22] Sir David Baird has left an exact plan of his prison. With this plan in our hand, Captain Malet and I spent two days in endeavouring to find the building. At last we succeeded. It is one of the mud houses, now in ruins, which were erected on the prolongation towards the inner rampart of the walls of the Sultan's palace.

Immediately after passing the vault just alluded to the traveller finds himself facing the enclosure in which still stands the famous temple of Sri Ranga, long since abandoned. There also he sees the wall which once enclosed the palace of the

[20] Lord Valentia's Travels, Vol I, page 374
[21] *Vide* Buchanan, Valentia, *Asiatic Annual Register* and others.
[22] Vol. I, page 41.

Hindu Rajas, demolished in 1800, in order to build with the materials a new palace at Mysore. The enclosure was converted after the siege into a manufactory of gun carriages. It is now a heap of ruins.

On the other side of the road which leads to the north-west angle are the walls which once enclosed the palaces of Haidar and of Tipu Not a vestige of either remains, but the place is now used as a depot for sandalwood. The minarets and the immensely strong fortifications on the eastern face speak for themselves. The town is poor, dirty, and uninteresting. Its splendid houses have disappeared Amongst the sights shewn to travellers is a *mamelon* upon which rises a flagstaff placed there by Colonel Wellesley's orders; and an ingenious bridge, built by Captain de Havilland, which illustrates Lord Palmerston's motto, '*flecti non frangi.*'

There are two other buildings, connected with the dynasty of Haidar, which it is impossible that the traveller should leave unexplored. These are the palace and garden called *Darya-daolat*, and the *Lal Bagh* containing the mausoleum of Haidar Ali and of Tipu Sultan.

The palace of the Darya-daolat was simply the country house of the Sultan whither he was wont to repair for recreation. But he never slept in it. At sunset he used to return to the fortress. The palace is a good illustration of the Indian ornamental style. The walls on one side exhibit in grotesque paintings the victory gained by Haidar and Tipu over Colonel Baillie in 1780; those on the other are apparently intended to portray the various phases in the life of a Muhamedan gentleman of rank The house is ornamented throughout with a paper covered with false gilding,[23] the effect of which is extremely good. The house and garden are kept up by the Mysore Government.

Colonel Wellesley occupied the house in 1800-1. It was visited by the Marquis of Dalhousie in 1855, upon which occasion that nobleman recorded a striking minute regarding it and the mausoleum of Haidar Ali and of Tipu [24] Not only for the reasons urged by Lord Dalhousie, but as the specimen of a building unique of its kind, and as the only place of rest for the traveller who may visit the famous fortress, its maintenance would seem desirable.

Driving from the Darya-daolat through the village of Ganjam, to the east end of the island, the traveller reaches the Lal Bagh—no longer the beautiful garden painted in enthusiastic terms by Major Dirom—but famed as containing within its borders the mausoleum of Haidar Ali, of Tipu, and of the wife of the former. The building would disappoint those who might

[23] *Vide* Buchanan, who gives a recipe for its preparation
[24] *Vide* Appendix.

hope to witness a renewal of the glories of the Taj Mahal, for though the foundation is stone the upper portion is stucco. Still it is in many respects worthy of a visit. Its pillars of black marble, its doors of rosewood inlaid with ivory, the magnificent shawls over the tombs[25] form in themselves objects of real beauty. Nor can be witnessed without feeling the reverence still displayed by pious Muhamedans towards the memory of one, who though he might not deserve the epithet of martyr applied to him by his adherents, was still the champion of their cause and faith in Southern India, and who died fighting, as he believed, for both.

Of the other objects which call for attention are Colonel Baillie's tomp, erected by his nephew in 1816, Colonel Baillie having died a prisoner in 1782; an insignificant obelisk erected to the memory of the officers of the 12th and 74th regiments who perished in the siege of 1799; the tombs at Palhali of others who fell in that year; the burial ground of the garrison after the occupation of the fortress in 1799, and Colonel Scott's bungalow on the banks of the Kaveri.

This bungalow derives its notoriety from the following circumstance: Colonel Scott was placed in charge of the gun carriage manufactory in the Fort in 1800, and afterwards commanded the garrison. He is mentioned by Lord Valentia in 1801 as Captain Scott who had just exerted himself "with the highest credit" to establish that manufactory. It would appear that the Raja of Mysore built for him a bungalow in an extremely pretty locality on the banks of the river about a quarter of a mile from the elephant gate. The loss of his wife and children in this spot in 1817 caused him, however, suddenly to quit it, to resign his appointment, and to return to England, leaving all his furniture standing in the house. The curious part of the story remains to be told. The late Maharaja of Mysore, hearing of this sad occurrence, directed that the house should for ever remain in *statu quo;* that none of the furniture should be removed. And so in fact it has remained The traveller who may visit it will see the beds with their torn and antiquated mosquito curtains; the carpets crumbling with age: two voiceless pianos, the tables and chairs of a bygone era.

To return to the fortunes of Seringapatam. Occupied by a garrison of combined British and Indian troops the fortress almost immediately lost its warlike character. In a few years it was found practicable to withdraw all the European Infantry but two weak companies of the 80th regiment, numbering 100 men, thus leaving the place to be garrisoned by two Indian

[25] A present from the prince well-nown in Calcutta as the "last surviving son of Tipu Sultan," Prince Ghulam Mahomed He died in 1872

regiments, and between two and three hundred European artillery men.

It happened, however, in 1809, that a foolish ruling of the Court of Directors, and the still more foolish and tyrannical proceedings[26] of Sir George Barlow, then Governor of Madras, had produced a general feeling of strong indignation amongst the officers of the coast army. They convened committees in all the principal stations in the Presidency, and universally or all but universally resolved to oppose the execution of the obnoxious orders, if necessary by force. This determination to resist was not less strong amongst the officers of the Company's Army stationed in the Mysore province than elsewhere. It shewed itself first at Seringapatam where Lieutenant-Colonel Bell, of the Artillery, was still in command. He was one of the officers whose removal had been directed by Sir George Barlow for having signed a paper expressive of his sympathy with the Deputy Adjutant-General, who had himself just been suspended for executing the orders of the Commander-in-Chief, General Macdowal Colonel Bell and the officers of the Seringapatam garrison manifested their feeling so openly, that at the end of July, Cole, the then Assistant Resident, reported to Government that any attempt on their part to enforce their orders would be met by open revolt, and that the feeling was universal amongst the officers of the province

But before this despatch could reach the Madras Government, the first blow had been struck On the 29th July the garrison took forcible possession of the collector's treasury in Seringapatam. They likewise were placed under restraint, and in a few days later expelled from the fort, the hundred men of the 80th regiment, who had remained there on duty.

Upon these overt acts of violence becoming known to Cole, he, acting in unison with Purnia, the Dewan of the Raja of Mysore—a man who after having faithfully served Haidar Ali and Tipu, had transferred his allegiance and his fidelity to the Hindu dynasty—at once took measures for surrounding the island to prevent the ingress of supplies of any sort

Colonel Bell met this measure by stationing guards on the mainland to ensure the transmission of whatever supplies might be needed ; and, learning that a treasure escort would pass near the fort on the night of the 1st August, he even detached a

26 Amongst these proceedings may be enumerated .

1.—The depriving the Commander-in-Chief of a seat in Council

2—The transfer of all important commands to Officers of the Royal army.

3.—The abolition of the Tent Contract

4.—The suspension of Captain Bowles. Dy. Adjutant-General, for carrying out the orders of the Commander-in-Chief

5.—The suspension of Colonel St Leger, Major de Morgan, and

company of Indian infantry to sieze the treasure[27] and bring it within the fort, a feat which was successfully accomplished.

This daring measure, accompanied by the stoppage of the post, and the rumour of the preparation of a battering train, led Cole to fear that the mutineers might march on Mysore, where he would have had to rely solely upon the native troops of the Raja. The only troops in the neighbourhood upon whom dependance could be placed were a detachment of the 25th Light Dragoons and 59th Foot. But these were at Mandia, fifteen miles to the north of Seringapatam.

Whilst this was the state of affairs in the Mysore territory the Government of Madras had, by timely offers of pardon, persuaded the officers at the Mount to sign the test, and to return to their duty. Similar offers of forgiveness had been likewise expedited by the hands of Colonel Davies, commanding in Mysore, to the garrison of Seringapatam But Davies on reaching the place had been at once placed in confinement, and when released after a few hours' detention, had been dismissed without a reply. Colonel Bell and the officers acting with him intended, indeed, no reply unless the obnoxious orders should be withdrawn and the suspended officers reinstated. On the 2nd August they "annexed" the Paymaster's treasure, amounting to about 45,000 rupees, and on the night of the same day they detached 500 men with guns to meet and escort two native corps which they had summoned from the fort of Chitaldrug to reinforce the garrison.

Intelligence of these proceedings having reached Cole he at once despatched 1,000 of the Mysore Horse to hover about and harass the enemy's detachment, by cutting off their supplies, though avoiding as far as possible any overt act of violence. At the same time he despatched messengers on the Bangalore road to expedite the march of the European troops summoned from that station, and expected to reach the vicinity of Seringapatam on the 4th August.

Matters were protracted for some days by the refusal of Colonel Gibbs commanding at Bangalore to allow the European troops to leave the station without an express order from the

Captains Marshall and Grant; the removal of Colonels Bell, Chalmers, Cuppage, and Captain Coombs, the supersession of Majors Keasberry, Muirhead, Haslewood, and of Captain Smith; for expressing sympathy with Captain Bowles.

6.—The issue of instructions by the Government requiring all their officers to sign a test-pledge engaging themselves to support the measures of Government under penalty of being sent from their Regiments, and "interned" in stations of the coast.

[27] About 120,000 rupees.

Government of Fort St. George; and by the delay in the march of the native corps from Chitaldrug.

However annoyed Cole may have been by what he considered the backwardness of Colonel Gibbs, he was sensibly relieved by the receipt on the evening of the 5th August of a letter from Colonel Bell which betrayed evidence of a desire to come to terms Cole took it upon himself once again to offer oblivion of the past on the condition that the officers of the garrison should sign the test. To this proposition, however, Colonel Bell replied by a letter characterized by Cole as "compound of incomprehensible confusion of matter, aimed evidently to gain time and to fabricate excuses for conduct which the brightest genius could not palliate." In his letter Colonel Bell had amongst other things requested that military proceedings against him might be for the present stayed.

Before the receipt of Colonel Bell's letter information had reached Cole that the two battalions at Chitaldrug, after plundering the treasury of about 80,000 rupees, and having been reinforced by a third corps, had begun their march for Seringapatam. Cole at once despatched 1,500 peons armed with matchlocks and 3,000 Silladar Horse to manoeuvre between them and the fortress.

Meanwhile Colonel Bell, having stored a quantity of grain sufficient for several months' consumption, wrote to Cole threatening to destroy the bridges over the Kaveri and to cut off all communication with Mysore unless he should withdraw his troops from the field He also placed a guard over Purnia's house in Seringapatam, in which his collections of twenty years had been stored, in revenge for the rejection of an overture he had made to that Dewan It was clear that, counting upon his strong position, upon the universally spread disaffection, and upon the rumoured action of the officers of the Hydrabad contingent, he and his colleagues had cast away the scabbard, not to sheath it until the opinion of the Governor-General, Lord Minto, should have been pronounced upon the proceedings of Sir George Barlow.

All this time the two battalions from Chataldrug, unaided by the third to which I referred, were advancing. They were met on the 7th August by the peons and the Mysore horse, but these latter fell back before them. There was an unwillingness on both sides to begin a contest. They reached the neighbourhood of Seringapatam on the 10th August. The Mysore Irregulars were there joined by the 25th dragoons, the 59th regiment, a detachment of native cavalry, and an Indian battalion whose officers had been interned on the coast. Encouraged by this reinforcement the Mysore horse advanced to check the mutinous battalions. These however fired upon and repulsed them. Upon this the 25th Dragoons came to the rescue. The men of the battalions, who had been ordered not to fire upon Europeans, did not wait their charge, but, dispersing, made for a part of the river commanded by the fire of the fort. Under that fire the greater part of them succeeded in entering Seringapatam.[28] Their commandant, however, was wounded and made prisoner, and one officer was killed. During the night Colonel Gibbs' encampment was cannonaded from the fortress, and compelled to move backwards.

Subsequently, on the 14th August, a conference was held between Colonel Davies on the one side and Lieutenant-Colonel Bell and two other officers on the other. The result was unsatisfactory, Colonel Bell and his associates professing their determination to adhere to their attitude 'until the arrival of Lord Minto.'

But a heavy blow was awaiting them. The officers of the Hydrabad Contingent who had been the loudest in their denunciation of the conduct of the Government of Fort Saint George,[29] had yielded, on the 11th August, to the representations of Colonel Close, sent specially for that purpose from Puna They had written a penitential letter to Lord Minto, then expected at Madras , had signed the test, and had subscribed a paper to be circulated to the army generally in which they stated that imperious circumstances and mature reflection had induced them to sign the test paper, and they earnestly entreated their brother-officers to follow their example. This paper reached Cole on the 18th August. He at once transmitted it 'to the officers composing the garrison of Seringapatam' with a very few lines from himself.

This communication after having been long and anxiously considered, was personally replied to on the 21st. On the morning of that day two officers[30] from the fort came into Mysore under a flag of truce. They were received by Colonel Davies and Cole. They stated that an address similar to the Hydrabad address was in course of signature, and they urged that until the signature should be completed, which might be expected in a few hours, hostilities on the part of the Government forces might cease. To this the two representatives of the

[28] Their returns were · 9 killed, 150 wounded, 281 missing

[29] They had published a letter to the army and to the suspended officers, declaring their entire disapprobation of the suspension and removal of so many valuable officers from the service and their commands; their willingness to contribute to the support of these officers; and their determination to co-operate with the army in all legal measures for the removal of the cause of the present discontent, and the restoration of their brother-officers to the honourable situations from which they had been removed—*Mill.*

[30] Captain de Havilland and Captain Cadell

Government replied that beyond a cessation of hostilities during the night they would listen to nothing except that which involved "the actual delivery of the fort and the arms of its present retainers;" further, that they would hold no communication with Colonel Bell.

The following day all the officers signed the address and the test; on the 23rd they surrendered the fortress, and the arms of themselves and their men, the latter were at once marched off the island in four bodies to separate positions The fort was occupied by H. M.'s troops the same day.

The fate of the officers may possibly excite some interest. I supply it, therefore, so far as I have been able to collect information on the subject. Colonel Bell was brought to a Court Martial, and sentenced to be cashiered,[31] the others, I believe all of them, were interned in stations on the coast. These latter, however, were restored to active service in 1811; Colonel Bell and other officers who had suffered similarly for their conduct in other stations, were restored at subsequent dates. The matter then passed into such oblivion that with the exception of Mill, no Indian historian has noticed it.[32] Yet it was a very serious business. "The East India Company" wrote Lord Minto, "and, I may add, the British Empire in all its parts, never, I believe, was exposed to greater or more imminent danger." Nor was it creditable to any of the leading parties in the transaction. If the conduct of the officers was mutinous, that of Sir George Barlow was tyrannical. This was evidently the opinion of Lord Minto. For, whilst he condemned unequivocally the conduct of the officers, he refrained from exercising that arbitrary and absolute power the misuse of which by Sir George Barlow had led them to mutiny. He pardoned many, and left the others to be tried by their own ordinary tribunals.

The main results were practically unfavourable to Sir George Barlow. Almost the grievances complained of by the officers were silently remedied, and if it may be said that their leaders were cashiered—only however to be restored—it may be urged on the other hand that the recall of Sir George Barlow a year later was due to the conduct which had roused all the officers of a large army beyond their power of self-control.

With this episode terminates the sensational history of Seringapatam. Abandoned as a military station, on account of the malaria which prevailed there, some years subsequently to

[31] The Government, not considering the sentence sufficiently severe, sent it back for revision, but the Court adhered to it—*Mill.*

[32] It is referred to by Krishna Rao, in his little history of Mysore

the events last recorded ; the gun carriage manufactory broken up, and the ramparts dismantled ; it has remained thenceforth, as it remains still, an object of wonder and of interest. There are those, I have been told, who can see it for the first time unmoved, but I have not met them on the spot..

APPENDIX

Minute by the Most Noble the Governor-General. Dated 2nd November, 1855 on Seringapatam

1.—My journey through the Mysore territories has afforded me an opportunity of visiting this memorable fortress, the scene of events most glorious to the British name, and of happy augury for the people of Mysore.

2.—There are two objects within the Island which are well worthy of the protection of the Supreme Government, and which call for its respectful care.

3.—The first of these objects is the Tomb in which rest the remains of Hydar Ali Khan and of Tipu Sultan. The structure is well preserved, as far as the means of its guardians will permit, its interior and the gardens by which it is surrounded are well kept, and it is under the immediate charge of one Tipu Sultan's family. But it already feels the pressure of the hand of Time. The endowments are insufficient for maintaining it in complete repair, and some portions of it, more especially the inlaid doors, have already become dilapidated.

4.—The Tomb is itself an imposing structure, and an interesting specimen of the style of art which marked the days and the dynasties that are past. The Court of Directors have most cheerfully and liberally given their sanction to the general expenditure which I proposed to make for the purpose of preserving such works of Art, for the instruction and gratification of the generations that shall come after. In this particular instance I feel certain that I correctly interpret the sentiments of the Honourable Court when recording my belief that it would be their especial desire to manifest an enduring respect for the last resting place of brave and fallen enemies.

5.—I shall therefore request the Commissioner to take measures for replacing the worn-out inlaid doors of the Tomb, and for expending such sums upon it from time to time as may be required for its proper repair, whenever the funds of the endowments may be inadequate to meet such expense

6.—The second object on the Island to which I have alluded is the House in Dowlat Bagh which was long occupied by the Duke of Wellington, then Colonel Wellesley, after the fall of Seringapatam, and when he held charge of the Mysore Territories.

7.—This mansion, formerly a Garden House of Tipu Sultan, is traditionally known on the spot as the residence of Wesly Sahib, and I have just now seen and talked with an aged man, who remembers and describes his residing in it. This building, which has been unoccupied for some time past, and in which I now write these words, is visibly falling into decay. It is a purely Eastern residence; and some of the walls are covered with paintings, executed by the orders of Tipu and still traceable, though greatly faded, which represent the defeat of the British Force, under the command of Colonel Baillie The paintings were partially obliterated by Tipu during the last siege of Seringapatam, and were in the first instance restored by Colonel Wellesley himself.

8.—In all respects this struture is one full of interest, but it is most especially worthy of our reverential care, as the material object, which, more than any other now remaining in India, most immediately and most vividly brings before us of this day the memory of that great man, with the early period of whose glorious career the East India Company must ever be proud to connect the history of its rule.

9.—I request therefore that the Commissioner will cause this House to be put into proper repair and to be maintained in that condition for the future. It should be upheld as nearly as possible in the condition in which it was left by Colonel Wellesley, and in which it still is. The paintings on the walls to which I have alluded above should be restored, if, as I am assured, their correct restoration can be effected by the aid of persons still living who remember them in their completeness. In further aid of the main object now held in view the enclosure of the Dowlut Bagh shall not be suffered to fall into decay.

10.—The Commissioner will be so good as to place this Minute upon his records, and upon those of the office of the Superintendent, Ashtagram Division, who will consider this building as at all times an object of his special attention.

11—When the separate Department of Public Works shall have been organized in Mysore, Colonel Wellesley's House in the Dowlut Bagh at Seringapatam will form a separate head of account, and a separate head in each Annual Report of the Chief Engineer

12.—By this means I trust that the building with all its memories and associations may long be preserved for the contemplation and reverence of generations to come.

(*Signed*) DALHOUSIE.

Letter from Colonel Wellesley to Colonel Rose, dated Trincomalee, December 30th, 1800, preserved in original in the records of the Commissioner's Office at Bangalore : "I have received a letter from Lord Wellesley in which he talks of going through Mysore in the next season.* * He proposes to inhabit the Dowlut Bagh at Seringapatam, and although I think it very probable that the plan will never be put in execution, I shall be obliged to you if you will now and then take a look at my house, and urge forward the painting of it."

TIPU'S COLLECTION OF ORIENTAL BOOKS

Reprinted from The British Critic, December, 1809

A Descriptive Catalogue of the Oriental Library of the late Tipu Sultan of Mysore, to which are prefixed Memoirs of Hydar Ali Khan and his son Tipu Sultan, by Charles Stewart, late Major on the Bengal Establishment, and professor of Oriental Languages in the Honourable East India Company's College at Hertford. London, Longman & Co. 1809.

The short memoirs of Hydar Ali Khan and of his son Tipu Sultan are extremely interesting. Had not the plans laid by the latter been seen and counteracted by the active vigilance and penetration of Marquis Wellesley, we should have had ere this to lament the loss of our possessions in India. The pleasures we have experienced in perusing these sheets has been considerably heightened by our confidence in the accuracy of the contents, (Major Stewart giving notes and references from the most authentic materials) and from the modest, unassuming manner in which the whole is written.

The work Major Stewart proposed to write (a Descriptive Catalogue of the Library of Sultan Tipu) was one of great curiosity to all classes of readers, and desideratum of real consequence to Oriental scholars. On the whole, we are much pleased with the execution. He appears to have consulted the best models, the Bibliotheque Orientale of Herbelot, and subsequently the catalogues of the Libraries of the Escurial, and of the King of France at Paris ; and although we coincide with him in opinion, that it would have required much time and a considerable expense to have adopted the plan of those works, we regret that a gentleman who appears every way capable of the task did not make his memoir of each important work, and of its author, a little more diffuse. His plan and arrangement are excellent, and, as far as we have been able to examine and collate, his accuracy is nearly unquestionable, as will be observed by the few corrections we have had to make during a minute perusal of the work.

As No. 1 of the class of Persian History is a book highly esteemed in the East, we concieved it will be indulging our readers to give an account of it in Major Stewart's own words.

"No. 1. *Tarikh Rozet al Suffa* Large folio, Nastalik character. This is the most esteemed history in the Persian language, and consists of an introduction, seven sections, and a conclusion.

"Introduction—on the utility of history in general, and more especially to sovereigns and rulers.

"Sect. 1. describes the creation of the world, and the deluge, details the lives of the patriarchs and prophets; and contains the ancient history of Persia, to the conquest of that country by the Mohammedans, A D 636.

"Sect 2. details the history of Mohammed, and the four first Khalifs, Abu Bekar, Omar, Osman (Othman) and Ali; with a particular account of their conquests to A D 664.

"Sect. 3 contains the lives of the twelve Imams, who are held in the highest veneration by the Persians. The first of these was Ali, and the last Mehedi. This person is said to be still living, and will appear again, before the coming of our Lord Jesus Crist, for the conversion of infidels to the Mohammedan religion. He was born A.D. 869, and is supposed to be concealed in a cave. This section comprises also the history of the Khalifs, from Moavia, A.D 661, to Mostafim Billah, 1258, when the Khalifat was overturned, on the taking of Baghdad by the Tartars, under Holagon Khan, grandson of Genghies (Chengez) Khan

"Sect. 4 includes memoirs of the dynasties of Thabarides, Sossarides, Samanides, Dilemahs, Buides, Seljukides, and Attabegs, who reigned over Persia, Transonania, Iraq, &c. from about the year 800 to 1263

"Sect. 5. presents the history of the celebrated conqueror Genghiez Khan, who was born A D. 1154, and died at the age of seventy-three; also memoirs of his descendants, who reigned over Persia till 1335.

"Sect 6. exhibits the history of the renowned Timour (Tamerlane), born A D. 1335, and died 1404; also of his sons and successors, to the year 1426

"Sect 7 In this section are preserved the memoirs of Sultan Hussein Mirza Abul Ghazi Bhahadur, forth in descent from Timur, who reigned with great reput over Khorassan for thirty-four years, and died A.D. 1505. The encouragement which this prince gave to learning will appear by the number of authors in this Catalogue, who lived at his court, and dedicated their works either to him or his ministers.

Conclusion—contains a description of the city of Herat (then the capital of Khorassan), and of several other places of that kingdom.

The author of this esteemed work was the celebrated Mohammed Mir Khavund Shah, who died in Khorassan, A.D. 1497. It is dedicated to Ali Shir, Vizier of Sultan Hussein, the patron of the learned of his time, and himself a poet and author of note.

We think Major Stewart should have given a translation of the titles of every book, (of some he has) as well as an account of their contents. The title of this work is very apposite for general history, *Rozer at Suffa menus*, "The Garden of Purity or Truth."

In describing No. 15 of this class, the *Nizam al Tuarikh,* a most excellent and useful little book, we conceive Major Stewart has been much too concise. He merely calls it "An Epitome of Oriental History from Adam to the Overthrow of the Khalifat by the Tartars under Holagu Khan, A.D. 1258. The author was Abu Sayed Byzavy, A D. 1275. We therefore subjoin a table of its contents from a copy of the work itself.

The Nizam al Tawarikh, written by Abu Sayed Abdullah ben Abi al Kasim Omar ben Mahammed ben al Baizavi on the 21st of Moherrem, 694 of the Hijra, is an abridged account of the kings and rulers of the countries comprehended between the rivers Forat (Euphrates) and Jihon (Bactrus) to the west and east and the kingdom of Khejend and Arabia to the north and south, and takes in a space of time from Adam to the year 694 of Hijra. It is divided into four chapters.

The Chapter 1st contains an account of the prophets and rulers from Adam to Noah inclusive, comprising ten persons and space of about 2500 years.

Chapter 2nd. An account of the kings of Persia and the illustrious men and philosophers contemporary with them; comprizing the reigns of seventy-three kings, and a space of 4181 years and one month, subdivided into four dynasties, viz. 1 Peshdadians. 2. Caianians. 3. Ashcanians. 4. Sasanians—from Cayuinurs to Zezdejerd ben Sheheryar.

Chapter 3rd. An account of the Khalifs, comprising a space of 645 years, in three successions—1st of thirty years duration, commencing with Abubekar, and ending with Amir el Momenin, Hussein the son of Ali. 2nd Beni Onniah, of 95 years duration, and thirteen reigns, from Moaviah to Merwan ben Mohammed. 3rd. Beni Abas, of 520 years duration, and thirty-seven reigns, from Al Sifaj Abu al Abas Abdullah to al Motaafem.

Chapter 4th. An account of the kings and Sultans of different provinces of Iran, contemporary with the Abbasides, divided into nine dynasties, viz. 1. Sasariah. 2. Samaniah. 3. Ghazneviah and Ghoriah. 4. Dilemiah. 5. Siljukiah. 6. Malahedah or of Kohestan. 7. Silghoriah. 8. Khoarizmiah; and 9. Mughal. The 1st comprising three reigns and a period of 50 years. 2nd ten reigns and 102 years. 3rd. twelve reigns and 161 years. 4th. sixteen reigns and 126 years. 5th. fourteen reigns and nearly 160 years. 6th. twenty reigns and 171 years, and four months 7th. eleven reigns and 131 years, to the period of writing this book. 8th. eight reigns and 128 years 9th. the Mughals, originally descended from Chengez Khan, commencing from Holagu Khan, A. H. 654, and ending with the reign of Sultan Abdil Abusaaed Khan Bahadur.

As a specimen of Indian History, we conceive our reader will not be displeased at our giving them Major Stewart's description of No 29 of that class—Finshtch's History

12

"A General History of India, on which the author was employed for twenty years; containing an Introduction, twelve books, and a conclusion.

"Introduction contains the ancient history of India, and a short account of the Hindoos

"Book 1. Memoirs of the Kings of Ghizri, commencing with Nasir Uddin Subactagy, and terminating with Mohammed Ghori, from A.D. 975 to 1186.

"Book 2. Memoirs of the kings of *Dhely*, from the accession of Kutub Uddin Aibek, A.D. 1205, to the death of Akbar in 1605.

"A very good version of these two books has been given by Colonel Dow, which is generally known.

"Book 3. Memoirs of a very excellent translation of this book by Jonathan Scott. Any further description of it here is thought unnecessary.

"Book 4. Memoirs of the Princes of Gujerat.

"Book 5 Memoirs of the Princes of Malwa. Vide 4th and 6th. sections of the Tabkaati Akbari

"Book 6. Memoirs of the Princes of Khandeish (now in possession of the Mahrattas) till reduced by the Emperor Akbar

"Book 7. The History of Bengal. This province was first reduced by the Muhammadans, during the reign of Mohammed Ghori, about the end of the 12th. century, without an effort on the part of its dastardly inhabitants for the preservation of their liberty and their temples, by an officer named Bukhtiar Khiljy, and since that period, has in general been subject to the empire of Dehli; but being at a distance from the capital, the governors have frequently arrogated to themselves independence. Three of its sovereigns, in succession, were either eunuchs or Abyssinian slaves, who, having murdered their masters, assumed the reigns of authority, and decorated themselves with lofty titles; but since the accession of the great Akbar to the throne of Hindusthan, it has been regularly governed by a viceroy. Having been the object of ambition of all the Omrahs, it was distinguished by the appellation of Jennebal Balad, or the Paradise of Regions.

"Book 8. Memoirs of the Princes of Multan.

"Book 9. Memoirs of the Princes of Sinde. Vide 7th and 9th. sections of the *Tabkati Akbari*.

"Book 10. History of Cashmir. The ancient state of this delightful region is much disfigured by fable. By many it is supposed the Hindu religion originated here, every river, mountain, and fountain being sacred to some deity It is however certain, that Cashmir was long governed by a line of its native princes; and the first time we hear of its having been overrun by foreign armies was in the year of the Hijra 724, or A.D. 1323, when it was invaded by an army of 70,000 Turks, who, with their usual cruelty demolished the temples, and tinged the rivers with blood. Their chief, Sultan Kudder Khan Runju, established himself on the throne, and was soon after converted to Mahommedanism. He was succeeded by his Vizier, Shahmir, a Derveish, A.D. 1341, under whose posterity it remained till the year 1541, when it was taken possession of by Mirza Hydar, in the name of the Emperor, Humayun of Hindusthan; and in the year 1588 it was annexed to the empire by the great Akbar.

"Book 11. The History of the Zamorins of Malabar, a race of princes whose memoirs are very interesting to us, having been the first Indians who entered into treaty with, or waged war against, Europeans. Unfortunately Ferishtah did not consider them from the same point of view, and his detail of their actions is rather concise.

"Book 12. Gives us an account of the arrival of the Portugese, and of the other Europeans in India, and describes the first settlement of the English at Surat.

"Conclusion, respects the geography, topography, and climate of India.

"The author of this very elaborate work was Mohammed Kasim Ferishta, of Ahmednagar in the Dekhan, dedicated to Sultan Abul Muzuffer Ibrahim Adil Shah the second, of Bijapore, A D. 1609.

Ecclesiastical History, No. 62, page 23. Rouzet al Shohada, or the Garden of Martyrs. As Major Stewart has not in our opinion been sufficiently particular in his account of this work, we subjoin a table of its contents, as being a book of great note amongst Mussulmans, and written in a peculiarly simple and interesting style. It is divided into ten chapters and a conclusion.

Chapter 1st. An account of the Prophets from Adam to Mohammed, in the commencement of which is a very affecting narrative of the death of Abel by the hand of Cain, and the lamentations of Adam over the body of his favourite child.

Chapter 2nd. The enmity of the tribe of Koreish to Mohammed, and the martyrdom of Hamjah and Janfer.

Chapter 3rd. The death of the prophet.

Chapter 4th. An account of Fatima, the daughter of the Prophet, from her birth to her death.

Chapter 5th. An account of Murteza Ali, from his birth to the hour of his martyrdom.

Chapter 6th. The excellencies of Imam Hassan, and an account of his actions from his birth to his death.

Chapter 7th. The praises of Imam Hussein, and what happened after his brother Hassan's death.

Chapter 8th. The martyrdom of Moselm ben Akil, ben Abi Taleb, and the murder of his children.

Chapter 9th. The arrival of Hussein at Karbala, his battle with his enemies there, and the consequent martyrdom of him, his children, relations and followers.

Chapter 10. What happened to the people of Mecca after Hussein's death, and the fate of those who fought against him at Karbala

Conclusion. Some account of the descendants of the Prophet, and their genealogies.

We should be very glad to see a good version of this most affecting volume in an English dress.

Either Major Stewart has made a mistake in his account of the *Akhlak Nasery* in the division of Ethics, No. 9, page 51, or the copy in Tipu Sultan's collection, differs from several manuscripts of that work which we have had an opportunity of examining. We believe the proper reading of the name of the author of *Ketab al Teharet* (the original Arabic work) is Abu Ali Mohammed Ben Messaviah, and not Mekavieh. The arrangement of the chapters too is widely different; Major Stewart makes them fix, but we can only find three which are divided and subdivided in the following manner.

Three Makalah, chapters of divisions.

Makala 1st. consists of two divisions—division 1st subdivided into seven sections—division 2nd. into ten sections.

Makalah 2nd. consists of five sections.

Makalah 3rd. contains eight sections, concluding with the advice of Plato, &c.

In the division of Poetry we quote the notices given by Major Stewart, of Sadi and Hafiz, and regret that he has not indulged the public with short accounts of all the authors of the different works, and with such little anecdotes would enable the reader to form some idea of their respective characters He could have procured the memoirs of all the best authors (particularly of poets) in the Biographers, or Tezkerehs of Dowlat Shah, Taki Auhadi, Sirajuddin Ali, Ali Kuli, Sam Mirza. &c. &c and he has shown us how very capable he is of selecting and arranging them.

"Kulliat Sadi. The works of Sadi, containing seventeen books, all of which are held in great estimation. The author was the celebrated Moshlehuddin Shaikh Sadi of Shiraz. He died A.D. 1290, aged 102 years. During his youth he served as a soldier both against the Hindus and Christians; by the latter he was taken prisoner, and obliged to work at the fortifications of Tripoli, whence he was liberated by a person who gave him his daughter in marriage; but the lady was of so bad temper, that the poet complained he had exchanged his slavery for worse bondage.

He was a great traveller, and made the pilgrimage of Mecca fourteen times When advanced in years, he devoted much of his time to solitude and religious contemplation. He was a disciple of the venerated Sufi, Abd-al Kader Ghilani, or, at least, adopted his opinions. During the period of his retirement he was visited by Princes and the great men of the age, and was held in the highest degree of veneration by the people His tomb is still to be seen in the neighbourhood of Shiraz

"A very good edition of Sadi's works was published in Calcutta about twelve years ago, by Harrington; with an English Preface, containing the memoirs of the Author, and many other interesting anecotes."

No. 50 of the division of Poetry, page 64, is the Duwan Khuage.

"The celebrated collection of mystical and other poems of Hafiz, most of which have been at different times translated into some of the European languages At the head of the English translators stand W. Jones, Richardson and Carlyle The two former, however, acknowledge their obligations to Baron Revitsky, whose *Specimina Poeseos Persicae* were published at Vienna in the year 1770. Vide Sir W. Jones's works, Vol. 2nd. page 321; Vol. 5th. page 484.

"The author of these Poems was Mohammed Shems-uddin-Hafiz, of Shiraz He died A.D. 1394, and was buried with considerable pomp His tomb is still to be seen in the neighbourhood of his native city

"A few of his poems may be understood in a literal sense, but in general they are figurative, and allude to the Sufi doctrines. Had wealth or sensual enjoyments been the wish of Hafiz, they might have been gratified, as most liberal offers, both from the princes of Persia and India, were held out to him, but he preferred a life of poverty and retirement. He was eminent for his piety, and passed much of his time in solitude, devoting himself to the service of God, and reflecting on the Divine Nature By the general consent of his countrymen he is classed among their inspired and holy men; and his works, held as inferior only to the Koran, are frequently consulted by divines. The userper Nadir Shah never undertook any arduous enterprise unless he found a happy omen in these mysterious poems."

In this division (poetry) where the works of Jami are mentioned, vide Nos 52 and 54, we find the same mistake in the title of one of the poems, as crept into Sir William Jones's Grammar We allude to that named by Major Stewart *Sejyet-al Abrar* (The Manners of the Just), but which in every manusript we have ever seen (and we have seen some good and valuable copies) is written *Sabhat-al Abrar*. The Difference in Persian characters, as the Oriental scholar will soon discover, is not easily discerned, but we will venture to say, that after reading this notice there are few readers of Persian who will fail to percieve, on examining their copies of this poem, that the first diacritical point in the word is the distinguishing mark of Be and not of Jim. Besides the meaning of the word Sabbat (a rosary) is much more apposite than that of Sejyet, (manners) as the book consists of a string of forty separate prayers, or sermons. Should there still be a doubt on the subject, it must be done away by reading the author's preface, where, by scanning the lines in which the title of the book is introduced, it will be found that Sejyet would be a syllable too long for the metre. Jami, moreover, in recommending the persual of his book to the virtuous, plays on the title by requesting they will wear his resary round their necks.

We now take leave of Major Stewart, highly pleased with his interesting catalogue, but cannot pass by the few errata which, we presume, has escaped his notice.

In the word Hind, in Persian characters, the letters *Ye* should be omitted. Vide Indian History, No. 42, page 17.

The word Maarij should be spelt with an Ain instead of a Vaw. Vide Ecclesiastical History, No. 57, page 22.

For Joy Bussunt read Joy Bashisht. Vide Ethics, No 21, page 53.

Corabidin, in Persian Characters, has *Ye* instead of *Be*. Vide Physic, No. 20, page 110.

Sherch, in Persian, has Sin instead of a Shin. Vide Philosophy, No. 3, page 117.

The word *Nahu* has a *Hamza* instead of a *He*. Vide Turkish Books, No. 2, page 184, and Arabic Books, No. 5, page 188.

As specimens of Major Stewart's style, we subjoin a few extracts from his *Memoirs of Hyder Aly Khan,* and of *Tippu Sultan,* and also a few passages from his translations in the appendix.

From the Memories of Hydar Ali Khan

Hydar Ali now perceived, with triumph, his ambitious views ripening to maturity, and, under pretence of securing his conquests, augmented his old corps, and took into his service an additional body of troops, on whose attachment he could depend.

"These circumstances being reported to the Delaway, he began to repent of the blind partiality which had induced him to raise Hydar Ali to so dangerous a height of power and authority, and proposed to the Raja to inveigle him to Seringapatam, and to secure his person. In prosecution of this design, a letter, replete with thanks and flattery, was written by the Delaway to Hydar, inviting him to return to court, to receive some distinguished mark of honour, in reward for his brilliant services.

"Hydar, who was well versed in all the intrigues and politics of an oriental court, constantly retained a private agent at Seringapatam, to whom he paid a liberal allowance for furnishing him with intelligence. From this person he learnt the insidious purport of the letter before it arrived. After considering the steps it became necessary to take, he marched from Batapore to Bangalore, and saving collected all his forces, proceeded at their head to Seringapatam, where he encamped in the neighbourhood of the city. In the evening he went to pay his respects to the minister, attended by a few trusty followers ; but although everything had previously been arranged for seizing or putting him to death, the opportunity was suffered to escape, and no attempt was made. The next visit was fixed for the perpetration of the act, but the attachment which some persons, acquainted with the intentions of he Delway, bore to Hydar, induced them to apprize him of the plans in agitation against him. Although previouffsly aware of the hostile designs of the minister, he affected much surprise and alarms at this intelligence ; and, having consulted with his friends, resolved to depose the Delway. To accomplish this object, he proceeded, a few days afterwards, under pretence of paying the promised visit, to the residence of the minister, and, stationing a party of soldiers at the door, entered the house with a select guard, and, without opposition, took him prisoner. A detachment was then sent to reduce the palace ; but the Raja submitted voluntarily, and, sending for Hydar Ali, received him most graciously, and declared, before the whole court, that the conduct of Josachuri Nundoraj having for some time past given him great offence, it had been his serious intention to depose him from the office of Delaway, and to confer that honour on his general, Hydar Ali ; but that measure being now happily effected without his interference, he had much pleasure in placing the reins of government in so able hands. Hydar seeing the Rajah sufficiently intimidated, was profuse in his protestations of fidelity and attachment, and alleged the minister's design upon his life as the sole cause of the commotion which had taken place. Next day, however, he repaired to court, and demanded a patent or commission conferring on him and his posterity the perpetual office of Delaway. The Raja, reading the consequences of a refusal, acquiesced in this demand, and contented himself with requiring a written engagement, stipulating that he and his posterity should prove themselves loyal and obedient subjects Thus Hydar Ali acquired the *real* sovereignty of Mysore, but for some time continued his respectful behaviour to the Raja. All the public acts of government were made in the name of the prince ; and, on occasion of any new conquests, congratulatory letters and presents were sent to him. This event happened in the year 1759.

"The first act of Hydar Ali's authority was to get possession of the fort of Mysore. To this place he sent his prisoner, the late Delaway, with his two sons, Viraj and Tadaraj, but allowed them a comfortable pension The father survived his disgrace thirteen years ; and one of the sons lived long enough to witness the restoration of the royal family to the throne, and the destruction of the son of the usurper

'Hydar, having thus disposed of his rival, usurped all the

official powers of government, and seldom condescended even to consult the Raja Many of the distant Zemindars, however, refused to acknowledge his authority, and there was still a strong party against him about the court. The latter he appears to have held in too much contempt, for in the month of May, of the year 1760, he suffered himself to be prevailed on, by the offers of M. Lally, governor of Pondicherry, to detach, to the assistance of the French, nearly the whole of his regular troops, amounting to 2000 cavalry and 3000 infantry, with some artillery, under the command of his wife's brother, Mukhdum Sahib. Even after the departure of these troops, such was his confidence, that he continued to reside at Deria Bagh, a garden distant about three miles from the fort of Seringapatam, attended only by a guard of 300 chosen horse."

FROM THE MEMOIRS OF TIPU SULTAN

"A.D. 1796. In the year 1796, the Mysore Raja Chiaum Raij died, leaving an only son, then an infant of three years old, to inherit the dignity of his ancestors. But the haughty Sultan would not now condescend to acknowledge even a nominal superior, and, far from exalting the boy to the throne of his forefathers, barely allowed him to exist in squalid poverty, and humiliating contempt

"A.D. 1797. In the end of this year, or the commencement of 1797, an army of Afghans crossed the river Attock, and attempted to proceed towards Delhi. They were, however, so warmly opposed by the Seik chiefs, that after losing a considerable number of men, they were obliged to retreat. This expedition was probably undertaken by Zeman Shah, in compliance with the proposals made by Tipu to that prince, in his first plan[1] for attacking the English; and it so far alarmed the British government, that a large force was assembled at Mindy Jhat, on the western bank of the Ganges, avowedly for the purpose of opposing the invasion.

"The intrigues and military movements of Tipu at this period, (although his correspondence with the Shah was not then known) rendering it probable, that he meant to take advantage of these circumstances to invade the Carnatac, the Madras army was also ordered to take the field; and an expedition, which was sitting out against the spanish islands in the China seas, was in consequence relinquished.

"The retreat of Zeman Shah's army from Hindusthan, the premature discovery of the intrigues of Feridun Jah,[2] and the menacing position of the English armies, combined to prevent Tipu from engaging in any open scene of hostility, or any overt

[1] Vide Tipu's correspondence with Zeman Shah, Nos. 22 and 26, Beatson's *War in Mysore*, and *Asiatic Register* for 1789 .

[2] He was seized and confined by his father

act of insult against the British nation; although several months previous to this period, he had privately dispatched ambassadors to the Mauritius to renew his connections with France, and to solicit the aid of 10,000 European and 30,000 Negro troops. The discovery of this transaction and the ineffectual assistance sent him by his friends, drew again on the Sultan the vengeance of the British arms, before he was properly prepared to resist him.

"A.D. 1798. In the month of June, 1798, the Governor-General of India[3] received an authentic account of the arrival of Tipu's ambassadors at the Mauritius, and of all their proceedings. This glaring proof of the Sultan's intentions leaving no room for doubt or hesitation, orders were immediately issued for assembling the armies; and the most active preparations for war were made throughout British India The Governor-General did not, however, continue his precautions to his own territories; effectual measures were at the same time taken to annihilate the party of Tipu and the French at the court of Hyderabad, and to enable the Nizam to co-operate against the common enemy[1]. An attempt was also made to unite the discordant parties at the court of Puna, but the mutual jealousies of the Mahratta chiefs, some of whom were probably in the interest of the Sultan, rendered it impossible for the Peshwa to fulfil his engagements, or to take any part in this war.

"The Governor-General being thus prepared to punish the Sultan for his breach of faith, but averse to rush unnecessarily into an expensive and uncertain war, deemed it proper, first to admonish him, and to leave it in his power to terminate the differences between the two governments in an amicable manner, by proper apologies, and new stipulations. He, in consequence, addressed several letters to the Sultan, in which he carefully avoided every hostile expression, merely apprizing him that his intercourse with the French was perfectly known, and proposing that Major Doveton might be sent to him on the part of the allies, for the purpose of forming an amicable arrangement[5]. The answers to the letters were replete with prevarication, and the proposal respecting Major Doveton entirely evaded.

"During this period, intelligence reached the Governor-General of the operations of the French in Egypt, and of the embarkation of Monsieur Dubuc at Tranquebar, as ambassador from Tipu Sultan to the French Government.[6] A knowledge of these circumstances rendered any further delay inexpedient: and orders were in consequence issued, on the 3rd. of February,

[3] Marquis Wellesiley, then Lord Mornington.

[4] The corps under the command of Monsieur Raymond, and other French officers, were disarmed, and the battalions placed under the control of English officers, in October, 1798.

[5] Vide Appendix to the *War in Mysore,* No 8, and following.

[6] Vide Appendix to the *War in Mysore,* No. 13.

1799, for the armies and those of the allies, immediately to invade the Sultan's dominions. Ten days subsequent to these orders, a letter was received by the Governor-General from the Sultan, in which the latter stated, that 'being frequently disposed to make excursions and hunt, he was accordingly proceeding upon a hunting excursion, and that his lordship might dispatch Major Doveton to him slightly attended.

"On the 11th. of February, the grand army, under the command of General Harris, marched from Vellore, and, on the 28th. of the same month, was joined at Karimunglum, by the Nizam's forces, with 6000 subsidiary British troops in his highness's pay

"On the 4th. of March, the combined armies encamped near Ryacotta, on the frontier of Mysore; whence a letter from the Governor-General was dispatched to the Sultan, acknowledging the receipt of his last epistle, and referring him to General Harris for further explanation."

EXTRACT OF MAJOR STEWART'S TRANSLATION FROM THE TARIKH TABBERY

"Omar, (on whom be the grace of God!) in the same year, being the fifteenth (of the Hijra) A.D. 636-7, sent Saad Ben Aby Waccas with an army to Gufa, with orders to halt there Afterwards he wrote to the General: 'As your troops have new recovered from their fatigues, and the Almighty God has spread the Musalmans all over the world, and the Persians continue inactive at Madain, let not their inactivity prevent your exertion, but attack them, and if God give you the victory, inform me'

"Saad immediately marched with his army, which then only consisted of 20,000 men, but from every city numbers joined him, convinced there would not be any fighting, (because Yezdigerd had not any person remaining fit to be appointed commander of his army) and before Saad arrived at Madain, the Arabs were increased to 60,000

"When Saad arrived at Amba, Yezdigerd, who had heard of his approach, collected all his troops, and consulted with his ministers whom he should appoint Generalissimo, in the room of Rustam; but as none of his officers would accept the post, they advised him to quit Madain, and to retire to Khorassan, Pars, or Carmania, all which were under his authority; and added, that they also would abandon the city to the enemy, and accompany him The king was much distressed at the idea of quitting his capital, but there being no other remedy, he obliged to comply. During this time, the Arabian general advanced by easy marches, supposing that the Persians were coming to meet him When he arrived at Sahat, which is only one day's journey from Madain, Yezdegerd (who was very undetermined) had only time to pack up and take with him a small portion of his treasure and valuable effects. The inhabitants of Madain also, whether soldier or citizen, noble or mean, all fled. No person paid any attention to their property, but abandoned the whole of their possessions.

"As soon as Saad was informed of this circumstances, he detached Cacaa Ben Amru with a party in pursuit of the fugitives. This officer, having marched through Madain without stopping, followed the king; but being unable to come up with him, he took and put to death a great number of the Persians who had fallen behind, and collected much plunder. At the same time that the Arabian general detached Cacaa, he proceeded with the remainder of the army to Madain, and, on his arrival there, found it entirely evacuated Saad was much delighted at the sight of the palaces and beautiful gardens.; but not wishing then to enter the city, he encamped at the porch or hall of Casrow, which is still to be seen at Madain. The extent of it is, in breadth one hundred and twenty cubits, and in length six hundred cubits : instead of brick, it is built of hewn stone ; and along the front are twelve columns, one hundred cubits in height, all built of hewn stone. This edifice was erected by Kefra Ben Cobad Firoy, who, when arrived at the pinnacle of his greatness, placed here the golden throne.

"Saad drew up the army around the porch when he entered the building; and, in gratitude for the victory, repeated eight prayers; and, at the end of each prayer, prostrated himself on the ground. This he did in imitation of the prophet (on whom, and his posterity, be the blessing of God!) who, on the day that he took Mecca, entered the Caaba, and repeated these eight prayers with their prostrations; to which he added, his benediction for the saints, the first and other chapters of the Koran at the end of each prayer, together with the creed four times This is called the Service for Victory. Saad, having performed this act of religious duty, appointed Amru Ben Mocurreb superintendent of the plunder, and directed a crier to proclaim, that whoever found any thing should bring it to Amru, that the whole being collected might be equally divided Some time after, the General mounting (his horse) went into the city, and took up his residence at the palace of Cosroes. Then he saw tables (the number of which God only knows) covered with gold, silver, cloths, jewels, armour, carpets, and vessels of various kinds.

"The troops, having dispersed themseves in different places, collected every thing that was valuable, and brought it to Amru Cacaa, who had pursued (the king) as far as the Nehruan bridge, brought back also many valuable articles. The quantity of plunder was so great, that after deducting one-fifth (for religious purposes) and many presents, each man of the sixty thousand received twelve thousand dirhems[7]. Besides these, many things

[7] A silver coin, eight of which weighed an ounce.

were gratuitously sent to the Khalif; of these, some could not be broken; others were so superb as to be useless to any other person.[8] Of this kind was the camel load of goods taken by Cacaa at the Nehruan bridge, which consisted of a wardrobe and a vase, containing a dress of Cosroes, wrought with pearls, and between every two pearls there was a ruby, besides several other dresses of cloth wrought with gold. They also found the royal crown, and the king's rings, and ten other suits of clothes, all of (*gerbast*) cloth wrought with gold; the whole of which was sent to Omar

"In the armoury, they discovered a press, lined with cloth wrought with gold, containing the armour of Cosres, inlaid with jewels. The helmet, coat of mail, cuishes, and cuirasses, were all of gold There were likewise six suits of Daudy armour, and nine scymitars of great value, which were also sent to the Khalif In addition to these, there were found in the treasury a horse made of gold, having on a silver saddle set with jewels, and a camel made of silver, with a gold saddle Among the stores was found a carpet three hundred cubits long, and sixty cubits wide This was called the Winter Carpet, because the kings of Persia used to have it spread to sit on in that season, when neither flowers nor any verdure was to be seen, and its borders being wrought with emaralds, it appeared like a field of variegated crops, or of green corn, interspersed with numerous flowers and blossoms, composed of jewels. and other precious stones.

"There were also found many bottles filled with camphire. amber, musk, and all kinds of perfumes, and various other articles, all of which Saad sent to the Khalif.

"When these commodities arrived at Medinah, Omar (upon whom be the grace of God!) ordered them to be deposited in the mosque, and when the people of Medineh saw them, they were astonished. After some days, the Khalif ordered them to be divided, to each person according to his office. The commander of the Faithful, Ali, the son of Aby Talib, (upon whom be the favour of God!) received a small portion of the carpet, which he sold for eight thousand dirhems; and people came from all quarters, from India, from Africa, from Egypt, and Yemen, to Medinah, to buy the gold, silver, jewels, and precious stuffs The conquest of Madain happened in the month Sufer (second month) of the sixteenth year of the Hijra, A.D 637."

Our readers cannot fail to see from these specimens, that this work is extremely valuable.